Motivation Management

Motivation Management

*Fueling Performance by Discovering
What People Believe About
Themselves and Their Organizations*

Thad Green

Davies-Black Publishing
Palo Alto, California

PUBLISHED BY DAVIES-BLACK PUBLISHING,
an imprint of Consulting Psychologists Press, Inc.
3803 East Bayshore Road
Palo Alto, CA 94303; 800-624-1765.

*Special discounts on bulk quantities of Davies-Black books are available
to corporations, professional associations, and other organizations. For details,
contact the Director of Book Sales at Davies-Black Publishing, an imprint of
Consulting Psychologists Press, Inc., 3803 East Bayshore Road, Palo Alto, CA
94303; 650-691-9123; fax 650-623-9271.*

Visit the Davies-Black Publishing web site at www.daviesblack.com.

04 03 02 01 00   10 9 8 7 6 5 4 3 2 1

Printed in the United States of America

Library of Congress Cataloging-in-Publication Data
Green, Thad B.
   Motivation management : fueling performance by discovering what
   people believe about themselves and their organizations / Thad
   Green.—1st ed.
      p. cm.
   Includes bibliographical references and index.
   ISBN 0-89106-143-6
   1. Employee motivation. 2. Psychology, Industrial. 3. Industrial
   management. I. Title.
   HF5549.5.M63 M7473 2000
   658.3′14—dc21
                                                            99-086822

FIRST EDITION
First printing 2000

Dedicated to Mama, Alice, and Bates

Contents

List of Stories

Introduction

Twenty years ago I had the greatest job in the world. I was a university professor teaching management and behavioral courses to business students. I loved teaching and loved interacting with the students—helping them grow, helping them learn to deal with the present and prepare for the future.

Little did I know my life was about to be turned around—by a mathematical formula.

A colleague, Walt Newsom, and I were writing a principles of management textbook for the introductory course that thousands of business majors were required to take each year. Walt's background was in organization behavior, mine was in computers and statistics. One day Walt rushed into my office waving a handful of papers. "Let's build the motivation chapter around Victor Vroom's expectancy theory."

"Victor who's, expectancy what?"

Walt explained. Vroom, a professor at Yale University, had developed a complex mathematical model to explain motivation in the workplace.

$$F = \Sigma (E \times V)$$

That sounded contradictory to me. How could mathematics explain human behavior? I spent days poring over the research and countless books and journal articles discussing expectancy theory.

Vroom had laid it all out, and the practicality of it was clear once I sifted through the mathematics. I wondered, "Why haven't I heard of this before?"

Scholars in both management and psychology agreed—as much as they ever do—that expectancy theory of motivation was (and still is) the most theoretically sound approach to motivation and performance. They also agreed that in spite of its strong theoretical underpinnings, expectancy theory did not have much practical value.

I disagreed (though with some hesitancy since my view was at odds with the entire academic community). It was clear to me that this theory presented a rock-solid approach that offered greater power than anything I had ever seen before. It was tailor-made for anyone whose success depended on motivating and influencing others. It was equally useful to those who occasionally needed a jump-start themselves. I was intrigued. I set about testing whether real-world managers could make it work. I found that they could.

That did it. The entrepreneurial spirit that had been dormant in me for years took over. I resigned my position as a full professor with tenure to start a business—without knowing what I was going to do and with no business experience.

I had gone to college for nine straight years. I finished my Ph.D. degree when I was 26 and went right into teaching. As my brother-in-law said, "Thad, you've never had a real job." And I wanted to be *president* of the company!

With a partner, I started a company to train people who were out of work, to help them develop the skills they needed to get and keep productive jobs. We used expectancy theory as the foundation for managing, and the company grew to more than 200 employees. It was exciting. My only regret was that I never finished the manuscript for that textbook.

Throughout the ensuing years, we learned one thing for certain: Expectancy theory worked. It guided our hiring practices and helped us choose people who could do the work, who would enjoy doing it, and who were motivated in the environment we offered.

Of course, we had some problems, but our insights into motivation helped us spot and resolve them quickly and prevent others. Building solid, high-performing teams was easier because of our knowledge of human behavior. Decision making improved by anticipating behavioral issues. Managing change was more effective with an eye on motivation.

Expectancy theory taught us that sound management principles hold up in practice. There is a critical connection between motivation and performance. Employees *are* the best source of solutions to their own motivation and performance problems. Managing is a shared responsibility. It takes *more* than offering people what they want to unleash their motivation to perform. It is on this latter point where expectancy theory diverges from all other theories of motivation and performance, where it sets itself apart, where it offers the power to release a mighty force within each of us, and where I discovered how to run a business.

But eventually the excitement of the early years disappeared. The daily grind caught up. The stress of working hard and traveling a lot accumulated. I had been reasonably successful, so I decided to retire. I was 43.

I did not exactly pick up where I had left off in my teaching days, but I did go back to writing. In *Motivation and Performance Strategies for Today's Workforce* I described how we used expectancy theory in our company. The book got some attention. A corporate executive asked, "How can we apply this to employees at the first level in our organization?" I did not know the answer.

My previous application of expectancy theory was a step-by-step process that was used mainly as a one-on-one approach between manager and employee. It was not designed for entire organizations. But I believed in the potential power of the theory and I loved a challenge. I organized a team and we implemented, tested, and gathered data to measure results in the corporate environment. Everyone was flabbergasted by the success.

I documented the results in my second book, *Manage to the Individual.* It explains how expectancy theory convinced managers and employees that managing to the individual works better than treating everyone the same. And best of all, it shows how managers discovered that expectancy theory does not require a major commitment of resources.

Managers and employees liked the book, accepted it, and used it. Their communication, interpersonal, and motivational issues dissolved. Individual and organizational performance made a sharp turn upward.

Other organizations became interested. Once again, I had the greatest job in the world—teaching, helping people deal with their problems, reach their goals, feel good, be happy.

Expectancy theory had taught me that people are at their best when they have confidence in themselves, trust in their manager, and are satisfied in their work. And most important, it taught me that you can have this for yourself, you can help others get it, and it can turn lives around.

The hundreds of people I have worked with helped me more than I ever helped them. Through them I realized the wide range of applications, in large and small organizations, in personal relationships beyond the workplace, and in my own family. Through them I discovered the full and awesome power of expectancy theory.

I present it to you in this book.

Although expectancy theory is a complex mathematical model, as I mentioned earlier, that is not what you will see in this book. My work with expectancy theory has removed the mathematics and simplified the theory. I have changed the appearance of the model; I have not altered the substance of it. Where Vroom says people have *expectations* that determine their motivation at work, I simply say they have *beliefs.* Where he measures expectations in the form of *probabilities,* I measure beliefs on simple *10-point rating scales.* Where his mathematical model is called *expectancy theory,* I call my easier-to-understand version the *Belief System of Motivation and Performance*™. In other words, my goal has been to simplify Vroom's theoretical model and give it the language of managers.

At this point my work begins to differ from Vroom's landmark contribution. Vroom offers only a *theoretical model,* while I present an *application model.* The model is a refinement of the approach I developed during my days as an entrepreneur; it allows managers to apply the Belief System in daily interactions with employees. I also introduce an *implementation model.* This model is the product of my later work as a management consultant; it enables managers to implement the Belief System with full teams, multiple layers in selected units, or entire organizations.

This book, however, has a broader focus than the Belief System of Motivation and Performance. *This book is really about motivation management.* Motivation management is managing with motivation in mind. It is a management approach that focuses on the motivation to perform. Specifically, motivation management is managing in a way that creates the conditions required for motivation. The end result of motivation management is fewer problems, stronger motivation, and improved performance.

Motivation management is important because the weight of performance demands has taken its toll. Managers see employees who are tired, discouraged, and disillusioned. Employee tolerance for "more, faster, better" has weakened. Cracks have appeared in their motivation to perform. Employees see no way out, no light at the end of the tunnel. They are trudging along an uncertain path, no longer stimulated to do their best. Rather than examining ways to perform better, the workforce is engaged in a battle to survive, seeking answers to troubling questions such as, "How much more can they expect of me? How much longer can I stand the strain?" Motivation is the fuel for their performance, but the fuel gauge no longer registers a full tank. Performance is sputtering to the demands of a long, stressful, uphill climb. Managers need ways to boost the power to perform and to do so within the limits of the resources and authority available to them. That is what this book offers.

Whether you are a manager or supervisor, or someone who wants to be, this book is written for you. It also is very useful for employees who want to gain more control over their own lives at work.

The book takes you on a curiously interesting journey through the Belief System. Intriguing stories are woven throughout to illustrate pertinent points and demonstrate the application of major concepts. The stories are based on real situations and constitute approximately 40 percent of the book. If you prefer interesting, application oriented reading, focus on the stories. If stories don't grab your attention, concentrate on the textual material.

Chapter 1 summarizes the Belief System of Motivation and Performance. This chapter is the foundation of the book: It provides the nuts and bolts. Chapters 2 through 6 are devoted to the application model for the Belief System. Chapter 2 shows how to use the Belief System to quickly identify motivation problems before they get out of control. Chapters 3 and 4 explain how to work with employees to uncover *true* problem causes and discover solutions that will work. Chapter 5 offers a practical, step-by-step approach that tells managers what to say and do for a successful march from problem, to cause, to a solution that will get performance back on track. Chapter 6 provides an approach managers can use to effectively handle difficult motivation and performance problems, the kind that seem to defy resolution.

Chapter 7 describes the implemention model for the Belief System and presents the tools (including written instruments) managers can use to take the Belief System to their own teams and larger parts of the organization. Chapter 8 summarizes five approaches to motivation management from which managers can choose. Data collected over a seven-year period to measure the effectiveness of the Belief System are presented in the Appendix.

This book offers the Belief System of Motivation and Performance—with its structure, process, and guidelines—as the foundation for motivation management for those who want to start managing with motivation in mind.

I urge you to read this book, use the Belief System, and become a motivation manager.

Acknowledgments

I want to thank the following:

Walt Newsom, management professor and former colleague, for starting me on the trail that eventually led to this book.

Bill Barkley, Vice President, AT&T, for giving me the first opportunity to use motivation management in a large organization and nudging me to develop the implementation model for the Belief System of Motivation and Performance.

Ray Butkus, Vice President, AT&T, for giving me my second opportunity to use motivation management in a large corporate environment and allowing for the collection of data to measure its effectiveness.

John Willig, literary agent, for his invaluable help in developing this book, encouraging me to include some storytelling, and finding a first-rate publisher, and in general for pushing my literary career along.

Melinda Adams Merino, former Acquisitions Editor, Davies-Black Publishing, for seeing the value in this book and providing expert advice in developing it.

Ryan Ramsey, human resources professional, for first encouraging me to use the term *motivation management*.

Grace Hawthorne, expert storyteller, for teaching me the art of storytelling and helping shape the stories in this book.

John Thompson, a football teammate from the University of Florida and the best creative writer I know, for getting me to develop the 10-step formula for the Belief System and providing some exceptional editing in the early stages of this book.

Merwyn Hayes, international management consultant, for insisting I develop the chapter on handling difficult problems.

Lee Langhammer Law and her excellent staff at Davies-Black Publishing, particularly Jill Anderson-Wilson, Managing Editor, who did an outstanding job of shepherding *Motivation Management* through the editorial and production process.

Shannon Green, Associate Consultant, the HayGroup, Metro New York Office, for her timely, comprehensive review of the manuscript for this book and making many helpful suggestions. Eslie Green, David Murphy, and Jay and Sandy Knippen, also for reviewing the book.

Special clients—Rock Anderson, Dave Bogue, Sandra Bond, Gary Boren, Carlos Cantu, LeAnn Coe, Jim Croll, Ian Cunningham, Vince Donnelly, Warren Dodge, Paul Ferreri, Pat Gorman, Ken Hannan, Doris Jean Head, Carol Heller, Don Howard, Lucy Kratovil, Ann Kroupa, Alan Kuritsky, Diane Lapore, Mercedes Lytle, Tony Miranda, Joe Massimo, Marty McCommons, Aloise McNichols, Joe O'Brien, Gary Phipps, Carol Richardson, Doug Ripley, Jane Sanders, Art Sparks, Wayne Thrasher, and Dan Wyatt.

Special people who have had a major influence on my thinking and career—Herb Hannah, Minton Williams, Tommy Baker, Howard Baker, Homer Pharr, Scooter Dickerson, Lowell Vancil, David Harris, Bobbie Lee Rainey, Wayne Johnson, Gus White, Ray Graves, Jack Green, John Donaldson, John Eibner, Jim Bernhardt, Floyd Dean, John Wells, William Wilmot, H. R. Smith, Everette Hong, Mort Cotlar, Frank Schilagi, George deLodzia, Bill Ruble, John Harper, Roy Rein, Andy Cutler, Lynda Hart, Jim Lowe, Marva Smalls, Jay Knippen, Buddy King, Kurt Sutton, Leif Roland, and Shirley Cooper.

Special relatives—Pa, Ida, Sonny, and Neena.

Very special family—my wife, Joyce; children, Stacy, Shannon, and Eslie; and grandchildren, Frances Helen and Bates

About the Author

At 37 he was a full professor with tenure teaching management courses.
Then he left to practice what he preached.
He was a millionaire within one year of starting his own company.
Then he left to preach what he practiced.

Based on his success as a college professor and as the president of his own company, Thad Green began his third prosperous career as the author of *Performance and Motivation Strategies for Today's Workforce* (1992). The book received considerable attention in the corporate world and was quickly followed by an equally successful book, *Managing to the Individual* (1994, with Bill Barkley).

His most recent books include *Developing and Leading the Sales Organization* (1998), *Motivation, Beliefs, and Organizational Transformation* (1999, with Raymond T. Butkus), and *Breaking the Barrier to Upward Communication* (1999, with Jay T. Knippen).

In *Motivation Management,* Green explores yet another area of expertise—storytelling. The anecdotes drawn from his years of experience not only are engaging, but each carries a powerful lesson not easy to forget. The narratives combine the best of the ancient art of teaching through stories with invaluable insight into motivation management, illustrating how applying these principles will result in fewer communication and interpersonal problems, stronger motivation, and improved performance.

Green divides his time between research and writing and serving as a management consultant. As head of The Belief System Institute, which he founded in 1994, he helps individuals and organizations reach their goals and provides motivation and performance systems *that people use.* The Institute works primarily with large corporate clients such as AT&T, Lucent Technologies, Metropolitan Life Insurance, Delta Air Lines, Bank of America, National Data Corporation, and Andersen Consulting.

In addition to his many successful books, Green has published over 150 articles and research papers, many in national journals including *Training and Development, Supervisory Management, Personnel Journal, Journal of Business,* and *Academy of Management Journal.*

Green received his B.S. degree in statistics and an M.A.degree in management from the University of Florida and his Ph.D. degree in management at age 26 from the University of Georgia. He was on the faculty of the University of Georgia, Auburn University, Mississippi State University, and Emory University.

CHAPTER 1

The Offering Is Never Enough

"The key to motivation and performance lies in each person's head."

A BRIEFING SESSION

Managers are unhappy with motivation strategies that work only part-time.

This chapter shows why they work in one situation, yet fail miserably in others.

It explains how managers can get more consistent results.

Motivation is future oriented, always.

Employees are motivated by what they believe is going to happen, not by what managers promise will happen.

This chapter gives managers a way to look ahead, get in tune with employees, and stop guessing how to motivate them.

Motivation management is managing in a way that creates the conditions required for motivation.

This chapter spells out those conditions, three in all.

The remainder of the book shows managers how to create them.

LEADER IS AS LEADER DOES

Preston Turner skipped lunch as usual and hurried to make a 1:30 appointment. It had been a long day already. He reached down without looking, touched the hard, reddish-brown wood of his mahogany desk, and rolled open the bottom drawer. He reached in, pulled out a freshly pressed shirt, and took care not to crumple up the front as he put it on.

It embarrassed him to be concerned about looking good for the 21-year-old college student he would be talking with for the next hour. He decided to be two minutes late.

"Why did I volunteer for this interview?" he muttered to himself as he retied his tie. He slipped on the jacket of a suit that had been tailor-made on Savile Row during a business trip to London. He buttoned it, quickly checked his watch, then the mirror, carefully, and left his office.

He walked into the chairman's private conference room. It was elegant and intimate. He was surprised and somewhat irritated that she was not there. A backpack, he noticed, was in a chair, and a notepad and pen in her school's colors rested on the handsome teakwood tabletop. He heard laughter coming from the adjoining office. That would be Alice Johnson talking with her uncle.

"I think he's here now. Thanks for arranging the interview. It will help me complete my last paper, and in a few weeks I'll have my journalism degree. Oh, Dad said to tell you to stop working all the time and come visit us. He misses you, you know."

She walked in, smiling, hand out. She greeted Preston, but he did not hear what she said.

Twenty-five years ago Preston had been a confident, self-assured college senior with uncompromising principles, inner peace, and joy. He knew who he was and where he was going.

In that moment, holding her hand, he could see all that in her. She had now what he had had then. He wondered what had happened.

They sat. "Mr. Turner, I know your son, Ralph. We're in school together."

"How is he?"

"He's fine. I told him I was meeting with you for an hour today."

"What did he say?"

"That he was jealous." She paused long enough to make the point. "He asked me to tell you hello."

"Yeah, well, we're both busy."

"And my dad said to tell you hello, too."

He frowned and cocked his head to the left. "Do I know your dad?"

"Bill Johnson. You went to high school together. Held the ball on extra points for you. He's kept up with you over the years. He does that with a lot of people."

"Bookworm Bill? Second-string quarterback? Married the home-coming queen?"

"That's him, and my mom. Still in love."

Preston was already saying, "Well, I'll be darned," when her last three words registered. He paused and remembered the early years in his own marriage, and then continued with, "Your dad was smart. I guess he's successful like your uncle now."

"Not really, not by most standards. He could have been. He's a writer. Had a chance to go to Hollywood as a screenwriter, but he wasn't willing to move the family out there or to be away from us. Said he needed us and we needed him. In my book he's the most successful person I know. He's comfortable with himself, likes his work, loves his family, has balance in his life. What more could a person ask for? How about you? Are you successful?"

Preston shifted in his chair, took his eyes off her, and said, "By conventional standards I suppose I am."

"I'm sorry." She waited and watched his reaction. "Shall we start the interview? My uncle tells me you're one of the key players running the company now. What's been the secret in getting to the top?"

"There is so much pressure in corporate America now. And not enough time to really manage anymore. The pressure comes down on me and I pass it on to others. I communicate the goals and expect the cream to rise to the top. Good people step forward and get the job done. It seems like the greater the pressure, the better people perform."

"So what you're saying is that you got to the top because you put pressure on people?"

"That's not exactly the way I'd put it, but you've summed up the basic approach."

"Doesn't that eventually take its toll on people?"

"Sure, but that's just the way things are now."

She paused to take notes. Preston waited uncomfortably.

"Who is the best leader you've ever been around?"

"That's easy. My high school football coach. Coach…um…"

"Mason. That's what my dad says, too. Why was he so good?"

"After the end of the year, he called all the seniors in, reminded us why we'd had a championship season, and gave us words of wisdom for the future. He said three things mattered. First, you have to help people believe in themselves. Second, they have to trust you to give them what they deserve. Third..."

"Third, remember that everybody's different, that what's satisfying to one may not be to another."

Preston was taken aback. These were Coach Mason's exact words. Twenty-five years later.

"My dad lives those three principles every day, at home and at work."

She flipped back through her notepad, found a couple of hurriedly scrawled lines, and said, "Mr. Turner, do you live them, too?"

He did not answer, and yet he knew he had answered by his silence.

She stood, smiling, hand out. She thanked him, but he did not hear what she said.

• • •

MOTIVATION IS THE FUEL

Unfortunately, too few people understand the connection between motivation and performance. Motivation is the fuel for performance. Without motivation, performance suffers. That is why gifted people are not always high performers and those with good skills sometimes fail. With motivation, people reach their potential, even exceed it. That's why people with average ability become top-notch performers, and the reason those with modest skills become solid employees.

To extract top performance from employees, managers need to see the critical connection between motivation and performance. Employees must have fuel to power them into action. No gas, no go. Managers can become better equipped to provide the impetus for performance by understanding the basics of motivation.

SEEING IS BELIEVING

Modern management strategies relating to employee motivation and performance are rooted in theories that say, in essence, "Offer people something they want as an incentive to perform and they will work hard to get it." The only trouble is, as any seasoned manager will tell you, the theories don't always work. Were you ever offered an all-expenses-paid vacation for a performance you felt should have earned a raise instead? Did that motivate you to work even harder? Have you ever been offered a bonus for a performance level you knew was impossible to achieve? How motivated were you to chase that reward? Were you ever party to a reward offered but never delivered? What happened the next time that reward was held out as incentive to perform well? Where is the motivation in a father's offer of a new car to his academically deficient son if the 16-year-old makes the dean's list next semester? Think about it: How many times are people offered attractive rewards that fail to produce the performance necessary to get them? It happens all too frequently. Why?

This question has intrigued me throughout my career, first as a university professor, and then as a consultant and hands-on businessman. The trouble with popular theories of motivation, including those by the likes of Abraham Maslow and Frederick Herzberg, is that they do not translate well to the realities of the workplace. Specifically, the motivation theories in wide use today are incomplete; they proceed from a single truth when there are three; and they come with no practical guide for utilization. Theory rarely holds form under pressure to shape it into a useful tool of production.

The Belief System of Motivation and Performance changes that. It is a monumental step forward in the imperfect art and science of human motivation. This book conveys a vital, simple truth: What employees *believe* is infinitely more important than what is being offered to motivate them.

THE CHAIN OF EVENTS

The Belief System for motivation management explains how people determine (1) how hard they will work and (2) how well they will perform. These decisions spring from a process or chain of events that goes like this: *Effort* leads to *performance,* which leads to *outcomes,* which result in *satisfaction.* An employee's effort can be a little or a lot, resulting in performance that is good or bad, begetting outcomes big or small that produce high or low levels of satisfaction or dissatisfaction. Whatever the variables, the principle remains the same.

Effort ······> Performance ······> Outcomes ······> Satisfaction

Figure 1   THE BELIEF SYSTEM MODEL

The popular theories of motivation focus solely on the end of the process—the relationship between *outcomes* and *satisfaction*—as the way to motivate employees to perform. Performance is best achieved, according to these theories, by offering employees something they want so they will work hard to get it. The other side of this tactic is to offer employees something they *don't* want—unemployment, perhaps—so they will work hard to avoid getting it.

The problem with simply offering employees something they want (desirable outcomes) as an inducement to work harder and perform better is that part of the basic equation is ignored—the product that follows is unpredictable. The Belief System does not dispute the importance of offering employees what they want; it merely points out that the offering alone is not enough.

Employees must first *believe* certain specific things before the offering of desirable outcomes will produce the motivation managers desire and expect. The beliefs—three in all—are the key to motivating employees, and all three must be "believed" or everyone loses to some extent or another.

The First Belief—Confidence

"Can I do it?" *Confidence,* the first belief, deals with the relationship between employee effort and performance. What must be believed is that one's effort will lead to performance. Without this belief, there is a motivation problem, and perhaps a big one. Consciously or unconsciously, people always ask themselves, "If I give it my best, will the effort lead to the performance desired?" In other words, "Can I do it?" The question demands an answer: "Yes, I can," or "No, I can't."

Suppose a person is offered a desirable reward but concludes, "I really want that reward, but no matter how hard I try, I can't perform well enough to get it." What happens to motivation? It plummets. It happens in corporate downsizing when jobs are combined and heaped on overworked employees. It happens when sales or production quotas are raised to improbable levels. It happens when people are placed in positions of responsibility when they do not have the necessary training or experience. Even though employees in situations like these may be offered something they want, motivation does not result because they believe "I can't do it." People must believe that the effort they are capable of giving will be sufficient to perform as expected.

In the next story, two special people, Juanita and Gary, gave me an interesting insight into confidence and the impact it has on motivation and performance.

A CONTRAST IN CONFIDENCE

Juanita had gotten herself into deep trouble. Her manager was annoyed because she always resisted new assignments. My job was to figure out why. Juanita was a sweet-looking woman with beautiful white hair. She was nearing retirement. Her kind nature gave me a warm feeling, and a vulnerability about her cautioned me to be gentle.

She finally opened up when I asked, "Did anything happen in your past that had a major impact on your self-confidence?" I could see the pain in her face, hear it in her voice as she quietly answered.

"All of my life when there was any mention of me doing something new, my mother always said, 'You'll never be able to do it.' Eventually I believed her. So when I'm faced with doing something new here at work, I'm filled with this horrible fear. My first reaction always is that I can't do it, so I resist. I'm 61 years old, my mother is in her eighties, and she's still telling me I can't." She was crying.

Several years before I met Juanita, a self-assured cowboy named Gary worked for me. He would tackle any problem. I asked him one day where he got his confidence.

"I got it from my grandfather. Any time I doubted myself, he'd say, 'You're as good as the best and better than the rest.' I believed him."

• • •

```
Confidence

Effort ······> Performance ······> Outcomes ······> Satisfaction

    "I can perform as expected."
    "I cannot perform as expected."
    "Not sure I can perform as expected."
```

Figure 2 CONFIDENCE (BELIEF 1) "CAN I DO IT?"

Because I grew up in a family of strong, confident people who built my confidence, I assumed others were from similar environments and had the confidence to tackle most anything. During my early years as a consultant I learned a lot about how pervasive confidence problems are in the workplace.

IT'S EVERYWHERE

My jaw dropped. Not once, but over and over. It began when I started facilitating one-on-one sessions with managers and employees who met to resolve motivation and performance issues. Every single person had at least one significant confidence problem.

At the time I was surprised that the number and magnitude of confidence issues tended to be greater as people moved to higher levels in the organization. However, this makes sense because as responsibilities widen, so does the range of skills required, and therefore the greater the likelihood of feeling ill-equipped and uncomfortable, and lacking in confidence. Life is complicated, and jobs are demanding. People cannot be good at everything and when they are not, confidence is an issue. It happens to all of us.

• • •

Unfortunately, confidence problems usually go undetected, principally because people do not find them easy to discuss. People generally do not like to confess their shortcomings. It is human nature. In the minds of many, feelings of inadequacy and weakness are attached to such admissions. So the problems are covered up.

Not only do people tend to cover up confidence problems, they even deny their existence. As a consultant I often hear, "Sure, I can do it," when the truth turns out to be quite the opposite. Why? Fear of the consequences. "If the boss thinks I can't do the job, he'll find someone who can," or "It will hold back my advancement." These are typical reasons for denying a lack of confidence. The guilty party is the corporate culture that does not permit employees to talk openly about confidence problems. A high-level executive in one of the largest corporations in the world confessed in an interview that he was "over his head" in his new position. "I can't do it," he said. Yet he could not bring himself to express this to anyone for fear that the organization would not want to hear it. Neither employee nor employer is well served in a situation like this.

The irony in the cover-up of confidence problems is that they tend to be relatively easy to remedy—easy compared to the problems they can cause. Like a small nick on the arm that goes untreated, confidence problems can fester into debilitating afflictions of the first order. Look for the "confidence nicks" in your workforce and treat the problems early so they do not get out of hand. In this book you will learn how to treat them.

Clear up confidence problems and the way is opened for motivation to wield its power on performance; allow the problems to fester and motivation never gets out of the starting gate.

The Second Belief—Trust

"Will outcomes be tied to my performance?" *Trust*, the second belief, deals with the relationship between performance and outcomes. Employees must believe that outcomes will be tied to their performance. In other words, employees must trust their manager to give them what their performance merits.

Suppose an employee is offered an outcome and believes, "That reward would be very satisfying and I can do the job," but concludes, "My manager is always promising things but never delivers. I don't believe I will get the reward even if I perform well." What happens to the employee's motivation? Needless to say, it is diminished. Even when employees are offered what they want (satisfaction) and believe they can do the job (confidence), they are not motivated when they believe that "outcomes will not be tied to my performance" (trust).

DO WHAT I SAY

Lucy was beside herself. A first-time manager, she pictured her group at work like her children who ignored her most of the time. "I tell my employees what to do, and they just don't do it," she said. I asked if she followed up and held them accountable.

"No. I don't like to look over their shoulders and check on them all the time. I just expect them to do what I say."

• • •

I was reminded how easy it is for all of us to deceive ourselves and fail to get a firm grip on the situation. Employees can clearly sense it when their manager is not going to follow through and when there will be no consequences one way or the other. Therefore, they are not motivated to do what they are asked to do.

Confidence	Trust		
Effort ·····> Performance ·····> Outcomes ·····> Satisfaction			
	"Outcomes *will* be tied to my performance." "Outcomes *will not* be tied to my performance." "*Not sure* outcomes will be tied to my performance."		

Figure 3   TRUST (BELIEF 2) "WILL OUTCOMES BE TIED TO MY PERFORMANCE?"

YES, THEY DO

I was doing research to determine how many employees believed they were getting what they deserved on the basis of their performance.

First, I asked top executives. "No," they answered, "I generally don't get what I deserve."

"How about the people you manage?"

"Oh, yes," they all agreed. "My people get what they deserve because I see to it."

Next I spoke to middle management, and they said, "No, I don't get what I deserve."

"How about the people you manage?"

"Oh, yes, absolutely. My people get what they deserve. I make sure of it."

I moved down one management level and asked the question again.

"No, I don't get what I deserve."

"What about the people you manage?"

"Oh, sure, they get what they deserve. You can count on that."

I continued down the hierarchy and, almost without exception, the response was always the same. Managers believed they were giving people what they deserved. Yet, the consensus among employees was, "You can't trust the people above you to give you what your performance merits."

• • •

People often do not get appropriately rewarded for their performance. It is a fact of life. Consider, for example, the following scenarios: A sales organization in the telecommunications industry had little turnover in 80 sales positions during a four-year period. Yet, most of the salespeople never met their annual sales quotas. The few who did left for better jobs. One former salesperson who had been there for years said, "It didn't matter whether you did a good job or not. Everybody was treated the same. Management took care of you."

Wayne retired after working 30 years at an automobile assembly plant. He described the reward system at the plant as one in which "all that mattered was how long you'd been there."

A services unit in an international corporation downsized from 400 to 200 workers. One employee described what happened: "Many of the people who were asked to leave were high-performing employees. Yet, a significant number of poor performers who had neither the skills nor the motivation the organization needed were retained."

Trust problems are widespread in the workplace for several reasons:

- It is not always easy to tie outcomes to performance.

- In many instances, performance is difficult to measure.

- There are not always desirable outcomes to give for performance, particularly in hard times.

- Sometimes people have an inflated sense of their own worth and when the outcomes actually match their performance, they do not see it that way.

11

• Sometimes people misconstrue and expect outcomes based on effort rather than performance. Effort should not earn outcomes, performance should.

Unlike confidence problems, trust issues are openly discussed by employees—at least among themselves. Unfortunately, expressions of trust problems are often interpreted by management as something else: complaining. "My performance evaluation was not fair. The system of rewards around here stinks. You don't get what you deserve here no matter how well you perform." To construe these as mere grumbling, offhand comments may be to miss a deeper meaning, which is "Outcomes are not tied to performance." If that is believed, employee motivation and performance are at risk.

Trust problems are serious business and can take a long time to correct. Fail to deliver on an annual performance bonus and it's another year before it can be corrected; miss again because of an off year in corporate earnings, and a pattern is established in the employee's mind that will take at least a couple of years of "doing as promised" to overcome.

LOOKING

I walked into a new client's office and found her assistant, Ginger, in tears, with mascara streaming down her face. She made no effort to hide her feelings or her face.

"I've just about had it with her, boss or no boss."

I did not have to ask what the problem was. She told me straight away.

"Janet is the most ungrateful person I've ever known. She never appreciates anything. Never a word of praise, not even a thank-you. I can't take it much longer."

I had not been working with this client long, but stories about Janet were beginning to form a pattern. Janet pushed people to perform but gave little in return.

"What happened?"

Ginger dried her eyes and made an effort to fix her makeup. "I completed nine of ten things she'd asked me to do. She commented only on the one I hadn't done yet. Janet's idea of motivation is to tell people to get with it or get out."

She was feeling better and even beginning to laugh a little. "If the truth be known, about as many people get out as get with it. Turnover's high. With Janet, getting fired is a relief."

"What are you going to do, Ginger?"

"I don't know. It's hard to give your best when you aren't appreciated. I'll give it a little more time. If things don't get better, I'll start looking for something else."

Janet was making a serious mistake. When people perform, you have to reward them.

· · ·

The Third Belief—Satisfaction

"Will the outcomes be satisfying to me?" *Satisfaction*, the third belief, deals with the relationship between outcomes and satisfaction. This is the classic notion that offering outcomes deemed to be satisfying will produce motivation.

Suppose a person believes, "I can do the job and I will get the outcomes if I do," but realizes that the outcomes would not be satisfying. What happens to the motivation of this person? No doubt, it suffers. People may believe that they can do the job (confidence) and that outcomes will be tied to performance (trust), but they will not be motivated if they believe the outcomes will be dissatisfying. It does not make sense for anyone to work hard for something he or she doesn't want.

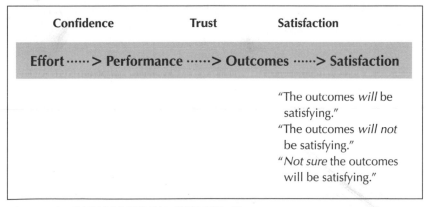

Figure 4 SATISFACTION (BELIEF 3)
"WILL THE OUTCOMES BE SATISFYING TO ME?"

Think about empowerment—a popular concept in the early 1990s. It illustrates a satisfaction problem that many people experience. Give employees more say-so in how they do their jobs. Everyone wants to be empowered, right? Not true. Empowerment may be satisfying to people who like the added responsibility and know how to handle it, but not everyone falls into that category. Many people—good workers, valued employees—do not want to be bothered with added decision-making responsibility. They want to clock in, do the job they know by heart, and clock out—no fuss, no bother.

Many organizations that pushed through empowerment programs in recent years with great expectations found themselves coming back to undo the damage caused by assuming that everyone wants the same thing. Empowering people who do not want the power is a good way to end up with satisfaction problems.

REALITY CHECK

Myth   Everybody is motivated by the same thing.

Reality   An outcome that is satisfying to one person may not be satisfying to another. If you want to know what will be satisfying to someone, ask.

Nobody is left out when it comes to employee dissatisfaction. I surveyed countless people about their level of satisfaction with their job. I pored over their questionnaires. I interviewed them in depth. Following are the results.

1. Every employee said, "I am dissatisfied with parts of my job, and it holds back my performance." However, the primary source of dissatisfaction seldom revolved around money, promotion, or job security. Everyone said "money is important," but most quickly pointed out that "other things are more important." The majority stated that "getting promoted is less attractive than it once was." It was generally recognized that "job security is a thing of the past."

2. People reported that dissatisfaction came from not getting something they wanted. The desired items most frequently mentioned were respect, being valued, meaningful work, feedback

on performance, coaching, clear direction and expectations, praise and recognition, being kept informed, time for family, fair treatment, and a boss who cares.

3. They said dissatisfaction also stemmed from getting things they did not want. Commonly cited were long hours, fast pace, pressure, conflict, uncertainty, criticism, and stress. Most people indicated that their dissatisfaction was the result of only a handful of things. However, the sources of dissatisfaction varied widely from one person to another.

4. People in the survey typically said that dissatisfaction was primarily a result of what their manager said and did, or failed to say and do. For this reason, they pointed out that "My manager has the power to change all of this, and it would not cost a dime."

Why are satisfaction problems a common occurrence in the workplace?

- Managers offer outcomes that are satisfying to themselves in the belief that employees will want the same things.

- Everyone is offered the same outcome when in reality different things motivate different people.

- The "big three" outcomes—money, advancement, and job security—are assumed to negate the need for praise, recognition, openness, honesty, and other important motivating outcomes.

AFTER THE SHOCK WORE OFF

Suzanne, a 40-year-old manager with an old-fashioned work ethic, was struggling to understand young people in the workplace. She had observed a steady decline in performance from her two most recent hires, both in their late twenties. She called me in a panic.

"What should I do? I'm afraid I'll lose both of them soon if I don't get things back on track. They both came in and hit the ground running, excited about their jobs, doing great work from day one."

"When did you first notice a change in their performance?"

"About two months ago, I guess. They've been here for six months."

"Did their jobs change in any way after the first two or three months?"

She hesitated before she said, "I did give both of them a couple of special projects beyond the normal workload. Their plates were more than full by the third month."

"Do you think the additional responsibility could have anything to do with the problem?"

"Surely not. They're both so talented and ambitious. The special projects were...well, that was my way of giving them a chance to show what they could do, of giving them some exposure to a few of our key executives, puting them in the spotlight."

"Is that what they want?"

"I assume they do. They're very eager to please. At least they were."

"There's a way to find out what they want."

"How?"

"Ask them."

Silence.

"Suzanne?"

"I'm here. Good idea."

She thanked me, then met with her employees that afternoon. She called me a few days later, after the shock had worn off.

"I couldn't believe it. I met with each of them separately, but the message was the same. They felt that I had unfairly overloaded them with work. They didn't see at all what I was trying to do for them. They helped me understand, in a professional way, that they were ambitious but didn't want to achieve success at the expense of everything else in their lives."

"Now you know."

"Right. I didn't make any rash promises, though. They'll still be overworked some, just like everybody else. But I'll keep their workloads more in line with the rest of the team, I assured them of that." She paused. "You know, you can really foul things up when you give people something you *think* they want."

Suzanne had gotten overly enthusiastic in her misguided zeal to help two people. Good intentions gone awry. Not the first manager to make that mistake.

Motivation management is a tricky business, unless you go to the source and ask employees what they want.

• • •

Employees do not necessarily hide satisfaction problems, but they tend to be vague about them. There is good reason: They know exactly what is causing their dissatisfaction, they know the remedy, but they need to be *asked*. It is not the kind of information most people are comfortable volunteering to their boss, who, after all, had some hand in establishing the rejected "reward" to begin with. I have learned over the years that employees are willing to talk about these things if management asks. Most managers just never ask, and so satisfaction problems gnaw away at organization after organization. The lost performance can only be estimated, but the estimates are staggering.

The record shows that motivation management using the Belief System can help restore much of this performance.

THE BOTTOM LINE

It is not what is offered but what is believed that counts in the serious business of motivation. Certainly, people must be offered what they want, as the popular theories of motivation emphasize; but, alone, the offering is not enough. Employees must believe—in the three ways defined—that they will actually get

> **LEARNING LESSON**
>
> In the serious business of motivation, it is not what is offered but what is *believed* that counts.

what is being offered. Only then does motivation occur. That is the bottom line. Employees are not motivated when managers focus on the offering and ignore the believing.

In the Belief System approach to motivation management, three conditions must exist for people to be motivated. They must believe

1. "I can do the job." (Confidence)

2. "I will get the outcomes if I perform well." (Trust)

3. "The outcomes will be satisfying." (Satisfaction)

Confidence	Trust	Satisfaction
Effort ······> Performance ······> Outcomes ······> Satisfaction		
"I can do it."	*"Outcomes will be tied to my performance."*	*"The outcomes will be satisfying to me."*

Figure 5 CONDITIONS FOR MOTIVATION

Many managers do not realize they can take steps to elevate the motivation and performance of others. They do not realize they should. My view is that motivation management—making sure the three conditions for motivation exist for each employee—is the job of every manager. Success in motivating people to perform is greater when this view is held.

WHAT KIND OF MANAGER ARE YOU?

Typical Manager	**Motivation Manager**
Belief: Just as cream rises to the top, so do good employees.	*Belief:* Cream rises to the top when the *conditions* are right.
The Manager's Job: Let high performers emerge and carry an inordinate workload.	*The Manager's Job:* Create the *conditions for motivation* for all employees.
Result: Managerial success depends on how much cream happens to be in the mix.	*Result:* Managers have greater control over their own successes.

SOMETHING TO THINK ABOUT

One thing I have learned is that working hard is not enough—you have to work *smart*. That means you have to keep on learning. One good way to work smart is to learn something new and apply it to yourself. Start now by assessing your own motivation.

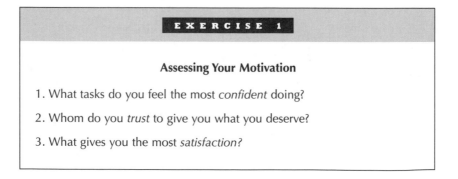

EXERCISE 1

Assessing Your Motivation

1. What tasks do you feel the most *confident* doing?

2. Whom do you *trust* to give you what you deserve?

3. What gives you the most *satisfaction*?

Your answers to these questions show you some of the strongest sources of your own motivation. It is possible to widen these sources. You have more control over these matters than you imagine. If you want to develop confidence over a broader range, find more people you can trust to give you what you deserve, and improve your overall satisfaction. Keep reading; this book will show you how.

MOVING AHEAD

By now, you may want to start thinking about how you will use the Belief System. As you realize the value it can bring, consider one of my favorite stories. It has helped me think about opportunities and how to approach them in a new way.

GLAD AND SAD

The human resources department had scheduled Warren for a management training program he did not want to attend. He thought he could get out of it. He discussed it with Trudy, his manager.

"What's the problem, Warren?"

"There's so much going on. It's hard to find the time to go to an outside training session. I just feel like what I'm doing now has more value to the company than what it will gain if I go."

"I understand what you're saying, Warren. I used to feel that way myself. I never went to training programs. I didn't read management books, either."

Warren frowned. "You're certainly not like that now. What caused you to change?"

"I heard a story."

"A story?" Warren laughed. "You changed because of a story?"

"Yes, I did. It was about a man in the desert. It took a while for the story to sink in, but when it did, I found myself on the learning side of the fence. I pick up every bit of knowledge I can now."

Warren scratched his head.

"Would you like to hear it?"

"Sure. I'd love to."

Trudy leaned back in her chair and began. "A traveler walking across the desert met a stranger who said, 'Straight ahead, over that large sand dune, is an area with many small stones. Pick up as many as you want because the winds you hear now soon will cover them. But I must warn you, if you do this, you will feel both glad and sad.'

"The traveler continued his journey and late in the day came to the flat, sandy area with the small stones. Although he was in a hurry and his mind was occupied with many things, he stopped, bent over, and picked up as many stones as were easily within his reach. Then he walked on as the wind howled and whipped the hot desert air around his body.

"Days later he remembered the stones, reached into his pocket, and pulled them out. In the brightness of the midday sun he looked at them and realized they were diamonds. Immediately, he remembered what the stranger had said, 'If you pick up the stones, you will be both glad and sad.'

"And he was. Glad he had picked up as many as he had, sad that he hadn't gotten more."

A smile came to Warren's face. "Interesting story. Do the diamonds represent…"

Trudy quickly held up her hand and stopped him. "Warren, you'll get more out of the story if you mull it over for a while. Take your time and think about it, okay?"

"Okay."

"And Warren, about that training program…"

"You've convinced me. I'll go."

• • •

CHAPTER 2

What's the Problem?

"If you want to know, ask."

A BRIEFING SESSION

Talking with the person who has a problem is the recommended way to determine what the problem is.

Three answers must be obtained (these are not the actual questions to ask):

Does the person believe effort will lead to the performance? (Confidence)

Does the person believe outcomes will be tied to performance? (Trust)

Does the person believe the outcomes will be satisfying? (Satisfaction)

Remember, the bottom line is this: To be motivated, people must have

Confidence in themselves to meet performance expectations

Trust in others to tie outcomes to their performance

Satisfaction with the outcomes they expect to receive

Motivation management using the Belief System is a simple, practical, and effective way for managers to easily identify motivation problems and to do so before they get out of hand.

THE GIFT

She took a deep breath, let it out slowly, and tried to let the tension slip away. It was 6:30 Friday night, the first time she had slowed down all day—all week, actually. She looked at her clean desk, decided to enjoy it for a minute and then go home. Jason, her youngest, would be there, his first visit since he had started law school two months ago. Then she remembered: She hadn't checked her voice mail or e-mail messages since early afternoon.

She planned to check a few of the messages and leave. Fifty minutes later she finished. She thought of Jason and felt guilty.

Still, she was glad she had plowed through all the messages. Most were customer complaints and internal problems screaming for immediate attention. The one that worried her most was the last. Her boss had filled her in on another problem with Carlos; this time he was late finishing his assignment on an interdepartmental team project.

She would deal with Carlos first thing Monday. He had once been the most dependable person reporting directly to her, but no longer was. He occupied her mind and tied her stomach into knots all the way home.

When she walked in, she gave Jason a broad but tired smile and a warm, clinging hug.

"What's the matter, Mom? You look frazzled."

"This job's making an old woman out of me. I'm not sure being a manager's worth it."

"Did something happen today?"

"Let's get dinner started. We'll talk about it later."

"Okay. I'm starving."

"You boil the shrimp and I'll make the roux. Want to watch?"

"Sure."

"The roux is the secret to shrimp creole. An iron skillet works best." She put the skillet on moderate heat, added some oil and flour, and started browning it.

They talked about school for a while. He was doing fine, studying hard, having fun.

Then he said, "You haven't answered my question."

"What question?"

"Mom!"

"Okay, okay. I have a problem employee. Carlos."

"What's he done?"

She cut a large onion and tossed it into the skillet.

"He started moping around a few weeks ago, looking unhappy and discouraged."

She took the shrimp he'd boiled and added it to the skillet.

"Anything more tangible?"

"He's turning in assignments late and the quality of his work has gone down."

"So you *have* seen something concrete." Jason had always had a knack for gently, yet effectively, pushing people and getting to the bottom of things.

Jokingly and with pride in her voice she said, "What are you, the lawyer already?"

"Just trying to help."

"You are. Those definitely are symptoms that something's wrong."

"So what's the problem?"

"I asked several people who work closely with him. No one knows."

"What do you think?"

She added the peppers and tomatoes.

"At first I thought he might be upset about money or a promotion, but it's not that. Then I thought it was the change in his responsibilities, but he's the one who wanted the change."

"Mom, is this beginning to sound familiar?"

"What do you mean?"

"Remember when I was in the seventh grade? I'd always been an A student. Then I started making B's and C's. You asked everybody what the problem was—my teacher, the counselor, the principal, even a couple of my friends. Nobody knew."

"Yes, I remember."

"Then you and Dad decided I needed glasses; then you thought it was my IQ; finally you concluded I was just lazy. Do you remember how it ended?"

"How could I forget? You told us it wasn't cool to be smart. When you were an A student, people made fun of you and you didn't like that. When you started making B's, you got your friends back."

"Mom, why didn't you ask *me* what was wrong? You asked everybody else."

"At first I didn't think to ask you. Then I was afraid to ask. Afraid of what you might say. Afraid it was my fault. Afraid I wouldn't know what to do."

"Could that be why you haven't gotten a handle on what Carlos's problem is?"

"You mean ask him?"

"Sounds like a plan to me." He leaned over the pot, "This stuff smells great; when do we eat?"

"How about now?"

As they ate, she reflected on the gift she had received, and she relaxed for the first time in days.

• • •

READING THE SIGNS AND SYMPTOMS

Motivation is the fuel, the energy, the power to perform. When managers do not see the connection between motivation and performance, they focus on performance. This is dangerous, like driving a car without a fuel gauge. If all you do is watch the road, you may run out of gas and not reach your destination. Keeping an eye on performance is not enough; managers need to monitor the gauge on employee motivation. This allows them to anticipate problems, shore them up, and stay on the road to success.

When the office computer crashes or the elevator lurches to a stop between floors 16 and 17, you are immediately notified that there is a problem. Not so with motivation. The problem may have been building for some time and may be deeply entrenched by the time it becomes obvious. Indeed, the first step in solving motivation problems is recognizing when there is a problem. Quick recognition is important. The difficulty is that managers often do not take the time to read the signs—lack of effort, lagging performance, employee dissatisfaction, tardiness, absenteeism, missed deadlines, and other rather obvious indications that something is wrong. These indicators are not the problem; they are only the symptoms.

IDENTIFYING THE PROBLEM

Symptoms tell us when something is wrong, but, unfortunately, they don't tell us *what* is wrong. That's the next step—identifying the problem. My experience has taught me that identifying motivation problems is anything but easy. The key is knowing what to look for.

The Belief System helps take the guesswork, false starts, and missed opportunities out of the search for motivation problems. Specifically, the Belief System alerts management to one or more of the three basic types of employee motivation problems:

1. *Lack of confidence*, a Belief 1 problem ("I can't meet the performance expectations.")

2. *Lack of trust*, a Belief 2 problem ("The outcomes will not be tied to my performance.")

3. *Lack of satisfaction*, a Belief 3 problem ("The outcomes offered will not be satisfying to me.")

Confidence	Trust	Satisfaction
Effort ·····> Performance ·····> Outcomes ·····> Satisfaction		
Lack of Confidence *"I can't meet the performance expectations."*	**Lack of Trust** *"The outcomes will not be tied to my performance."*	**Lack of Satisfaction** *"The outcomes offered will not be satisfying to me."*

Figure 6 TYPES OF MOTIVATION PROBLEMS

Managers who use the Belief System often are surprised to learn that many of their employees have a *confidence problem*. "I didn't realize how many of my people were unmotivated because they didn't believe they could do what was expected," noted one senior executive of a large service company. "Some people weren't clear about what to do; others simply were not sure how to get it done. My mistake was I assumed they could do it. I thought because they were bright and had good work histories they would naturally be motivated. I was wrong."

The pervasiveness of confidence problems stems largely from three conditions that are prevalent in the corporate environment today: (1) *Downsizing* results in altered and expanded job responsibilities with little training provided to prepare employees for their new roles. (2) The *rapid pace of change* makes it difficult for employees to keep up with new technology and new ways of doing their jobs. (3) *Intense competition* has caused companies to raise the bar on individual performance without adequately preparing employees to meet the new standards.

The *trust problem* also is widespread. Repeatedly, I see managers telling employees that if they do well they will be rewarded, but the rewards often do not come. Whatever the reasons for this, it is my experience that when commitments become hollow promises, a general lack of trust develops. This is a quick way to destroy an organization.

THE EASY WAY OUT

A participant in one of my training sessions had the group nodding in agreement when she shared her observations about trust problems. "In spite of all the talk about giving employees what they deserve, many companies simply can't overcome a long-standing culture to the contrary. They continue to take the easy way out and treat people basically the same no matter what their performance. Women continue to be paid less for the same performance as men. Strict seniority systems in business, education, and government prevent organizations from tying outcomes to performance."

• • •

Another twist on the trust problem is readily apparent in public reaction to media reports about the earnings of senior executives in major corporations. Survey after survey shows that employees do not think the disparity in income levels between "them and us" is justified. "Performance does not warrant the outcomes enjoyed by senior executives" is the message.

OPTIONS OF DISTRUST

With anger in his voice, Robert, a high-level manager not eligible for stock options, told me, "While companies are downsizing and pinching pennies with everyone on the payroll, executives and directors are getting rich."

He showed me a newspaper article about a vice president of human resources who had amassed nearly $24 million in stock in his company since 1990. His latest addition was in mid-1998, when he exercised an option to buy shares totaling $58,017, which immediately were worth $868,644.

As I finished reading it, Robert said, "Look at this!" and shoved another newspaper clipping in front of me. A person who became a director in a company in 1997 exercised an option in 1998 to buy shares totaling $1,869,331 and sold them immediately for $2,845,353. Another who became a director in 1996 exercised an option in 1998 to buy shares totaling $163,840, and then sold them right away for $1,718,323.

When I looked up, Robert said, "It's not illegal for executives and directors to make money exercising stock options, but it does send a message. Management is letting these guys get rich quick and holding salaries down on the rest of us. Employees don't trust management anymore. People aren't getting what they deserve."

· · ·

The prevalence of *satisfaction problems* comes as a surprise to many first-time users of the Belief System. It is no surprise to me. I see it frequently in the best and the worst of organizations. One manager recently trained in the use of the Belief System noticed it, too. "Once I started focusing on the individuality of my employees, I was shocked to find how diverse they are in terms of what motivates them. I'd been working hard to treat everybody the same. All I did was create a lot of dissatisfaction. It was a huge mistake to assume the *same* incentives would have the *same* impact on everybody. I really felt foolish when I realized I had been causing so many problems. Makes you wonder how many other managers out there are making the same mistake."

A friend told me he had been doing this for years until his wife helped him "see the light." "She taught me that what is satisfying to one may be a curse to another. I love red beans and rice, creole-style…love the smell of them cooking. My wife likes them, too, but can't stand the smell in the house. 'Permeates the upholstery,' she says."

> **LEARNING LESSON**
> Motivation problems are everywhere—some obvious, some *sitting in silence.*

GETTING TO THE PROBLEM

So now you know what to look for: confidence, trust, and satisfaction problems. But *how* do you find them? Keeping your eyes open is not enough. You cannot be everywhere at once and see everything.

There is one best answer to the question of how to identify motivation problems: Go to the source, to the one with the problem—the employee. Simply put, *if you want to know what the problem is, ask the person who has the problem.* After more than 30 years of experience in working with managers, I remain intrigued by the unwillingness of managers to simply ask employees what is behind rather conspicuous motivation problems. Perhaps part of the answer lies in this response from the general manager of a large TV station: "I don't ask because I'm afraid I'll find out! And then I'll have to deal with it."

> **GETTING STARTED**
>
> If you want to know what the problem is, go to the person with the problem and ask.

Most people are glad to tell you what the problem is, especially when they believe you want to help. All you have to do is get the answers to a few thoughtful questions.

Managers must look for the answers to three core questions, each one a derivation of the confidence, trust, or satisfaction problem. How the questions are worded can vary, but the objective remains the same: to get specific, truthful answers to these questions.

1. Does the person believe his or her effort will lead to the expected performance? (Confidence)

2. Does the person believe the outcomes will be tied to his or her performance? (Trust)

3. Does the person believe the outcomes will be satisfying? (Satisfaction)

Confidence	Trust	Satisfaction
Effort ······> Performance ······> Outcomes ······> Satisfaction		
"Does the person believe his or her effort will lead to performance?"	*"Does the person believe the outcomes will be tied to performance?"*	*"Does the person believe the outcomes will be satisfying?"*

Figure 7 CORE QUESTIONS TO BE ANSWERED

WOULD YOU TELL HIM?

I was working with Gorham, a manager who wanted his team members to perform better. He wanted them to speak up, get more involved, and contribute more. He asked me to help.

Gorham suggested I start by talking to Michaela, a soft-spoken but very direct member of the team. I did. She had several legitimate concerns.

"Have you mentioned these to Gorham?"

"No."

"Would you tell him if he asked?"

"No."

"Why?"

"It wouldn't do any good; might even do harm."

• • •

This is a common response, and it is a problem—a serious one—if managers want to get to the root of problems their employees face.

Getting to the answers is a two-step process. First, you have to prepare employees to talk—help them feel confident that it is okay to give honest answers, that they will not get fired or suffer by communicating openly. Second, you must ask employees the right questions that will extract the truth.

Step 1: Prepare People to Talk

What can managers do to get reluctant employees to talk? It helps to keep in mind that employees want solutions to the problems they face. They want help, but they want it to be *safe* help.

My experience with the Belief System is that managers get a positive response when they turn to employees and convey a simple message: "I want to help, but you have to help me help you."

SAMPLE SCRIPT

Preparing People to Talk

Manager: I know you're facing some tough issues. I'd like to help and I believe that I can, but I can't do it alone. You'll have to talk to me. I'll keep whatever you say confidential and will use it only to help you. Will you *help me help you*?

Step 2: Ask the Right Questions

Managers have questions. Employees have answers. Remember, some questions beg for an answer; some answers beg for a question. Employees are waiting for you to ask.

Getting honest answers is a product of asking the right questions in the right way. It is true in the Belief System, true wherever truth is sought. Here are some questions that get to the truth of the matter with motivation and performance problems.

For answers to the confidence (Belief 1) question, managers might ask these questions:

"Do you know what is expected?"

"Do you think what's expected is attainable?"

"Can you do what is being asked of you?"

"Can you finish the work on time?"

"Do you see any problem in doing what you're being asked to do?"

Answers to the trust (Belief 2) question can come from queries such as these:

"What is being offered for good performance?"

"In your opinion, have we come through on our promises in the past?"

"Do you expect to get what is being offered?"

"What do you expect to get if you do a good job?"

"What do you expect to happen if you perform poorly?"

For answers to the satisfaction (Belief 3) question, these questions work well:

"What would be satisfying to you?"

"Is the work meaningful to you?"

"Is there anything you don't want?"

"Do you want the things being offered?"

"Do you want something that is not being offered?"

Keep in mind that the right question asked at the wrong time will not produce the desired results. Questions must be asked in the context of the situation at hand. How, then, do you decide which questions to use? One guideline is especially helpful: Select questions in relation to employee actions and words. That is, ask questions based on what employees are *saying* and *doing*. Here are some examples.

You noticed an employee was delaying the start of a new assignment; or he started the assignment but put off finishing it. Procrastination often signals a confidence (Belief 1) problem. This is not a time for managers to yell and scream or put pressure on the employee to "get with it." Instead, recognize that procrastination contains a message. Zero in on the situation. Find out what is happening. How? Ask. Give employees an easy opportunity to reveal confidence problems. How do you decide what to ask? In this case, form a question based on what you have *observed*—the procrastination, the fact that the employee is delaying, that there has been little progress. You might say, "I was wondering about the new project— how's it going?" or "I've noticed you haven't been spending a lot of time on the new project; is there anything I can do to help?" or "I'm not sure where you are on the new project, but I was wondering, do you have any questions?" Here is a second guideline: Avoid questions that might cause employees to get defensive, and instead ask questions that encourage them to speak freely.

Okay, you asked a good question and the employee's response was, "I guess I'm not quite sure how to get started on it." Bingo. That sounds like a confidence problem. To find out for sure, ask another question. How do you decide what to ask this time? Structure a question that is related to what the employee just *said,* such as, "What do you mean, 'not quite sure'?" or "Did I confuse you about what to do?" or "Have you ever done that before?" Listen to what employees are saying and ask questions that are prompted by the words they are using. This employee likely will confirm, "I can't do it."

What if the employee were to respond differently? What if he said, "It's not that I need any help. I'm just having trouble getting started on it, I guess"? Ah, now this does not have the ring of a confidence problem. Procrastination may also signal a satisfaction (Belief 3) problem. The employee may not be delaying because he *can't* do the work; instead, it may be because he *dislikes* the work. Does this employee have a satisfaction problem or not? If you want to know, ask. Come up with a question based on what the employee has said, such as, "What do you mean, 'having trouble getting started'?" or "If you don't need any help, then what's the problem?" or "Is something going on that I need to know about?"

Remember, the employee responded to an earlier question. The goal now is to keep him talking. If you do, you *will* find out what the problem is. The employee may respond to your question with, "I never have liked dealing with customer complaints. Unhappy customers are too contentious, and I hate conflict." Now you know. The employee has a satisfaction problem.

Consider another situation in which questions might be formed to match employee actions and words. A manager realizes an employee's motivation and performance need a boost. At the employee's request, the manager agrees that if she improves performance and sustains it for three months, he will take away some of her boring, routine work and replace it with assignments that are creative and challenging. This is very motivating to her and she quickly steps up her performance and maintains it at a high level—for four months. Then her enthusiasm declines. Her manager notices the change and wonders what the problem is. He decides to talk with her and forms several possible questions based on what he has seen—a lack of enthusiasm. "I've noticed that your enthusiasm has dropped off. Is anything wrong?" "I was wondering, how do you feel about your job now?" "You seem concerned about something, are you okay?"

Suppose she were to respond with, "It's just not fair. I worked hard, got my performance up, and kept it there." The manager might ask, "What do you mean by, 'It's not fair'?" or "You seem upset, what's wrong?" "You've been doing a great job—what's the problem?" All of these questions flow naturally and logically from her comment. Any one of them is sure to keep the employee talking and the manager is certain to find out what the problem is. A likely employee response would be, "You didn't replace any of my routine work with challenging assignments like you promised. You never even said anything." The manager had forgotten his promise. The employee has a trust problem. The manager can do something about it now. Why? Because he knows what the problem is. He knows because he went to the employee, asked good questions, and listened.

When asking questions, keep in mind the following: No matter how good your questions may be, being sincere when asking them is essential. If people think you are asking without caring, they will not give much back. People simply are unwilling to respond openly and honestly when they detect insincerity.

Identifying the Problem

1. Think of someone in your personal life who is not motivated to do something he or she would like to do.

2. Structure one *confidence* question, one *trust* question, and one *satisfaction* question you could use with this person.

3. Start the process of finding out what the problem is by asking these questions.

RESPONSES TO EXPECT

The examples above give a clue as to what managers may hear in response to Belief System questions. Responses revolve around confidence, trust, and satisfaction issues and vary depending on the employee's motivation.

For any of the *confidence* questions, a confident person might respond with, "No problem. That's a piece of cake." Clearly, the person is saying, "I can do it." Confidence does not appear to be a problem.

But the answer may well be different: "I think I can do it. If everything goes well, I'll probably be able to...I guess." Uncertainty comes through in this response. The employee has doubts about being able to meet performance expectations. This is a potential problem.

A person who lacks confidence might say, "You've got to be kidding. I can't do that, no way." Here, there is a problem, a confidence problem. "I can't do it" comes through loud and clear. People who believe that they cannot meet performance expectations are hamstrung and so is the organization that employs them. The confidence problem may easily be solved, but until it is, motivation and performance suffer.

To the *trust* questions, people may respond in this way: "You can count on what's said here. Produce and you'll be well rewarded; fail to perform and you're out the door." These are people who believe that "Outcomes are tied to performance." No reason to believe that a lack of trust exists in such cases.

To the same questions, respondents might also say, "Sometimes it's hard to figure out what management is thinking. The reward system isn't consistent. Sometimes people get what they deserve, sometimes they don't." The trust level is weak here. This is a potential problem.

"Work hard, work smart, or goof off and talk the day away—it's all the same here. Nobody seems to care." What is expressed is plain: "Outcomes are not tied to performance." A trust problem is at work. Believing that outcomes will not be tied to performance holds people back and dampens motivation and performance. This is not a problem to be taken lightly.

Satisfaction questions could yield a response along these lines: "You do that for me, and I'll give this company my first-born child." Would you guess this employee believes that "The outcome will be satisfying?" No reason to believe otherwise.

But not so with this: "Would I support a golfing weekend as a reward to our team's success? It might be great for some of the guys, but I'm basically indifferent about it. I can take it or leave it." It is a potential satisfaction problem if employees view too many "rewards" this way.

A dissatisfied employee might say, "That's no reward for me because I don't want more responsibility." No guesswork in this instance: The outcome will not be satisfying. A satisfaction problem is indicated. It can weigh as heavily on employee motivation and performance as the other two problems.

Employee responses will not always be demonstrative and unmistakable, but the truth will be clear enough to the careful listener. It is in the manager's best interest to listen well and ferret out the truth. More on *how* to do this later.

WHEN RESPONSES SOUND LIKE COMPLAINTS

A word of caution is in order for managers when employees begin to respond earnestly to the kinds of questions prescribed here. Managers who do not have the high ground of motivation management and the Belief System from which to see could easily view the feedback as complaints and the respondents as complainers. This would be unfortunate because a litany of negative consequences could result. Valuable employees might be labeled as "complainers." What they say or do from then on might be discounted. They might be avoided thereafter (managers do not like to be around complainers any more than anyone else does). Less communication with these employees could occur in the future. These employees could be expected to get upset with the "distancing" of their manager. Then relations between employees and manager would surely deteriorate. Job satisfaction for both parties would go down. And so on, and so on.

TAKE THIS JOB AND...

Monty, a talented manager, got a new boss, Rick. When Rick came on board, Monty was putting the finishing touches on an aggressive, skillfully engineered turnaround of an organization that had been in deep trouble two years earlier. Monty was outspoken and confident. He had a knack for spotting motivation and performance problems across the larger organization before they became visible and damaging. He was focused on solving problems and getting results.

Rick saw Monty as arrogant, harsh, and critical. He could not see beyond Monty's personality and his direct, matter-of-fact way of communicating. Consequently, he never heard the nuggets of insight Monty offered. Soon Rick stopped listening to Monty altogether. He periodically accused Monty of having a bad attitude and not being a team player. Their working relationship deteriorated.

Monty had other job opportunities, and he decided to take one. He left singing Johnny Paycheck's famous song, "Take This Job and Shove It." Rick was removed from his position four months later.

• • •

Managers will want to be careful listeners and interpreters when employees respond openly. Put employees at ease. Sift through complaints and find the truth hidden beneath. Use the information wisely. Get employee problems on the table and work hand-in-hand to solve them. Show employees that being candid is in their best interest.

Managers operating under the tenets of the Belief System see things differently. Employee feedback, openly and honestly solicited and forthrightly given, is seen for what it is: an unparalleled

35

WHAT KIND OF MANAGER ARE YOU?

Typical Manager If employees don't have anything positive to say, I don't want to hear it.

Motivation Manager Employees are my best source of information, so I listen.

---

opportunity to set things right in the workforce. Comments that previously would have been viewed as indications of a bad attitude, resistance, or insubordination are viewed instead as valuable information, the vital ingredient in a plan of action that can correct motivation and performance problems before they drag down an organization. For these managers, it is not complaining for an employee to say, "You never get what you deserve around here," or "I don't like that part of my job"; there is no reason to doubt the capabilities of a person who says, "I don't know if I can do that or not."

With these answers, employees indicate problems on the job, and they are asking for help in solving them. Seen this way, managers should

- Listen carefully
- Ask more questions to better understand
- Determine what is wrong
- Seek employee solutions
- Thank employees for being open and honest
- Fix problems
- Watch happy employees work harder and perform better

RESPONSES IN COMBINATION

Sometimes the identity of a motivation problem is easier to determine when the results of trust (Belief 2) and satisfaction (Belief 3) questions are combined. For example, if a person says, "I'll get a raise if I perform well (trust), and I can sure use the extra money (satisfaction)," there is not a trust or satisfaction problem. On the other hand, the following response indicates a problem: "I'll get an all-e> ⁙e if I perform well (trust), but I get seasick stand-

ir ⁙ssatisfaction)." There is a satisfaction problem at

w

⁙G IS A PAINFUL WASTE OF TIME

I ⁙ the grounds of a conference center in central Florida with a longtime friend from my academic days. The sky was blue and a cool breeze tempered the warm morning sun. We were eagerly waiting for participants to arrive for our one-day management training program.

The first person parked, got out of her car, and walked briskly in our direction across thick grass growing in the gray sand. She was not smiling.

"Good morning," we said enthusiastically.

She looked straight ahead and walked by us. "That remains to be seen."

All 30 participants soon arrived. They did not smile. They did not speak. They did not even look at us.

We started the session. "Usually, we begin by saying 'good morning,' but today 'morning' seems more appropriate. **What's the problem?**"

No one spoke. I heard the breeze rustling through the palm trees. I heard myself breathing. I heard my heart beating.

Eventually, someone spoke. "We expect this to be a painful waste of time." Others nodded agreement.

"What's the solution? What can we do to make the day worthwhile?"

"Teach us something we can use."

"What are the biggest management issues you're facing now?"

The room buzzed. They told us their concerns. We called a break.

Their input was helpful. Although we had interviewed many of these managers as part of our preparation and already knew most of the problems they faced, we had not realized how big their problems were, nor how painful.

We made some needed adjustments and proposed a plan. "We recommend building the day around how to handle your five most pressing concerns." After mapping out the approach, we said, "If you like it, we'll do it. If you don't, we'll change it."

They liked it. We did it. They thanked us, sincerely. They had learned something they could use. So had we.

• • •

Any time people are asked to behave in a certain way (like happily attending a training program) and they expect an outcome they do not want (such as wasted time "because I will not learn anything of value"), you can expect motivation to take a downturn.

When a person thinks, "I won't get selected for the special projects team even if I perform well (lack of trust); but who cares, I want to avoid the extra hours and pressure anyway when I come back from maternity leave (satisfaction)," there is *not* a problem. People are thankful when unwanted outcomes are not tied to performance.

There is a problem, however, when someone concludes, "I don't believe I'll get the promotion I deserve (lack of trust), and I really want the chance to move up in the organization, have more responsibility, and make more money (satisfaction)." A trust problem is the culprit.

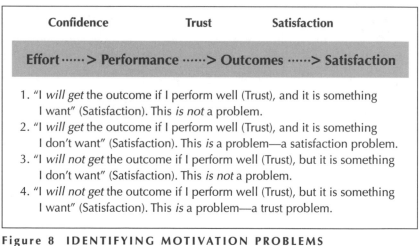

**Figure 8 IDENTIFYING MOTIVATION PROBLEMS
BY COMBINING TRUST (BELIEF 2)
AND SATISFACTION (BELIEF 3) QUESTIONS**

THE WASHING MACHINE

A college basketball coach who had just led his team to a national championship was having trouble recruiting one of the most sought-after high school players in the country. He drove his new luxury car to visit with David one last time. The final leg of the trip was a steep dirt road filled with sharp turns, potholes, and boulders. The shack David and his family called home was at the end of the road.

While he talked with David, the coach noticed a manual washing machine sitting beside them on the front porch. The coach smiled. "David, if you'll come play basketball for me, I'll buy your mama a new electric washing machine."

The coach was more than surprised when David did not respond.

Finally the coach gave up and got up to leave. Standing at the car door, one foot already inside, he said, "David, **is there anything I can do** to persuade you to play basketball for me?"

"Yes, sir. You could get us some electricity up here for that new washing machine."

• • •

INTERPRETING RESPONSES

Once a middle-aged father and corporate executive asked his teenage daughter for an opinion on a young man she knew. "Oh, he's bad, Dad; I mean, we're talking bad!" Whereupon the no-nonsense father struck the young man's name from the company's summer intern roll. Despite the chagrined daughter's subsequent protestations that bad is not bad, but *good,* there was no job to be had that summer for the bad (good) young man. The point? Make sure that what you hear is the message that is being conveyed. Remember, you, the manager, are trying to identify motivation and performance problems. Asking the right questions is crucial, but misinterpreting the answers will send you off in the wrong direction and doom your efforts.

Experience has taught me that the best way to avoid "missing the point" is to log employee responses onto simple rating scales. Precision is not a factor when using the scales. Thoughtful "guesstimates" work just fine. If you can rate a person's beliefs (confidence, trust, satisfaction), there is good reason to believe that you have learned what the person really believes. If you cannot with reasonable confidence rate the person's beliefs, you need more information. Using the rating scales helps you *know what you know.*

The confidence (Belief 1) rating scale has a range of 0 to 10. Zero represents the "I *cannot* perform as expected" belief. A rating of 10 indicates the expression that "I *can* perform as expected."

Can I Perform as Expected?

1	2	3	4	5	6	7	8	9	10

I *cannot* perform   Not sure   I *can* perform
as expected   as expected

Figure 9 CONFIDENCE (BELIEF 1) RATING SCALE

A similar scale is used for trust (Belief 2). The "I *will not* get outcomes based on my performance" belief is represented by a 0; the other end of the scale, a 10, indicates, "I *will* get outcomes based on performance."

Will the Outcomes Be Tied to My Performance?

1	2	3	4	5	6	7	8	9	10

Outcomes *will not* be   Not sure   Outcomes *will* be
tied to my performance   tied to my performance

Figure 10 TRUST (BELIEF 2) RATING SCALE

The satisfaction (Belief 3) rating scale differs from the previous two. It reflects the degree of satisfaction *or* dissatisfaction with an outcome or combination of outcomes. The satisfaction scale ranges from −10, the highest *dissatisfaction* rating, to +10, the highest *satisfaction* rating.

Will the Outcomes Be Satisfying to Me?

-10 -9 -8 -7 -6 -5 -4 -3 -2 -1 0 +1 +2 +3 +4 +5 +6 +7 +8 +9 +10

Outcomes will be   Not sure   Outcomes will be
dissatisfying to me   *satisfying* to me

Figure 11 SATISFACTION (BELIEF 3) RATING SCALE

Here, then, is how a manager might interpret confidence, trust, and satisfaction comments from employees.

1	2	3	4	5	6	7	8	9	10

I *cannot* perform as expected	Not sure	I *can* perform as expected
"I can't do it." "There's no way." "It's impossible." "I don't know how." "I haven't any idea what's expected of me."	"I'm not sure I can do it." "I might be able to." "Maybe I can." "The odds are even." "I'm not sure what's expected of me."	"I can do it." "No problem." "That's easy." "No sweat." "I know exactly what's expected of me."

Figure 12 INTERPRETING CONFIDENCE (BELIEF 1) STATEMENTS

1	2	3	4	5	6	7	8	9	10

Outcomes *will not* be tied to my performance	Not sure	Outcomes *will* be tied to my performance
"What you get is not based on how well you perform." "Everybody is treated the same no matter what knd of a job you do." "You never get what you deserve here." "Outcomes are never tied to performance."	"There is a 50-50 chance to get what you deserve if you do a good job." "Sometimes outcomes are tied to perfor- mance, sometimes they are not." "Wouldn't be surprised either way." "May get it. May not. You never know."	"If you do a good job, you can count on being rewarded." "If you perform well, they will take care of you." "You always get what you deserve here." "Outcomes are tied to performance."

Figure 13 INTERPRETING TRUST (BELIEF 2) STATEMENTS

-10 -9 -8 -7 -6 -5 -4 -3 -2 -1 0 +1 +2 +3 +4 +5 +6 +7 +8 +9 +10

Outcomes will be *dissatisfying* to me	Not sure	Outcomes will be *satisfying* to me
"I would hate that."	"Can take it or leave it."	"I would love it."
"Couldn't live with it."	"Either way is fine."	"I'd kill for it."
"That's the worst thing that could happen."	"It doesn't matter one way or the other."	"I want it more than anything."

Figure 14 INTERPRETING SATISFACTION (BELIEF 3) STATEMENTS

Okay, you have completed your ratings; now what are you looking at? How does this help you sort out motivation problems? The first step is to apply the following rules of thumb to the scale.

Rule of Thumb 1   If a rating is in the upper third of the rating scale, there is no problem.

Rule of Thumb 2   If a rating is in the middle third of the scale, there is a potential problem.

Rule of Thumb 3   If a rating is in the lower third of the scale, there definitely is a problem.

SAMPLE SCRIPT

Using Rating Scales and Rules of Thumb

Manager: You don't seem to be spending as much time learning the new computer software as you were last week. **Is everything okay?**

Employee: Well, . . . I, ah . . . nothing's wrong . . . it's not, really.

Manager: It's okay if it is. You can tell me. **What's the problem?**

Employee: Well, it's just so hard, especially trying to learn it without any help.

Manager: **On a scale of zero to ten**, with ten being "I can learn it on my own" and zero being "I'll never get it by myself," **how would you rate yourself?**

Employee: A big fat zero. I'm ready to give up.

Manager: I'd say that's a problem. Want to talk about it and see if we can figure out a way to turn things around?

Employee: Sure, if you think there's hope.

Here are some other examples. Suppose you were to interview a job applicant employing the Belief System of questioning and the rating scales for confidence, trust, and satisfaction. After a careful interview process, you conclude that the person's beliefs about the job available would be accurately stated by assigning a rating of 5 to confidence, a 9 to trust, and a +8 to satisfaction. The appropriate interpretation is that the person is not particularly confident about being able to do the job (confidence = 5). There is a potential motivation and performance problem here. The applicant is nearly certain of "getting the outcomes" if performance is good (trust = 9) and believes the "outcomes will be satisfying" (satisfaction = +8). Based on this, you would not expect this person to have a trust or satisfaction problem.

How about a top performer whose work has fallen off recently? After talking with this person and asking a few questions, you rate her at 9 for confidence, 10 for trust, and −8 for satisfaction. What do you conclude? The person believes "I can perform as expected" (confidence = 9), so there is not a confidence problem. The person is certain that outcomes will be based on performance (trust = 10), but the outcomes are viewed as very dissatisfying (satisfaction = -8). The person has a motivation problem, and you know what it is!

It may be that you have gathered all the information necessary to recognize a problem, but you still do not see it; the information is in hand, you just don't know you have it. Rating an employee's "three beliefs" is an excellent device that enables managers to determine whether they have learned all that they need to know. Furthermore, the rating scales bring out the full meaning of what you have learned. For example, a manager I know noticed that a new employee was having a little trouble catching on to some technical requirements of his job (confidence). The problem was not unusual and the manager, busy traveling, gave it no further thought. A couple of weeks later, the employee expressed dissatisfaction with how things were going with the job (satisfaction). Nothing else was said, and there ~~~ ~~~ ~~~ ~~~ ~~~ ~~~ lem for a time. Then the perso~~~ ~~~ ~~~ ~~~ ~~~ pset about the com-

~~~ at it all on the rating ~~~ ~~~ ~~~. The employee's confidence is ~~~ ~~~ ~~~ you do not know enough to rate it. Trust ~~~ pay ~~~ ~~~ ugh she did not say why. Satisfaction is negative, again for rea~~~ us that are not exactly clear. This information viewed in isolation does not suggest anything particularly troublesome, but when observed in sum it is clear that motivation is an issue with this employee. She is experiencing all three belief problems.

SOMETHING TO PRACTICE

During my years as a college professor I learned that there's a big difference between understanding something conceptually and feeling comfortable *using* it. This holds for most people when it comes to the rating scales. Exercise 3 gives you an opportunity to practice using each of the three scales and at the same time check your motivation to use the Belief System.

There is a pattern in the results I generally see when people complete this self-rating exercise. Confidence ratings usually fall in the 5-to-7 range—fairly confident, but still a little shaky on diagnosing motivation problems. This improves quickly with practice, if things hold true to form. Trust ratings tend to be very high—8 to 10. Most people believe that certain outcomes do spring from the ability to diagnose motivation problems. Satisfaction ratings normally range from 8 to 10, indicating that people believe the outcomes to be gained from using the Belief System will be very satisfying.

THE POSITIVE SIDE OF SELF-DOUBT

Although a moderate confidence level (in the middle third of the rating scale) typically signals a potential problem, it can also be highly motivating to individuals who like a big challenge or view proving "I can do it" as important to their self-esteem. Communication will tell you who these people are.

EXERCISE 3

Rating Confidence, Trust, and Satisfaction Levels

1. What is your *confidence* level for accurately diagnosing motivation
   problems using the Belief system? That is, can you do it?

1	2	3	4	5	6	7	8	9	10

I *cannot* perform   Not sure   I *can* perform
as expected   as expected

2. Do you believe that certain outcomes will be tied to your performance ? In other words, what is your *trust* level*?*

1	2	3	4	5	6	7	8	9	10

Outcomes *will not* be   Not sure   Outcomes *will* be
tied to my performance   tied to my performance

3. Will the outcomes be *satisfying* to you?

-10 -9 -8 -7 -6 -5 -4 -3 -2 -1 0 +1 +2 +3 +4 +5 +6 +7 +8 +9 +10

Outcomes will be   Not sure   Outcomes will be
dissatisfying to me   *satisfying* to me

MOTIVATION FROM UNLIKELY PLACES

Mary graduated from an Ivy League school with a 3.8 grade point average, and she was a good performer at work. When I asked for her secret,
she said, "The thing that motivates me most every day when I come to
work is proving to myself that I'm not stupid."

Pat, a high-performing sales manager, led a team that year after year
ranked at the top in an organization with more than 140 sales teams.
"I come to the office every day worrying that I won't be able to do it
again. That not only torments me, it motivates me, like gasoline fueling a
fire."

Linda looked at me, then at her manager, and said with a quivering
voice and tears in her eyes, "My mother and stepfather told me every day

when I was growing up that I'd never be successful. That hurt and I still doubt myself." Then she stopped crying, gritted her teeth, and said, "The thing that motivates me most is proving them wrong."

• • •

SIMPLICITY AND DEPTH

The Belief System of Motivation and Performance gives you the capacity to discern the true nature of almost any situation, and as you use it you will discover its many layers of insight.

MORE THAN YOU IMAGINE

I enjoy watching clients who have been introduced to the Belief System try it out with their own team for the first time. I sometimes learn unexpected things as I watch them teach what they have been taught.

Stacy had brought her team together for a motivation management seminar to introduce them to the Belief System. Midway through the seminar, one of her employees praised the Belief System as "great stuff because it's so simple." I cringed. My first reaction was to clarify the point, but this was not my show. I waited, and like a pro, Stacy, a Belief System graduate, came through.

"Great, yes. Simple, I'm not so sure. Let me tell you about an experience I had. I thought I knew baseball—after all, I had two brothers. They let me play in pickup games in the yard with them. And I attended their youth league and high school games for years.

"I was excited when my nine-year-old son, Joe, started playing in the Little League. By the time he was 12, I was frustrated. I couldn't follow the baseball conversations between Joe and my husband, Tom, anymore. And things happened in Joe's games that I didn't understand.

"I decided to dig in and learn. I read every book I could find on baseball history, strategy, and technique. Then I took a bold step. I started going to coaching clinics with the local high school baseball coach.

"It took me two years, but I know baseball now. It's wonderful. Watching Joe play is more fun than ever. He and Tom consider me an equal partner in their baseball conversations. And sometimes Joe even asks me for advice!

"The Belief System is like baseball. It's simple, yet there's much more to it than you imagine at first."

Everyone in the group nodded understanding.

Stacy looked pleased. I certainly was. Great story, good point. If you learn more about the Belief System, you will discover its depth and richness.

• • •

MOVING AHEAD

Motivation management is managing in a way that creates confidence, trust, and satisfaction—the conditions required for motivation. Using the Belief System approach outlined in this chapter to identify motivation problems is an excellent starting point for creating the three conditions for motivation.

As you move ahead in the direction of motivation management, here is a story with a familiar theme. It caused me to step back and reflect on some of my own tendencies.

HARD TO ADMIT

The management style William had successfully used to climb the corporate ladder was no longer working. He was having trouble deciding what to do. He needed to make a decision soon.

William had been with the company for 20 years. He had always performed well and he was proud of his success. This was the first time he had stood on the edge of failure. William looked to me for an answer.

I would not give him one. People have to come to their own conclusions on matters like this. I would try to help him find an answer.

"William, what do you think you should do?"

"I don't know, but I have to do something. We didn't meet our two most important goals last year—revenue growth and profit. My department heads aren't pushing; they aren't performing up to their potential."

"What will happen if you fail to meet your goals again this year?"

"They'll fire me, or shuffle me off into some meaningless job."

"That's a lot of pressure."

William gave a forced laugh. "That's an understatement."

"Do you think you can turn things around?"

"I honestly don't know. I want to, but....That's a good question."

"Well, let's see. What do you think the problem is?"

William sighed. "Okay, here's the way I see it. I have five department heads and they're all as different as day and night. One wants more freedom and independence to do her job. One comes to me with issues he should handle himself. Another needs my constant support and encouragement. Another is a perfectionist who drives me and everybody else crazy. And one is very creative but has trouble implementing his ideas."

"So what's the problem?"

"I like uniformity. I like for everybody to accept his or her goals and have a written plan for achieving them. Plan and execute. If plans change, I want to know—in advance. I like to stay on top of things. I have team meetings every Monday to check results so I can be sure we're on target. The problem is that my department heads don't like any of this. They complain about their goals, they resist having written plans, and they hate the weekly meetings. I don't see how I can manage if I don't have goals and plans and controls."

"Sounds like all five of them want you to use a different approach."

"I guess so, but I just wish they'd adjust to my approach and give it a chance. I keep hoping they'll change."

"How realistic is that—that all of them will change?"

William bounced a pencil eraser on his desk. He looked tired. "Wishful thinking, isn't it?"

"Is there another option?"

"What do you mean?"

"You've said one option is for them to adjust to you. Is there another alternative?"

"Like what?"

"That's what I'm asking you."

"You think I should adjust to them?"

I laughed. "What do you think? Should you?"

He walked to his office window. There was a long silence. Finally, he spoke softly. "It's hard to admit that what you're doing isn't working."

I nodded. "Yes it is."

"Maybe I should fine-tune what I'm doing, make it work better."

"Doing the same thing, only better, can work...sometimes."

"Can? What about in my case?"

"You're in a better position to answer that. What do you think?"

"That's what I've been trying to do for the last six months."

"Is it working? Are people responding better, performing better?"

"No. If anything, it's gotten worse. I guess I've taken my approach as far as I can."

"So what should you do?"

William's face flushed and he raised his voice: "I don't know." He closed his eyes and rubbed his forehead. He stood, paced behind his desk, and finally took his seat again. "I guess I've known all along. You can't keep doing the same thing and expect to get different results. I have to change."

"William, I'm wondering if that's really an option for you."

"I don't have a choice. I just hope it isn't too late."

William and I met several more times. He developed a plan. He would schedule an individual discussion with each of his department heads to determine what he could do to unleash their motivation and clear the path for them to reach their goals.

Within three months a turnaround was evident. When the year ended, every department head had exceeded his or her goals. The plan had worked!

William had changed. His department heads had changed. But one thing had remained unchanged—the principle, "If what you're doing isn't working, do something different."

• • •

CHAPTER 3

Uncovering Causes
Can Be Tricky

"Being certain doesn't mean you're right."

A BRIEFING SESSION

A common mistake when dealing with motivation problems is to quickly jump ahead to solutions without knowing what is causing the problem. This does not lead to *workable* solutions.

Motivation problems have specific, identifiable causes. Find out what they are if you want to solve the problem.

The best way to identify causes is to ask the person experiencing the problem.

Motivation management using the Belief System is a rock-solid way for managers to quickly and accurately uncover true causes of employee motivation problems.

THE MANAGER WHO KNEW TOO MUCH

The walls in his new office were paper thin. Even hushed voices in the adjacent offices were easy to hear, if you listened, and Ray Boulder was listening—hard. He felt uneasy, but he listened anyway.

He recognized Susan Kronkite's voice. She was his most loyal employee. She was talking with some man. Ray pushed his chair away from the desk, noticed that Linda, his assistant, had finished installing new computer software that he would never use, and put an ear close to the wall.

"What a jerk. Doesn't he know anything about managing?" Ray knew instantly it was Derek Johnson speaking.

Derek was the new hotshot MBA Ray's boss had pressured him into hiring.

"The problem is that his management style hasn't changed with the times. His career has stalled because of it."

Ray knew his career had stalled, but it was temporary. That was the reason he had decided to push everybody hard on the new project. It was his opportunity.

"Susan, what's the main thing I need to watch for?"

"Whatever you do, don't take problems to him."

"What does he do, beat you up instead of help?"

Ray smiled. He never beat his people up, unless they really deserved it.

"He tries to help, but his way of helping makes it worse."

"So, what does he do?"

"He takes the problem away from you, comes up with his own solution, and expects you to solve it his way."

Ray was aware that he did this occasionally, but only because he was more experienced.

"Sounds like he thinks he's always right."

"He does, and it makes you feel so...." She paused and searched for the right words. "It's like he has no confidence in any of us, like he doesn't value our opinions."

This reminded Ray of his last boss. He felt sick.

"Anything else?"

"When you try to tell him what the problem is, he cuts you off. He asks a few rapid-fire questions, bang, bang, bang, then gives you a solution. He doesn't really understand the problem, what's behind it, what's causing it. He jumps to conclusions and his solutions are always off the mark. You have to do it his way, and when it doesn't work, it's your fault. That's what drives people crazy."

"I get the message. Don't take problems to him."

"That's what we all say—don't take problems to Ray."

Ray's head jerked. He clenched his fists and almost hit the wall. "Why didn't somebody tell me?" Then he realized that someone probably *had* tried to tell him—his son and daughter. They were young adults now. He had tried to help them, too.

It was not Susan's voice anymore, it was his wife's. She had said it only once, but he heard it almost every day: "Ray, you've driven the children away."

• • •

COMMUNICATION IS THE KEY

Sitting face-to-face with her boss, discouraged and uncomfortable, she confessed, "I'm getting farther and farther behind. I don't think I can meet the deadline." He recognized the problem right away. She was young and inexperienced. He knew exactly what to do. All she needed was some encouragement. A good pep talk would do the trick. Four weeks later she resigned, leaving behind a project that never got off the ground.

One of the most common mistakes in handling motivation and performance problems is pouncing on the problem, and then jumping ahead to solutions without first determining the causes of the problem. Coming up with solutions that are not rooted in the causes is a hit-or-miss proposition. The odds for success are low. Solutions that do not grow out of causes are not solutions at all. They only compound the problem.

When the employee said, "I'm getting farther and farther behind," she was not looking for a pep talk. She knew what was causing the problem and how to solve it. All she needed was a little help to make her solution work. But her manager didn't listen. Instead, he quickly jumped ahead to *his* solution, as he usually did. She decided it was hopeless. The situation would have been far different had the manager focused first on what was *causing* the problem, rather than jumping ahead to a solution.

SAMPLE SCRIPT

Uncovering Causes

Employee: I don't know if I can meet the deadline.

Manager: **Why do you think you can't meet it?**

Employee: I've never used this software before. I'm learning, but it's going slowly.

Manager: **What's a solution that would work for you?**

Employee: If I could go to the two-day training on the software that HR offers, I know I'd get the project back on track.

Effective communication is the key to identifying the causes of motivation problems. With the Belief System, that means going to the source: *Ask the employee.*

Asking can take many forms—some that are effective, some that lead to employee distrust and less-than-candid answers. It is important that questions be neutral and probing; you want the truth—the facts—so sound decisions can be made. Be careful, therefore, to avoid leading questions. They beget answers employees think managers want to hear, not the ones on their minds or in their hearts. "You don't think the problem is really *that* serious, do you?" Or, "Now that the plant manager is gone, we won't have that problem again, will we?"

Here are some simple questions that have proven effective at uncovering the causes of a problem:

- Why do you feel that way?
- Can you tell me more?
- What's behind your thinking on this?
- What happened to make you feel that way?
- Can you tell me what's going on?
- Can you be more specific?

Asking is the way to uncover the causes of motivation problems. As simple and self-evident as that seems, the fact is that managers often do not ask. Some managers have an inflated opinion of themselves; they think they know it all and do not need to ask. Others are bound by tradition: "I'm in charge here; I'm supposed to decide these things." Fear—of dealing with unpleasant issues or of appearing incompetent—keeps many managers from asking. Clearing away such obstacles to effective manager-employee communication is one of the single most valuable benefits garnered from the Belief System.

REALITY CHECK

Myth Managers find out what they need to know. They ask when they need to ask.

Reality Managers are reluctant to ask employees about their motivation and performance problems.

WHAT WILL YOU FIND?

When you probe for the causes of motivation problems, what can you expect to find? It depends. The causes are different for each of the three types of motivation problems I have described—*lack of confidence* (Belief 1), *lack of trust* (Belief 2), and *lack of satisfaction* (Belief 3). Consider the causes of each.

Causes of Confidence Problems

What are the primary causes of confidence (Belief 1) problems? What causes employees to say, "I can't do it. I can't perform as expected."? Nine of the most common causes are discussed here.

Put-Downs
The teenaged daughter, proud of the best report card she had ever received, watched her mother review it with a frown, look up, and say, "I wish you could be a straight-A student like your brother!" The teacher ended a lecture on discipline by saying to the young boy, "You're just one of those people who always make bad choices." The young manager responded to an older employee's suggestion in a team meeting with, "No, I'm afraid your solution won't work," and muttered for only a few to hear, "as usual."

	Confidence	Trust	Satisfaction

Effort ·····> Performance ·····> Outcomes ·····> Satisfaction

- Put-downs
- Negative self-talk
- Inadequate skills
- Unrealistic expectations
- Unclear expectations
- History of failure
- Inadequate resources or authority
- Overdemanding management style
- Organizational factors

Figure 15   COMMON CAUSES OF CONFIDENCE (BELIEF 1) PROBLEMS

Put-downs come in a variety of forms. In her autobiography, *Managing Martians*, Donna Shirley, chosen Woman of the Year by *Glamour* and *Ms.* magazines and head of NASA's Mars exploration program, says that when she showed up at the University of Oklahoma to enroll in aeronautical engineering, her advisor snorted, "Girls can't be engineers." Bruce Clayton, in *Praying for Base Hits,* said his father, consumed by his own failings, could find only deficiencies in his son.

Put-downs are harmful in many ways. They influence the way we see ourselves, the way we feel about ourselves. When they pile up high enough, they diminish our self-confidence. Put-downs cause people to conclude, "I can't do it."

Negative Self-Talk
We all talk to ourselves. Some people talk *positively* to themselves. A customer service representative looked back on a problem she had created with a customer and said to herself, "I made a mistake. I'll learn from it and move on. I'm as capable as the next person." A young salesperson hung up the phone and said to himself, "I lost that sale. I'll just work harder and make the next one." A teenager anxious for a date asked two girls out, both turned him down, and he concluded, "There's nothing wrong with me. Next time I'll get a 'yes.'"

Many people in similar circumstances would engage in *negative* self-talk. "I mess up everything." "I'm no salesperson." "I'm a loser." Failure is a common cause of negative self-talk. Bruce Clayton, in *Praying for Base Hits*, illustrates this in his description of his father, Roy Roosevelt Clayton. He "was Buck's boy. And like Buck, who had never amounted to anything, neither had Roy Roosevelt. Who said so? The old man said so. And many, many times. 'I'm a failure. I've never accomplished anything and never will.'"

I have learned one thing over the years that I always try to remember: What we say to ourselves is very important. Talking to ourselves in a positive way lifts us up, makes us feel worthy, and gives us self-confidence. Negative self-talk pulls us down, creates self-doubt, and causes us to lose confidence in ourselves.

Inadequate Skills

When an employee does not have adequate skills for the job he or she is expected to perform, it should not be surprising that the employee concludes, "I can't do it." It is a common refrain in my consulting business. Organizations give employees considerable responsibility, but they don't always prepare them for it. This is not a situation that breeds confidence. I have found that motivation turns down and effort and performance decline with it. Particularly vulnerable to this problem are employees in work arrangements that are relatively self-managed and independent. Without the attendant skills for the job at hand, confidence sags and things bog down.

I LIKE MIKE

Bart shook hands with Mike, who was applying for the vacant management position. He ushered Mike into his office, told him about the job, and then quizzed him for nearly an hour on his education, background, and experience.

Bart liked Mike. The chemistry was there. Everything fit.

Bart wanted to do one more thing before concluding the interview. This would be his first time to use the Belief System with a job candidate. He had his questions ready. He started with a confidence question.

"How do you feel about what we would expect you to do?"

"To be honest with you, I don't have all the skills for the job, but I'm a fast learner and a hard worker. I'd do my best. I really want this job. I think I can do it."

Instead of hearing, "I *don't* have all the skills. I really *want* this job. I *think* I can do it," Bart heard only the positive, "I can do it." He rated Mike's confidence level as a 7 on the confidence rating scale.

Bart then asked a question intended to address the trust and satisfaction issues. "How would this position offer what you're looking for in a job?"

Mike answered in detail. It was clear to Bart that Mike believed he would get the outcomes if his performance was good (trust = 8 or 9) and that he believed the outcomes would be satisfying (satisfaction = +7 or +8). Bart decided these two beliefs could only strengthen Mike's motivation to perform.

Bart wanted to hire Mike and presented his case to his boss, Julianna. "I like Mike. He really wants the job and he'll work hard. I'll give him the training and coaching he needs, and I'll keep an eye on him until he's confident he can handle it." Julianna was not convinced, and cautioned Bart: "Are you sure you're being objective?"

Bart hired Mike anyway. He described what happened. "I watched Mike procrastinate on his first big decision. Then he was slow to tackle a sticky personnel situation. He kept dragging his feet on some of the skills he needed to develop. The biggest problem was that he distanced himself from me almost from the beginning. That's what people often do when they lack confidence. They try to hide it. Then it's hard to help them. My plans to train and coach him never materialized."

Two months into the job, Mike came into Bart's office, closed the door, and took the offered chair. "I made a big mistake. I don't have the skills for this job. I need to move on, get a job that matches the skills I do have, a job that calls for me to do what I naturally do well."

Bart should not have been surprised. Short on skills, short on confidence. Not a formula for success.

In the weeks that followed, Bart was hard on himself. "I asked the right questions, but I didn't listen. I heard what I wanted to hear."

• • •

Unrealistic Expectations

Organizations that stress performance, quality, and profitability often set standards so high that the stretch required of employees to meet them becomes a negative when employees conclude, "I can't do it." This is particularly common during economic downturns and downsizing. Workplace survivors are expected to carry heavier and heavier workloads. When employees start saying, "This is impossible," the tendency is to give up.

SAMPLE SCRIPT

Uncovering Causes of Confidence Problems

Manager: Since we reorganized, you've seemed discouraged, like you've given up. **What's wrong?**

Employee: I, ah…I don't know…. I just…I don't mean to complain, but I just don't feel like I can get everything done anymore.

Manager: **What's making you feel that way?**

Employee: Since you added the new workload on top of everything else I've been doing…well…it just seems hopeless. It seems like you're expecting too much.

Unclear Expectations

When people are not sure what is expected of them, they begin to doubt their ability to get the job done. The CEO who fails to give his direct reports proper guidance, for example, creates uncertainty about what is expected. Quite predictably, these people will begin to question themselves. Enthusiasm will wane, followed by a fall in performance, which can really set a company back. It is unreasonable to expect people to meet expectations if they do not know what they are.

FIND SOME ASPIRIN

LeAnn immediately went into a tailspin when she read the instructions her new manager, Dwight, had left for her. The note was clipped to a manila file folder. "LeAnn, take care of this." Inside were some sketchy instructions scrawled about a customer complaint.

She walked to Bob's cubicle. He was her peer and best friend at the office. She showed him the note and file.

"Bob, this is typical Dwight. A handful of words, a truckload of unanswered questions. What does 'take care of this' mean? What exactly is the customer's problem? What am I supposed to do? By when? There has to be more information than what he's given me."

Bob nodded.

LeAnn thought about her last manager. "When Beth assigned work, she was thorough and precise. She was patient and I always felt comfortable asking questions. Everything was completely clear before I tackled a new assignment."

She sighed. "Dwight is so different. He thinks he's put it all in writing, just like I like. He honestly believes he's been clear, that I'll know exactly what to do. People like Dwight don't understand people like me. You can't just toss a folder on somebody's desk, keep on walking, and say, 'On my way to the airport. See you in a couple of days.'"

LeAnn waved the note and file. "This is one of our biggest customers. If I foul this up, it'll be a disaster. What should I do, Bob?"

Bob looked over Dwight's instructions again. "Definitely not clear. Use his voice mail. Tell him you need to talk. He'll get back to you."

"I don't feel comfortable doing that. He expects me to be able to handle things like this."

"I'm sure you'll figure it out."

"Yeah, but what if I don't? What'll happen to me then?"

The next morning LeAnn stared out the window. She had not gotten any work done since the day before. Cars raced down the highway like the questions in her mind. She had a headache. She walked back to her desk to find some aspirin.

LeAnn eventually tackled the assignment and muddled through it. She stayed in a frenzy the entire time, doubting herself every step of the way. The customer, however, never sensed her anxiety and was pleased with the way she resolved the complaint. Dwight was pleased, too. He never knew how taxing his simple request had been for LeAnn, never realized how much of her time had been consumed by it.

• • •

History of Failure

People with a history of failure tend to say, "I can't do it," and give up. This is a complex issue that works to the detriment of a shocking number of employees. The pattern of failure can develop in childhood and carry over into the workplace, or it can spring from a single traumatic setback; it can manifest itself as subtle, nagging doubts about one's ability to do certain things (reducing confidence levels accordingly), or it can be a virtual brick wall (zero confidence) to one's value as an employee in specific situations. All of our past, failure included, hangs on. As Margaret Atwood points out, "You don't look back along time but down through it, like water. Sometimes this comes to the surface, sometimes that, sometimes nothing. Nothing goes away."

Inadequate Resources or Authority

You cannot cross a 10-foot crevasse on an 8-foot board, and you cannot do the job the boss wants if the resources needed to do it are not available. Resources include many things: facilities, equipment, personnel, information, finances, and *authority*. Having all the necessary tools at hand will not get the job done if the person responsible for the work lacks the authority to put things in motion. Expect debilitating confidence problems without it.

While it is obvious that people cannot get the job done without the resources and authority they need, it is surprising how many people will try. It also is surprising how often managers are unaware that employees are willing to go about their work ill-equipped, forging ahead in silence. The same employees continue to remain quiet as their confidence sinks and drags performance down with it. While every employee could yell for help when his or her toolbox is not full, many simply do not do so. Managers get better results from the workforce when they keep a watchful eye focused on giving employees the wherewithal to get the job done.

Overdemanding Management Style

Flaws and quirks in one's management style can be painful contributors to employee confidence problems. Project a tough perfectionist reputation with employees and watch confidence sag as one after another concludes, "I can't measure up; I can't do it." The same results follow when managers give harsh criticism of poor performance, fail to acknowledge good performance, allow poor matches between job requirements and employee skills, and do not provide enough structure in a job. ("I'm not sure what to do or how to do it or what you expect of me. I don't know if I can do it or not.") Digging out of one's own managerial shortcomings is not easy. It is hard to be objective, to see yourself as others do; but it is imperative if employees are adversely affected by your manner. Managers who diminish employee self-confidence always create performance problems. Employees don't perform at their best when this happens, and they may not get the job done at all.

THE MANAGER WHO WHITTLES IT AWAY

Mary Ellen was a brilliant, considerate woman who worked for a talented, inconsiderate manager. "He's a demanding perfectionist who in half a sentence can whittle you down to nothing," she said, "and often does. He shrinks your confidence until you can't wear it anymore. To this I come to work every day."

• • •

WHAT KIND OF MANAGER ARE YOU?

Typical Manager   I have my own management style and I expect employees to adapt to it.

Motivation Manager   I am willing to change my style of management if it helps employees perform better.

Organizational Factors

Circumstances within an organization play a big role in employee confidence. All things being equal, a well-trained employee is confident, and one who is not well trained is not confident. Is the company's rapid growth pushing employees beyond their training? If so, a Belief System manager will see it reflected in confidence problems. Rapid technological changes are a certain source of confidence problems if skills are not diligently updated. Hiring people with the wrong qualifications for the job will produce employees with low confidence levels. Understaffing will overload personnel, put them behind in their work, and dampen their confidence to get the job done. High employee turnover usually means less qualified (and less confident) people replace more qualified (and more confident) people; well-qualified (and confident) employees find themselves in tandem with increasingly less qualified (and less confident) associates, diminishing the former's belief that the work will get done correctly and on time. The overall result is the emergence of a wholesale belief that, "I (we) can't do it."

E X E R C I S E 4

Influencing Confidence in Others

1. Think of one person close to you (either at work or not) who is highly motivated and one who is not.

2. Do you ever *diminish* this person's self-confidence? How?

3. How do you *build* this person's confidence?

Causes of Trust Problems

What are the primary causes of trust (Belief 2) problems? What causes employees to say, "What I get is not based on my performance"? Three common causes are discussed here.

Confidence	Trust	Satisfaction

Effort ······> Performance ······> Outcomes ······> Satisfaction

- Outcomes are not tied to performance
- Misperception that outcomes are not tied to performance
- History of outcomes not being tied to performance

Figure 16   COMMON CAUSES OF TRUST
(BELIEF 2) PROBLEMS

Outcomes Are Not Tied to Performance

Some organizations don't have systems in place that reward people based on performance. Others promise to link rewards to performance but don't follow through. The practice of promising and not delivering can have a serious impact on a company, as previously noted.

Whether the problem is the absence of reward systems or systems that don't work, the end result is the same. High performers go unrewarded and poor performers are not penalized. The high performers ask, "Why should I do a good job when it doesn't pay off?" Poor performers say, "Why should I work harder if it doesn't matter?" This means managers must give proof that they can be trusted to give people what they deserve on the basis of their performance.

SAMPLE SCRIPT

Uncovering Causes of Trust Problems

Employee: I wanted to follow up with you on our discussion last week, the one about my pay raise.

Manager: **Okay, is anything wrong?**

Employee: I'm concerned about the rumors I've been hearing.

Manager: **What have you been hearing?**

Employee: You told me I was getting the biggest raise of anybody on our team and that I deserved it. But I've been hearing that everybody got a 4 percent increase.

Manager: That's right, they did.

Employee: But you told me I was getting the biggest raise.

Manager: You did. Your salary is the highest, so you got the biggest dollar increase.

Employee: That doesn't seem fair.

Manager: **What do you mean?**

Employee: Well, I feel like you misled me by saying that I was getting the biggest raise when you really gave everybody the same percentage increase. The other thing is that across-the-board raises reward people for just being here. They don't reward performance.

UNLIKELY CONFESSION

Terrence looked back on his 40-year career and discussed the shortcoming he lamented most, first as a manager and later as an executive.

"When people didn't perform well, I was quick to point it out. But when they did a good job, I didn't tell them. That was the biggest mistake I made in handling people. Of course, I didn't know it at the time."

"Why do you think that?" I asked.

"It held me back because it held others back. Most people want to be praised for what they do. If you withhold praise, you take away their motivation. Then performance starts to slide. Some good people even quit their jobs because I was so stingy with praise. Promotions saved me, though."

"I see that happening now. The manager leaves a group before problems get out of hand."

He laughed. "I always managed to stay one step ahead of the messes I made. I didn't plan it. The promotions just came at the right time."

"Why didn't you tell people when they did a good job?"

He paused, took a deep breath, and exhaled slowly. "Some people can't say 'Thank you,' and others can't say 'I love you.' Well, I can't say 'You did a good job,' not unless it's perfect, and nobody's perfect."

"So what advice would you offer other managers?"

He hesitated before answering. "The success of a manager always depends on the performance of others. If you want people to work hard for you, you have to give them what they deserve."

• • •

Misperception That Outcomes Are Not Tied to Performance

It is not unusual for managers and employees to define performance differently. Most managers define performance in terms of results—increased production, improved quality, reduced costs, and higher profit. Some employees define performance as coming to work every day, being on time, having a good attitude, and working hard; while these may lead to the kinds of results managers look for, they are not the same as results. Effort does not equal performance. Trying is not the same as getting the job done.

When managers and employees define performance differently, expect trust problems to occur. Employees who are never absent, who put in an honest day's work and keep their noses clean, expect to be rewarded for it. When the manager, who is looking for results, does not reward these employees, they feel cheated. "I didn't get what I deserved," is the conclusion, or, "Outcomes are not tied to my performance." This is a common problem. Even when outcomes are tied closely to performance, employees may perceive that they are not. The misperception causes a downturn in employee motivation with predictable effects on effort and performance.

History of Outcomes Not Being Tied to Performance

Employees who have a history of not getting what they deserve tend to hold well-entrenched beliefs that outcomes are not tied to performance. Bureaucracies, corporate and otherwise, often feel the bite of this problem. Outcomes must be tied closely to performance *over a long period* for people to change long-held beliefs that have been reinforced for years. Changing beliefs of distrust begins with a single opportunity. People want to trust their manager, but they have to have a reason to do so.

Managers sometimes are consistent in giving people what they deserve on one side of performance and not the other. For example, they may consistently give employees what they deserve for poor performance and do nothing when performance is good. This creates a trust problem.

HORSE IN THE BELL TOWER

In the early 1900s my grandfather was a freshman at Young Harris College, a sleepy little campus in the Blue Ridge Mountains of North Georgia. He said he and his friends occasionally saw some excitement, but only if they created it.

The bell tower in the chapel was an important part of campus life. The bell sounded to wake the students and faculty each morning, to call them to daily chapel, and to begin and end each class.

Late on a crisp winter night, my grandfather and his best friend, Harry, led a horse up the two flights of stairs to the top of the bell tower and left her there to be seen by one and all the next morning.

Harry rang in the new day and did not stop ringing the bell until everybody on campus came to see what was going on.

The young, citified president did not have a feel for horses at all except to know that they belonged on the ground. He grabbed two students and went with them up to the bell tower to get the horse down. But no matter how much they pushed and pulled, tugged and urged, coaxed and threatened, the horse simply would not budge.

Down from the bell tower the embarrassed president came to address the group. "The horse doesn't seem to like these two boys. I'm certain she'll come down if the right person will walk with her."

After this plea for help, my grandfather stepped forward.

He climbed the steps and in a matter of minutes led the horse down to safety.

The crowd clapped and cheered, "Yea, yea! Way to go, Jehu!"

The president thanked him and immediately began his unsuccessful attempt to identify the pranksters.

My grandfather ended the story there, but I had to know, "How did you do it? How did you get the horse down?"

"Horses aren't afraid to go up something steep because they can see where they're going," he said, "but coming down is a different matter. So I took off my shirt and tied it around her head, covering her eyes.

"I stood to her left with both of us facing down the stairs. I put my right arm under her neck and wrapped it up and around until my hand was on top, firmly grasping her mane. With my left hand, I caught a tight grip on the bridle. Then I leaned up and whispered in her ear.

"Together, slowly, we started. She'd lift one foot in the air, stretch it forward, search for a step, find it, shift her weight down on it, get a sure footing, then do it over again, and again, one step at a time, until we reached the bottom. I put my shirt back on and together we stepped out and faced an anxious president and a cheering crowd."

"What did you whisper in her ear?"

He paused and got a faraway look in his eyes. For an instant I was in the bell tower with him, decades ago.

"It wasn't *what* I whispered, it was my tone of voice, confident and caring. I wanted her to trust me. You can't lead horses unless they trust you. Same with people."

• • •

EXERCISE 5

Earning Trust from Others

1. Think of two employees, your best and your worst performers.

2. What are the differences in the outcomes (rewards and otherwise) you give them?

3. How closely are you tying outcomes to their performance? That is, are you giving them what they deserve on the basis of their performance?

Causes of Satisfaction Problems

What are the primary causes of satisfaction (Belief 3) problems? What causes employees to say, "The outcomes are not satisfying to me"? Eight causes are discussed here.

Confidence	Trust	Satisfaction
Effort ·····> Performance ·····> Outcomes ·····> Satisfaction		
		• Not receiving desired outcomes
		• Receiving unwanted outcomes
		• Undervaluing outcomes received
		• Overvaluing outcomes not received
		• Confusion over what is wanted
		• Preference changes
		• Conflicting desires
		• The work itself is not rewarding

Figure 17 COMMON CAUSES OF SATISFACTION (BELIEF 3) PROBLEMS

The most common of these causes are the first two on the list—not receiving desired outcomes and receiving unwanted outcomes—and the last—the work itself is not rewarding. The less common causes of satisfaction problems should not escape the manager's scrutiny, however. Managers can expect satisfaction problems when employees undervalue outcomes they receive, when they overvalue outcomes they don't receive, when they are confused about what they want, when they are undergoing preference changes, and when they experience conflicting desires.

Not Receiving Desired Outcomes

Satisfaction problems often arise simply because employees are not getting what they want. And it is not always the big or obvious things that are desired—more money, a big promotion, or improved job security. No serious student of human motivation fails to recognize the importance of "the little things" in prompting employees to extend themselves, little things like being treated with more respect, being given more responsibility, and getting management's attentive ear when there is a problem. To fail to extend these offerings as legitimate and coveted rewards for performance is to carry "half a quiver" into the hunt for managerial excellence. Remember, any time employees want something that they are not getting (satisfaction), motivation and performance are the losers.

Receiving Unwanted Outcomes

The second major cause of satisfaction problems is as basic as the first. Employees often are given outcomes they do not want. Not everyone desires additional responsibility, greater empowerment, or more overtime, for example. When people receive undesired outcomes for their performance, it should be no surprise to find that they are not as satisfied as they might be. Motivation, in this instance, cannot be expected to flourish.

SAMPLE SCRIPT

Uncovering Causes of Satisfaction Problems

Manager: I've noticed that since Marque retired last month you've seemed different. **Is anything wrong?**

Employee: Well, I, er…you know…. I don't mean to be different. Is there a problem with my work?

Manager: No, but I was wondering, **are you concerned about something?**

Employee: It's mainly…well…you know…it's the overtime, I guess.

Manager: I let the team decide whether to replace Marque right away or not. The group decided they'd rather hold off on a replacement and let everybody get in some extra overtime. **Is that something you don't want?**

Employee: Well…I didn't speak up when the group was deciding, but I wasn't in favor of more overtime. It's just not something I much wanted.

Everybody is different. People differ in what they want and need, and they differ in their likes and dislikes. People see the same thing differently, feel differently about it, and experience differing degrees of satisfaction and dissatisfaction from it. Although treating everybody the same is easier, it does not work. Managing to the individuality of each person yields better results.

Think about this: Young people today look for different things in a job than did people of previous genera-

> **LEARNING LESSON**
>
> The justification (if there ever was one) for treating everyone the same is gone.

tions; the justification (if there ever was one) for treating everyone the same is gone. Treat all employees alike today and you run the substantial risk of simultaneously denying them what they want and giving them things they do not want. That is a sure formula for trouble.

Undervaluing Outcomes Received

I know a manager who valued a young MBA so much that he gave him an assignment under the company's crusty manufacturing VP that was sure to put him on a fast track up the corporate ladder if he performed well. Concurrent with this assignment, the manager offered a more visible but less strategic promotion to another employee. You can imagine the manager's surprise when his protege floundered with satisfaction problems—the MBA wanted the promotion he did not get, and he did not see the value in the assignment he did get.

Overvaluing Outcomes Not Received
In a balancing act to keep two valued employees happy but with only one spot to fill on a key advisory committee, the manager gave the loser a reserved parking space near the branch office doorway. Unbeknownst to the manager, the winner of the committee seat coveted the parking space far beyond its value in the total scheme of things, and his satisfaction level actually fell.

Confusion over What Is Wanted
How about the person who was offered a new "territory" that would pay more and move him closer to the seat of corporate power, but would require that he relocate and would mean more pressure to perform? The potential satisfaction of more money and better exposure was very attractive, but the relocation and added pressure were not. What to do? The employee did not know. He could not make up his mind. He was confused about what he wanted, where he wanted to be, and where he wanted to go. Dissatisfaction seemed imminent whatever the decision.

Confusion of this type is no stranger to any of us.

Preference Changes
Then there was the case of the happy, hardworking, productive, newly married employee who lost enthusiasm for his travel-heavy job. Simply put, the value he had once placed on frequent excursions to San Francisco, Hong Kong, and Singapore gave way to a desire to be home more with his wife. He shifted from a high +9 or +10 on the satisfaction rating scale to a -3 or -4, and nothing had changed but his marital status. Unusual? Certainly not. Changed values are a major source of satisfaction problems in the workplace.

Values usually change slowly over time, although not always. Abrupt changes can occur, usually sparked by an event that is charged with emotion. The speed of the change matters little. The point is that once values change, satisfaction with one's circumstances changes as well, sometimes increasing, sometimes just the opposite.

Conflicting Desires
The manager of the newlywed in the previous example got to work right away accommodating his employee's understandable desire to

"get off the road" and spend more time with his new wife. The job the manager found seemed to fill the bill—same money, open-ended advancement possibilities, and regular hours with nothing more than an annual convention to take him out of town. There was just one snag: The employee had a sinking feeling that he would not like the work. "I've done that kind of work before," he explained, "and it's just not something I much enjoy. I don't know what to do." He was caught in a conflict of desires. "Enjoying the job" had long been a motivating factor in his life. Now he was faced with the prospect of doing work he didn't like because his values had changed. The conflicting desires played havoc with his satisfaction level.

The Work Itself Is Not Rewarding

Some employees like their jobs; others do not. A person who loves working with computers loves working with computers. A person who loves working with people loves working with people. Dealing with customer complaints would be an unpleasant job for a shy person who dislikes conflict. Being stuck working alone at a desk job would bring little joy to a natural-born salesperson. When the work itself is not rewarding, a satisfaction problem is sure to exist.

EXERCISE 6

Creating Satisfaction for Others

1. Identify two people who are very different from each other who have a similar relationship with you (two employees, two children, or two friends, for example).

2. What gives the first person the greatest satisfaction? Greatest dissatisfaction?

3. What is the source of the greatest satisfaction for the second person? Greatest dissatisfaction?

4. How much satisfaction and dissatisfaction are you creating for each person?

THE PERILS OF GUESSING

Uncovering causes can be tricky when you guess rather than talk to people who are in a position to know. With motivation and performance, it is the person experiencing the problem who is most likely to know what is causing it. Hold your course and refuse to move ahead to solutions until you know what is causing the problem.

IF THE CAR WON'T START, THE BATTERY MUST BE DEAD

Maurice was in a hurry to get home after a long customer meeting when he noticed he had left his lights on. He held his breath, but the car started and he got home okay. Next morning, when he turned the key in the ignition, there was no sound at all. Dead battery. Using his wife's car, he went out and bought a new battery and installed it in his car. The car still would not start. It caused Maurice to miss a plane and a big meeting at the corporate office.

He called his mechanic, who towed the car and fixed it. As Maurice was paying the bill, the mechanic said, "Wish you would've checked with me before you bought that new battery. The fusible link was causing the problem, not the battery!"

• • •

Jumping to solutions without first knowing the causes will inevitably lead to trouble. Many times I see managers needlessly replacing batteries. If managers want to avoid solutions that don't work, they can focus on motivation management, use the Belief System, and uncover causes that will lead to solutions that will work.

> **GETTING STARTED**
>
> If you want to know what is *causing* the problem, go to the person with the problem and ask.

MOVING AHEAD

I tend to get comfortable with the knowledge I have, and I tend to get a false sense of security with it. The result is a reluctance to open up to new knowledge. When this happens, I usually suffer.

LIKE A NEEDLE IN A RECORD

Everything was moving at a rapid pace, everyone had to produce more, and Freddie, a seasoned manager, was being pressured to change.

Freddie was a kind, hardworking manager. And he was a family man. He left his wife and two small children every morning to go to work. He was responsible for goals that he considered impossible to reach as he led his unit through turbulent times.

He was a steady worker and always did the best he knew how. He believed in good planning, a structured work environment, and sticking with proven methods and procedures.

Freddie trudged home at the end of a long day and sat down at the kitchen table with his wife. "I'm tired to the bone and they still want more. Top management is putting pressure on me to reorganize my department, to 'make it more efficient,' they say. We don't need to be changing everything. The way I've got it organized now is fine. I'm going to fight this."

Freddie did fight it. The case he stubbornly presented fell on deaf ears. He later told his wife, "It's a losing battle. I'm giving in on this one."

One evening a couple of weeks later, after they had gotten the children to bed, Freddie and his wife talked. "My nerves are raw. Get this, the latest 'news' at work. My supervisors have asked me to spend more time out in the field, listen more to our workers, interact more with our customers. I don't have the time. And besides, things are going pretty well the way I'm operating now."

The following Saturday, Freddie came home from the office in mid-afternoon, earlier than usual, threw his briefcase on the sofa, and paced back and forth while his wife listened. "My boss just told me he wants me to let go, delegate more, decentralize, push decisions down to lower levels. He says we need to improve the quality of service to our customers, reduce response time in meeting their needs, and provide service more efficiently. The system we're using now, I've had in place for a long time and it's served us well. I don't see a need to throw it out the window. This pressure they're putting on me to change this, change that, well, it's killing me."

The following Monday was a particularly frustrating day for Freddie. He came home, had dinner, kissed his wife and children good night, and went to bed early. He died during the night.

After the funeral, his wife reflected on their last conversations together. Freddie's exact words replayed in her mind for weeks, but they started to fade as a theme began to appear.

The realization hit her hard. She felt dizzy and sick. She experienced a sinking, pitiful feeling with more sadness than she had ever known.

"Freddie, you got stuck, like a needle in a record, playing the same thing over and over again, unable to get out of a familiar groove."

That night she sat in a chair, took both children in her lap, thought of Freddie, and cried...for him.

• • •

4

Discovering Solutions That Work

"Do only things you truly love."

Solution *approaches* for motivation problems tend to be self-evident once causes are identified. Specific solutions are less obvious.

The person experiencing a motivation problem is the best source of information about solutions that will work.

People usually are eager to help solve their own problems. All they need is opportunity, encouragement, and a feeling of security to open up.

Motivation management using the Belief System helps managers zero in on the real issues and discover solutions that work.

SOLUTION IN THE REARVIEW MIRROR

Ray Boulder knew exactly what had happened to him. "I've been clobbered with words, bludgeoned without mercy."

Two of his employees had landed solid blows to his ego and had fractured his spirit. Ray had heard them say he was a poor manager, one who took problems away from people, jumped to conclusions, and forced his solutions on everybody.

"They think they've got me pegged. Well, I'll show them. I'm not going to take this lying down."

Ray had a plan. He looked up his daughter's phone number, punched in the eleven digits, and waited. "I wonder if she lives so far away because of me?" He had never considered that before.

He thought of Karen and her twin brother, Rob. Karen was kind and gentle. Relationships were important to her. She always had trouble saying no. So she would meet with him, even if she didn't want to. No need to call her brother. He was filled with too much anger to help.

Ray sensed that Karen did not recognize his voice at first. It had been months since they last talked. Yes, it would be all right for him to come visit with her tomorrow if he wanted to; it was Saturday. Yes, she would meet him for lunch at noon at that little Greek restaurant. And yes, she would help him, if she could.

Karen was standing outside the restaurant when Ray arrived on time. He was surprised to see her finish one cigarette and light another as he pulled into the parking lot. He wondered if others looked for ways to calm their nerves before meeting with him.

Ray's first words were, "You look awful."

"Just a little under the weather. I'll be okay."

"What you need is some good food. Come on." They sat down, checked the menu, and ordered right away. Karen had skipped breakfast and had no appetite now, either. She decided on a small Greek salad and coffee. Ray insisted she would feel better if she ate more. "A well-rounded meal, Greek salad, moussaka, Greek fries, and a Coca-Cola™— Coke's good for you when you're not feeling well."

Ray always had a hearty appetite. He ordered the combo platter of moussaka, pastichio, spanakopita, Greek fries, Greek salad, and pita bread, a Coca-Cola, and baklava for dessert.

While they waited, Ray explained what his two employees had said. Karen sat upright in her chair to steady herself.

He knew she expected an explosion. Uncharacteristically he said, "They were right."

Ray was certain Karen would agree. Yes, they were right. He was back in the kitchen, watching her hold up the eighth-grade exam she had flunked. "You need to study more, Karen, that's all." In her junior year she was in the den, crushed, the night Johnny Johnson had dumped her, 24 hours before the prom. "You can go with Rob and his date. Come on, I'll tell him." Then there was the weekend she had come home from college and told him she hated her science courses and wanted to major in business. "No, Karen, we agreed. It's pre-med."

He remembered the kinds of things he had said to make her feel better after he got her back on track. "Karen, you're too young to make this kind of decision by yourself." Or, "Karen, I'm older and more experienced than you are. That's why I can solve problems better."

He noticed Karen watching him. She looked anxious. He saw her take a deep breath, the way she always did to let the tension pass.

Ray sampled everything on his plate, looked up at Karen, and made his plea. "Karen, you know my faults as well as anybody. What should I do?"

Karen was stunned. When it finally sank in that he was serious, she immediately brightened up. It struck Ray that he had never asked for her opinion before.

"I think I can help you, *if you'll let me.*" Ray was surprised at the confidence in her voice. "You remember that management skills course I took at the University of South Florida, the one Dr. Knippen taught?"

Ray nodded. How could he forget? That was all she had talked about the whole semester. And later she said, "Best course I ever had."

"Like everyone else, I was videotaped once each week practicing a skill, 15 skills in all. I racked up an A. I use that stuff every day." She paused and Ray watched her carefully choose her words. "Dad, **what exactly is the problem?**"

Ray started to give a quick answer, hesitated, then took a couple of bites of his food and a sip of Coca-Cola. "I always thought my job as a husband, a parent, and a manager was to solve problems. I'm beginning to think it's better to let people solve their own. The problem is, I don't know how to let them, and if I did, I don't know if I could bring myself to do it."

He could see her wheels turning as she readied her next question.

"Why do you doubt yourself?"

"I've done it my way for so long. I don't know if I have the skills to do it another way."

"Anything else?"

"You bet there is—and it's big. If I let people solve their own problems, will the problems really get solved?"

"That's a fair question," Karen replied. **"Any other reservations?"**

"Not really. That's it."

"Okay, let's take the next step. **What's the solution?** In other words, what's the best way to develop the skills you want to have?"

"That's the question I tried to answer coming up here this morning. It seems to boil down to two things. I guess I need to know the right questions to ask, questions that force people to think for themselves. And I need to listen rather than tell people what to do."

"If those are the skills you want, what's the best way to develop them?"

"Practice, I guess."

"**Can you be more specific?** How can you practice?"

Ray thought for a minute, then a smile crossed his face, and he said, "I'll look for opportunities at work and practice there."

"Let's take the final step. **Will this solution give you what you want?** In other words, if you develop the skills you need to let people solve their own problems, will their problems actually get solved?"

"Well, that remains to be seen, but I'm optimistic they will."

Ray was excited. He was confident he had a plan that would work. He noticed that Karen was beaming.

They finished their lunch, kept talking, and were surprised when the waitress told them it was 2:30 and asked if they needed anything else.

Karen gave Ray a warm smile and a hug. As he drove away, Ray watched her wave in his rearview mirror until she was out of sight.

Ray was almost home before he fully realized all that Karen had done to help him. He felt small for the way he had always seen her, but tall to be her father now.

• • •

SOLUTION APPROACHES ARE OBVIOUS

When the *causes* of motivation problems are identified, general solutions become self-evident. In other words, causes point the way to solutions. Notice that the solution approaches are a logical extension of the causes. Good solutions *always* address causes. When causes remain, problems remain. See Table 1 on the following pages.

Learning the causes of motivation problems also demystifies the approaches taken to solve them. My experience clearly shows that proceeding directly from the identification of a problem to its solution without first determining the causes creates an element of uncertainty, a mystery that can be unsettling for all concerned. Solution approaches suffer in an air of uncertainty. The mystery is removed by proceeding from the problem to the causes, and then to the solutions.

MANAGERS CONTROL SOLUTIONS

When I look over the full range of solution approaches, I feel an awesome burden. Most managers do. With few exceptions, managers control solutions; employees do not. Employees can ask for solutions they want and need, but when we look the facts squarely in the eye, it is clear that in most cases it is only managers who can make the solutions available.

However, managers operate under restrictions, too. Some solutions are not within their power. This is the case with trust and satisfaction problems, for example, when managers do not have control over the outcomes needed to solve the problem. I will comment on this in more detail later in the chapter.

Solutions to Confidence Problems

Solutions to confidence problems are often quick and easy.

- Managers can use *training programs* and *coaching* to rapidly give employees the skills they need.

- Managers can *communicate* with employees to instantly clarify performance expectations.

- Managers can *allocate resources* to swiftly give employees the wherewithal to get the job done.

- Managers can *delegate authority* to immediately authorize employees to make vital decisions.

TABLE 1		
Motivation Problems, Causes, and Solutions		
Motivation Problem	**Typical Causes**	**Obvious Solution Approaches**
Confidence (Belief 1) *"I can't do it."*	• Put-downs	• Encourage objective evaluation
	• Negative self-talk	• Encourage positive self-talk
	• Inadequate skills	• Give training, coaching, and other forms of skill building; redesign the job; transfer the employee
	• Unrealistic expectations	• Set realistic expectations, introduce more effective ways to meet expectations, provide more resources
	• Unclear expectations	• Establish and/or clarify expectations
	• History of failure	• Be supportive, create opportunities for success
	• Inadequate resources or authority	• Allocate necessary resources, delegate adequate authority
	• Overdemanding management style	• Loosen up, set expectations that fit reality, be supportive
	• Rapid growth and change	• Institute/upgrade training regimen
	• Wrong job qualifications	• Strengthen hiring practices
	• Understaffing	• Introduce labor/time-saving techniques, reduce workloads, increase staffing
	• High employee turnover	• Examine hiring process, management practices, employee satisfaction, and take action.

Motivation Problem	Typical Causes	Obvious Solution Approaches
Trust (Belief 2) *"Outcomes are not tied to my performance."*	• Outcomes are not tied to performance	• Tie outcomes to performance
	• Misperception that outcomes are not tied to performance	• Clarify performance expectations, actual performance, and outcomes received
	• History of outcomes not being tied to performance	• Consistently tie outcomes to performance
Satisfaction (Belief 3) *"The outcomes aren't satisfying to me."*	• Not receiving desired outcomes	• Give people outcomes they find satisfying, when appropriate
	• Receiving unwanted outcomes	• Withhold outcomes that are dissatisfying, when appropriate
	• Undervaluing outcomes received	• Show where value lies
	• Overvaluing outcomes not received	• Balance inflated perceptions with the facts
	• Confusion over what is wanted	• Lead employee through values clarification (why outcomes are desired, value and priority of each)
	• Preference changes	• Accommodate the changes where possible
	• Conflicting desires	• Lead employee through values clarification
	• The work itself is not rewarding	• Get people in jobs that match their skills, interests, and needs via job placement, transfers, and redesign of jobs

The toughest confidence problems for managers to deal with are those caused by negative self-talk and history of failure. Solutions are slow to take hold and sometimes there are no solutions, at least not in the workplace. Most managers, understandably, are not equipped to help people with firmly entrenched beliefs such as, "I'm not worthy" or "I'll always be a failure." It is often in the best interest of these employees to find alternative work environments where the pressure to perform is less intense.

The solution most often needed to overcome confidence problems is skill building. There are two principal reasons for this: (1) People are routinely placed in jobs that do not match their skills. This happens with initial hirings, job transfers, and promotions. (2) Even when skills are a good match for the job today, they likely will not be tomorrow. Skills become outdated quickly because tasks, work methods, and technologies change. It is easy for skills to lag behind. Managers who keep an eye open for skill deficiencies and do something to quickly remedy them are rewarded with substantial motivation and performance dividends.

PRACTICE MAKES PERFECT

Maggie, a bright, ambitious young manager, pushed the panic button when she was passed over for a promotion. Her anxiety was heightened when Keith, her manager, hinted that she needed to concentrate on developing her management skills. Keith suggested she talk with me.

When Maggie and I met, I noticed she was wearing a pin from the 1996 Olympic Games in Atlanta. Olympics are about skill development. That seemed like a good lead-in to the purpose of our discussion.

"Maggie, did you enjoy the Olympics?"

"They were great! I took two weeks of my vacation so I could attend events every day."

"What did you enjoy most?" I wanted to compare notes. My family and I had gone to events almost every day, too.

"I'm not what you'd call a sports nut, so I enjoyed the excitement of everything. Gymnastics was my favorite, though. Can you imagine how much those athletes had to practice to be the best in the world?"

"They train six to eight hours every day...for years."

She continued. "That reminds me of my 12-year-old niece. She practices the piano two hours a day during the school year, four in the summer."

"Successful people do that."

"I guess it's more obvious in some professions than others."

"Ever been to the ballet?"

She took a quick, deep breath. "Aren't their bodies gorgeous? Talk about training."

"Same thing with the symphony, the opera, modern dance."

"I've always admired performing artists—their talent, their dedication."

"The best always practice."

She stopped smiling. "I see what you're doing. We're talking business, aren't we?"

"Yes, we are."

"But I go to management training programs. I read all the latest management books. I know a lot about managing."

"Maggie, knowledge and skills are not the same thing."

"What?"

"Having knowledge about the piano is different from having the skill to play it."

"Okay, I see. So what am I supposed to do?"

"What do you think?"

"I guess I need to take the management knowledge I have and practice using it until I develop the skills I need."

"Makes you wonder, doesn't it, Maggie, how successful you might be, if you will practice your skills."

● ● ●

Many people transfer the practice model to their professional lives. Jim Carrey, the well-known comedian and actor, was asked how he learned to do the impressions that have earned him millions of dollars as a movie star. His response was, "I've spent half of my life in front of the mirror, practicing."

Although practicing one's skills is considered essential in some professions, not so in business. I conducted a seminar recently with a group of managers and encouraged them to practice their skills. A young woman in the group commented, "I've been a musician all my life, and I know the value of practice. I'm astounded that I never saw the connection to business."

> **LEARNING LESSON**
>
> You will perform better if you will practice and hone your skills.

Solutions to Trust Problems

It takes time to repair broken trust. Employees must see outcomes *repeatedly* tied to performance before they start trusting their managers. This means managers must show a *consistent* pattern in giving people what their performance deserves.

THE TRUST MASTER

Scooter Dickerson, my high school football coach, believed everybody should toe the line, and his was a very thin line. He did not just expect you to follow the straight and narrow, he demanded it.

He was the only person I have ever known whose presence caused people to simultaneously stand in awe and tremble.

His expectations were crystal clear, and you could always trust him to give you what you deserved, either way. If you did your best and followed the training rules, he let you know he was proud of you; if you did not, he punished you. If we had a good practice, he ended it on time; if we did not, he kept us until he was satisfied, and that was usually well after dark. If you played well in the Friday night games, he rewarded you by letting you play a lot; if you did not play well, you warmed the bench.

He believed you should say what you'll do, and do what you say. He did.

Every player on that team trusted him to tie outcomes to performance. I have never seen anyone better at it. We did not always like the consequences, but he dispensed them fairly and there was never any uncertainty about what the outcomes would be.

We defended him, we fought for him, we worked for him. We would have died for him. We felt like our lives had ended when he left his job as coach.

• • •

Giving employees what they deserve takes *courage*. This is especially true with employees who are not accustomed to having outcomes tied to performance. Managers face negative consequences when they give poor performers what they deserve. In some cases, it puts managers at loggerheads with grumbling, contentious slackers; in others, it means bringing disappointment to honest, hardworking employees whose performance simply does not measure up. Managers also can expect negative ramifications when they deliver appropriate rewards to high performers. Typically there is a backlash from jealous, disgruntled, poor-performing employees.

In view of the anticipated reaction from unhappy employees, managers often choose to minimize their own pain. Managers presume they will ruffle fewer feathers by treating everyone more or less the same. High performers abhor this; it causes some of them to become average performers ("Why should I work this hard if I don't get rewarded?") and pushes others to find employment elsewhere ("I'll get a job where I'm appreciated"). Poor performers love it when managers treat everybody the same; they can continue their substandard performance, yet be rewarded like everyone else. Average performers tend to dislike the sameness, although typically not enough to complain much; however, the sameness offers no incentive for them to perform better.

The bottom-line result is clear: Motivation and performance *always* suffer when managers do not give employees what their performance merits. Successful managers find a way to meet the challenge of tying outcomes to performance. Some managers who have struggled and found a way have told me, "You may have to go deep within yourself to search and find the courage that is lying there...waiting."

IT'S NOT THE DECISIONS YOU MAKE THAT KILL YOU

I interviewed the CEO of a major corporation not long ago as part of my research on motivation management. He was nearing the end of a remarkably successful five-year company turnaround, and I was anxious to hear his story.

When I walked into his office, he was sitting at a large mahogany table that he used as a desk, his family crest carved into the center.

When he stood I saw a strong, athletic man of medium build, wearing a tailor-made suit, looking relaxed and much younger than I had expected from seeing him on TV. He gave me a warm smile and a firm handshake that really did make me feel welcomed.

He glanced around the walnut-paneled room and said, "This is my home away from home, and it's filled with a lot of good memories." He proudly pointed to autographed pictures of himself with George Bush, Bill Clinton, Pavarotti, Alan Jackson, Bill Gates, Billy Graham, and others.

We walked across the beautiful hardwood floors covered with Persian rugs and took facing leather chairs in the sitting area. He tugged at his monogrammed shirtsleeves as he began telling the company's turnaround story, first reciting the profit figures over the last five years. It was hard not to be distracted by the Picasso and Matisse paintings displayed on the wall directly behind him.

He detailed the major decisions he had made, in the strong, confident voice of a man who knew who he was and where he was going. He said, "Most of the decisions seemed easy in light of the one that almost turned the company away from success."

He paused and was silent for a moment. As he started telling me about this decision, I noticed that his voice faltered and he looked more like I felt, having traveled through two airports that day to meet with him.

"One of my key executives wasn't doing his job, and it was holding the company back. He was a lifelong friend. Performance pulled me in one direction, the relationship in another. I needed to make a decision, but I couldn't do it."

He twisted in his chair, shifted positions, and continued. "Finally I realized how important it was to push aside my emotions so I could think clearly. Then it dawned on me. If everyone else knew his performance wasn't up to par, he must have known it, too. He had to be suffering. I'd been so concerned about my own pain, I hadn't seen his. When I approached him, we both knew something had to be done. The best part is that now he's happier than ever and we're still friends."

He smiled for the first time in several minutes and said, "Coming to grips with that decision was a pivotal point in the company's turnaround."

Then he looked me in the eye and said in the tone of a child reveling in a new discovery, "You know, it's not the decisions you make that kill you; it's the ones you don't make that hold you back."

• • •

REALITY CHECK

Myth Employees perform better when they are happy.

Reality Employees perform better when they get what their performance merits.

Solutions to Satisfaction Problems

Intentionally "offering" something not wanted is the old-school solution for getting people to work harder and perform better. The idea is that people will work hard to avoid negative consequences. And, yes, it is true. Most of us will do whatever it takes to avoid losing our job, to steer clear of harsh criticism, or to keep from being pulled off a plum project.

In his book *From Worst to First*, Gordon Bethune, CEO of Continental Airlines, tells about using the "offer something they don't want" approach. When he came on board as the new chief executive, Bethune ordered managers to speed up a stalled project. When a manager asked Bethune why he was so sure the new deadline could be met, he said, "Because I have a Beretta at home with a 15-round magazine, and if you don't get those airplanes painted I'm going to come in here and empty the clip."

Offering outcomes not wanted can work in the short run. The problem is that it works *only* in the short run. It causes too much damage to become an enduring solution. It stirs up resentment, spoils relationships, and creates job dissatisfaction. This wears thin with employees and works against, not for, their motivation and performance over the long haul.

Managers should withhold unwanted outcomes. They are stumbling blocks to performance and should be cleared away. One of the most common causes of satisfaction problems is managers unintentionally giving employees outcomes they don't want. Managers mistakenly think employees want something, such as more responsibility, and give it to them. At other times, managers simply are unaware that they are giving unwanted outcomes, such as when performance feedback intended to be positive is viewed as criticism.

Withholding these unwanted outcomes is an important solution to many satisfaction problems. It is a solution best accomplished with employee involvement. Employees know what is causing them to stumble, and they know the best way to smooth the path toward better performance.

LOCATION IS EVERYTHING

When Denise joined the sales force, she was assigned a desk in the corner of a big open room with waist-high cubicles. She was isolated from her 60 counterparts. Within months, Denise led the organization in sales. Her manager decided to reward her by moving her to a cubicle near her peers, in the thick of things.

People dropped by to chat. They interrupted her when she was talking with others. They wasted her time. She found it difficult to concentrate. It was impossible to talk comfortably on the phone with her customers, with the noise and lack of privacy.

Her sales decreased. She dreaded coming to work, developed a negative attitude, and was very frustrated. She kept her feelings bottled up and didn't know what to do.

Three months later, I met Denise in a meeting with her manager, Patrick, to discuss motivation and performance issues. Denise liked Patrick. He had pulled some strings to reward her with the new work area. She was reluctant to tell him she did not like it.

Patrick was concerned that her sales were slipping. He knew Denise was disappointed but working harder than ever. He was hesitant to confront her.

Finally he did. "Denise, **can we talk** about the fact that your sales have fallen off?" He stopped and waited.

Denise looked down and did not respond. She could tell the truth and likely solve her agonizing problem, but that would hurt Patrick. Or she could blame her decline in sales on something else. She decided, took a deep breath, and spoke. "Patrick, you've been very good to me. I have a problem now that I can't solve by myself. I'm afraid discussing it will hurt you and make you feel like I don't appreciate all you've done for me." With the stage set, she paused.

"Denise, **if there's a problem, I'd like to help you with it.**"

"Everyone around my cubicle wants to socialize. And I can hear everything. It interferes with my reason for being here. I want to sell, make money, and be the best. But since the move, I've been frustrated, miserable, hating my job. I'm not sure how much longer I can take it, having my desk where it is now."

Patrick was flabbergasted. After a brief recovery, and to his credit, he said, "Denise, you've taught me a valuable lesson. I'll never again make assumptions about how you want to be rewarded. Next time I'll ask. Now, **how can we solve this** mess I've put you in?"

"I'd like to move back to my desk in the corner"

He looked at her for a few seconds and decided.

"Shall we do it now?"

They did. Denise smiled all the way.

• • •

Withholding unwanted outcomes is one side of the coin. Giving people what they want is the other. I have found some confusion around the idea of giving people what they want. Actually, it means just what it says.

What do employees really want? It depends. No two people are alike. Just ask three people, or five or ten, to name what they want most from their job. Many managers, and certainly much of the management literature, would have us believe that there are certain outcomes that *everyone* wants, such as empowerment and money. I have worked with countless employees who find empowerment dissatisfying. And many have told me, "Money is important, but other things are more important to me." When the solution is to give people what they want, managers would do well to take time out and discuss the solution with employees to discover what they really want.

One thing most people want is to enjoy their work. However, many choose careers, accept jobs, and seek promotions only to realize that the work itself is not rewarding. When this interferes with motivation and performance, what can managers do? Dan Reeves, head football coach of the Atlanta Falcons professional football team, explains it well. He had a player who quit the team early in the season. Reeves' response was, "We tried everything we could to make him a player, but it's got to come from inside. You can't change a man's heart." Managers find it a losing battle when they try.

My daughter, Shannon, took Reeves' statement beyond sports when she said, "No, you can't change a person's heart. You can't make a woman love a man if she's not attracted to him. You can't make a man love to cook if he has no interest in it. You can't make people love a job if they dislike it." While it sometimes is possible to redesign jobs so people will enjoy their work, this seldom is a realistic alternative. This leaves but one solution approach: Get people into jobs they enjoy. While this is not always practical in the short run, remember this for long-term organizational success: People perform better when the work itself is rewarding.

MARCHING TO THE HUMDRUM

Erika joined the company five years and three jobs after graduating from college. She soon became the most talked-about salesperson since Fred Johnson came on the scene like a rocket in 1990.

Erika was an aggressive, no-nonsense, confident woman who quickly closed a couple of huge sales with stubborn customers. In her first full year, she had the highest sales volume for a rookie in the history of the company and was ranked fifth overall in an organization with more than 200 salespeople.

Midway through her second year, Erika was being talked about again, this time because her sales results had not kept the pace she had set in her first year. David, her sales manager, was puzzled and troubled. He decided to talk with her and invested some time planning his approach. Over lunch he asked Erika several open-ended Belief System questions he had carefully worded because, as he knew, "The words make all the difference."

"Erika, you continue to do good work for us. You consistently exceed your quota and you're ranked thirty-seventh in sales after the first six months this year. I don't have any complaints about that. Your results are off quite a bit from last year, though, and you don't seem as happy with your job as you used to be. I was wondering, **is anything wrong?**"

As David expected, she did not hesitate. He had asked her, so she was going to tell him. That was Erika. "I'm not having fun anymore. The sales approach we use is a good one, but it's the same old thing every day. I'm bored. I can't stand this humdrum existence much longer."

"So you're saying the problem is that liking your work is very important to you and you're not enjoying it anymore."

Erika's face was solemn as she nodded in agreement.

So Erika had a satisfaction problem. The cause: the work itself was not rewarding. David pictured the satisfaction rating scale with an "X" on the dissatisfaction side at about the –6 level. He wondered what the solution would be, but he had another question first.

"Erika, **is anything else bothering you?**"

"Not really. I proved I can do the job and I have no complaints about the way I'm being treated by you and the company."

David felt relieved. Confidence and trust ratings were at about the 9 level. Fortunately, there were no problems here. The satisfaction issue would be tough enough to solve, unless Erika had the answer.

"Okay, so you'd like to make your work more enjoyable. **Any solutions in mind?**"

She responded immediately. "I've been thinking about that. Is there any chance I could try winning back accounts the company has lost and go after some we've never had before? I'd enjoy the challenge of that. If I'm successful, maybe I can pass along some of my current accounts and spend more time in a new direction."

David chuckled, almost out loud, listening to Erika sell herself. How did Erika know that just last week he had been given the responsibility of winning back former customers and going after new ones?

"I'd be willing to give it a try, Erika, if you really want to do it."

"Great. Thanks for saying yes."

David wished all of his salespeople focused on closing the sale, as Erika was doing here. He wanted to get closure on a few things, too. "Winning back dissatisfied customers and taking new accounts away from our competition won't be easy. Are you willing to do what it'll take to be successful?"

Erika did not hesitate. "I'll do whatever it takes to pull this off. Whatever it takes!"

"How would you go about it?"

"I already know what I'd do. Can we get together tomorrow? I'll give you a detailed plan."

"Sounds fine to me. I'll be in all afternoon. Come by when you're ready. **Anything else I need to know?**"

"No, that's it." Erika paused and then thanked David. "One of my college professors used to say that people perform best when they like what they're doing. Thanks for giving me a chance to enjoy my work again."

David smiled as she wrapped up her sales pitch by mentioning how he would benefit—she would perform better.

He reflected on the way he had guided this discussion and was pleased.

• • •

David had been skeptical of the Belief System at first, but not after using it with Erika. He saw firsthand that the Belief System works. David asked good questions and got good results. He was successful in getting Erika to tell him what her problem was and what was causing it. David told me he had particularly liked having Erika come up with her own solution. He had enjoyed watching her sell him on what she wanted to do. He said, "It made me realize how unproductive it is when I try to sell employees on my solutions to their problems." He was impressed with the commitment Erika gave to making *her* solution work.

EXERCISE 7

Reaching Solutions That Match Problems and Causes

1. Think of a solution you recently used to solve a satisfaction problem.

2. Did the solution match the problem and its cause(s)?

3. What results did you get?

WHEN SOLUTIONS WILL NOT WORK

The solution approaches referenced thus far are inadequate in certain situations. For example, managers may not have the authority to redesign jobs, additional resources may not be available to give, organizations may not have reward systems that tie outcomes to performance, and managers may not have control over the outcomes employees want. What can managers do in these circumstances? This question is addressed extensively in Chapter 6, "Handling Difficult Problems." But know this about seemingly insoluble motivation problems: Managers tend to assume that employees want more than they are actually seeking.

In one company where I worked, for example, employees complained about not being able to see where to park. Management's response was, "Putting up lights in the parking lot is not feasible." But with a little Belief System probing into the causes of the dissatisfaction, it turned out that all the employees wanted was clear white lines on the asphalt to separate the parking spaces properly. Management, somewhat sheepishly, allowed that, yes, they could take care of the problem after all.

Of course, solutions will not work unless they match the problem *and* its causes. Offering more money (a satisfaction solution) will not motivate insecure employees with a long history of failure (a confidence problem). Tying outcomes to performance (a trust solution) will not motivate employees who hate the work they are doing (a satisfaction problem).

THINK, PEOPLE, THINK

James, a sales vice president who had 700 account executives in his organization, told me about the biggest problem he faced. "The pressure to perform has pushed expectations up so high that all of our account executives are saying there's no way they can make their sales quota this year.

"But we've come up with a plan." He was excited when he told me, "We just announced an incentive plan to motivate everybody to meet or exceed their quota for the first quarter. That way they'll see they can meet it for the rest of the year."

And I thought, "Or reinforce the belief that they can't."

"We're giving new cars to the eight people who sell the most. What do you think? Will it work?"

I know he wanted me to say, "Great idea." Instead, I asked, "How many of the 700 believe they have a chance to win a car?"

He did not look happy when finally he mumbled, "Probably around 20."

"How motivated do you think the other 680 will be?"

He opened his mouth to speak, but only silence came out.

• • •

Effective communication, asking the right questions of the right people, getting to the causes of problems so as to better see their solutions—nearly all motivation problems are solvable with the right approach.

DECIDING EXACTLY WHAT TO DO

Solution approaches provide general guidance in solving motivation problems. They point you in the right direction. That is important, but it's not enough. What about *specific* solutions? How are they derived?

While causes clearly guide you to solution approaches, specific solutions are not self-evident. This can be a problem—one that managers usually bring upon themselves. They see a motivation problem, identify the cause(s), and the solution approach becomes obvious. Then the manager tends to feel responsible for developing the specific solution, in all its detail, alone. This is the mistake. Think about it.

What happens when employees have motivation problems? They live with the problems every day. They think about what is wrong and how to fix it. They know the causes. They know the solution. Employees are the best source of information for solutions to their own motivation problems.

Employee solutions will not be acceptable to managers 100 percent of the time. Yet, they cannot be ignored. Solutions suggested by employees tend to be less complicated, less costly, and more effective than managers' solutions. Getting employees involved in solving their own motivation problems pays off. Because it pays off, and Belief System managers are quick to see it, many managers go beyond encouraging employee involvement in solving motivation and performance problems. These managers see the Belief System process as a *shared responsibility* between manager and employee and go to some pains to instill the thinking in all employees, managers or not. As Warren Bennis and Patricia Ward Biederman say in their book *Organizing Genius*, "In all but the rarest cases, one is too small a number to produce greatness."

WHAT KIND OF MANAGER ARE YOU?

Typical Manager   It is my responsibility to solve motivation and performance problems.

Motivation Manager   Solving motivation and performance problems is a shared responsibility between manager and employee.

AN ILLUSTRATION

A group of managers recently completed a training program on the Belief System approach. Here is a discussion that took place when one manager reported back to work.

SAMPLE SCRIPT

Listening for the Problem

Employee: You've always been pleased with my work, but now that my job's expanded, I'm not sure I can handle it. (Analysis: This sounds like a confidence problem—"I can't do it.")

The temptation for the manager was to lapse into a pep talk, something like, "Sure you can. It'll just take a little time. I can let somebody help you for a while until you get things under control." However, this would be jumping ahead to a solution without identifying the causes. The manager had a more appropriate response.

SAMPLE SCRIPT

Uncovering Causes

Manager: You've done good work, and I've never seen you question your ability to get the job done. **Why are you having doubts now?** (Analysis: If you want to know what is causing a motivation problem, *ask.*)

Employee: There aren't enough hours in the day to get everything done. (Analysis: The cause of the problem seems to be "unrealistic expectations.") And besides that, a couple of my new responsibilities are really technical, and I don't have the background to do them. (Analysis: "Inadequate skills" looks like a second cause.)

With the causes identified, solutions jumped out. A typical response would be for the manager to say, "It may be hard to change your responsibilities now, but I can get you some training right away." (Solution: "skill building.") This would be offering a solution without considering any ideas the employee might have. Fortunately, the manager resisted the tendency to solve the problem herself and, instead, turned to the employee.

SAMPLE SCRIPT

Discovering a Solution

Manager: **Do you have a solution in mind?** (Analysis: If you want to know how to solve a motivation problem, *ask*.)

Employee: When we were given new responsibilities, three of us ended up with things we don't feel comfortable doing. Maybe we could change some assignments around? (Analysis: "Job redesign" is the solution being offered.) I've talked with the other two. They think it's a good idea.

Manager: Okay, I'd like for the three of you to get together and decide exactly what you want to do. Then let's all meet and go over it.

According to the manager, this was not a solution she would have thought about. She had learned that when employees have a problem, they know the causes, and they have preferred solutions. While you may not always be able to live with employee suggestions, it pays to ask.

EXERCISE 8

Getting Employees to Share Responsibility

1. Identify an employee who is experiencing a motivation and performance problem.

2. Get the employee to share the responsibility for solving the problem.

3. See if you can make this approach work.

ONE SOLUTION FOR TWO PROBLEMS

Employees often feel the pressure of two motivation problems simultaneously, and sometimes they are connected. Confidence problems and satisfaction problems, for example, frequently are intertwined.

The two are woven together when a person's confidence level is low and the work itself is not rewarding. When this is the case, solving one may solve the other.

YOU CAN'T MAKE PEOPLE ENJOY THEIR WORK— OR CAN YOU?

"She's unhappy in her job and I'm afraid we're going to lose her." Clark had just finished briefing me when Jane, the object of our discussion, appeared at his office door.

At first glance, she looked every bit the confident, fast-track, career woman she was supposed to be. Then she gathered a strained smile, offered a warm, damp hand, and introduced herself to me. She was wearing a layer of uneasiness that did not match her natural pleasant manner. Her eyes were filled with doubt.

We all took our seats and Clark, her manager, said, "Jane, thanks for meeting with us. As I explained to you this morning, I wanted us to meet with Thad and see if we could work through the situation you came to me about yesterday. Would you tell him, **What's the problem?**"

Jane replied, "When I first got my promotion, I remember thinking that most people don't have job satisfaction, and I was one of the lucky ones. Becoming a manager was a dream come true. I got more money and more responsibility, and the best part was that I loved my job. I had it all."

When she paused, her shoulders sagged. "I've been in the job for only two months, and everything has fallen apart. My web site design team is missing deadlines, our customers are complaining, and employee morale is terrible. I hate my job, and I think it's time to leave it."

Clark turned to Jane and said, "You have the potential to be a good manager, and I don't want to lose you. But if you really do hate your job, maybe you should go. I want what's best for you, but I can't do anything to make you enjoy your work."

I thought I had heard enough to know what the problem was. If I was right, things would work out fine. If not, the solution could be difficult.

She needed to tell us more. "Jane, **what are you feeling now?**"

"I hurt all over. I've never failed at anything before, and I don't know how to turn it around."

She had concluded, "I can't do it." I wondered why. It was worth a guess. "**Do you have the skills you need for the job?**"

She shifted her eyes to Clark and looked uncomfortable.

He said, "It's okay to say it, Jane. Tell us."

"To be honest, I feel like I've been thrown to the wolves and left to make or break it on my own. I don't blame anyone but myself, though."

Her response to my next question would be telling. "Jane, suppose you could get things under control, make the problems go away. Projects are completed on time, customers are satisfied, and employees are motivated. **If you were performing well, how would you like your job?**"

"I'd love it. It would be a great job."

"So, **is it the job you hate, or the fear of failing?**"

She looked directly at me for what seemed a long time, then at Clark, and then at her hands gripped tightly in her lap. When she looked up she was talking to herself more than to either of us. "I've been running from the wrong thing, haven't I?" She turned to Clark. "When I learn how to be a better manager, I'll enjoy this job. Clark, will you help me?"

"Yes, I will, Jane. I want you to succeed. **What's the best way for me to help you?**"

She responded immediately. "I wanted to ask you this weeks ago, but you're so busy I just didn't." She looked down and paused. "I'd like to meet with you a couple of times a week. I can tell you what's going on and how I plan to handle things. You can give me your reaction and any coaching I need."

"I'm more than willing to do that, anytime you want. Ask Julie to put you on my calendar so I'll know when to be available. **Is there anything else?**"

"That's all I can think of now. This will be a great start."

Jane gave Clark a soft-spoken, sincere thanks and smiled.

• • •

The point is this: Sometimes the work itself is dissatisfying (a satisfaction problem) because the person is performing poorly (a confidence problem); however, the work becomes satisfying when performance gets on track and confidence is restored (a confidence solution)

E X E R C I S E   9

Applying the Belief System to Yourself

1. Think of something you currently are not motivated to do.

2. Do you have a confidence, trust, or satisfaction problem?

3. What is causing the problem?

4. What solution would work for you?

5. What steps must you take?

THE MOST IMPORTANT MESSAGE YOU CAN HEAR

When it comes to motivation and performance problems, an ounce of prevention is worth a pound of cure, and quick solutions are worth their weight in gold. Belief System managers use one approach for both. Consider:

What happens when you *let people do what they naturally do well?* First, they have confidence in themselves to get the job done. Second, dips in their confidence tend to be temporary when issues outside of their job skills (like unclear expectations or inadequate resources) infringe on their performance. Their overall positive self-assurance tends to spill over, and they believe they can resolve whatever issues they face. In other words, confidence breeds confidence. As a result, they move ahead quickly to get things back on track. In short, people who are assigned work they naturally do well are confident they can get the job done.

What happens when you *place people in jobs where they find the work itself rewarding?* (1) They enjoy their work; they wake up each morning looking forward to tackling the day. (2) When people, circumstances, and events cause dissatisfaction, they tend to be forgiving. Like anyone else, they feel disappointment if a pay raise falls short of expectations or if praise comes sparingly from the boss. But the disappointment does not linger and distract them. They are able to put their feelings behind them and sustain their motivation because they enjoy their work. In other words, satisfaction derived from the work itself tends to outweigh dissatisfaction thrown at them from other directions. The bottom line is that satisfaction derived from the work itself is a compelling force that spurs people on.

Think about your job as a manager and what it would be like if all employees simply loved their work. That is the best kind of motivation. If you must keep people motivated with external rewards—pay raises, promotions, and so on—it is tough to deliver all the time, you end up with unhappy employees, and their performance slips. But those people who love their jobs, cannot wait to get to work, and are the last ones out the door at night are the treasures.

Trust is never an issue with the work itself. To understand why, consider the difference between extrinsic and intrinsic outcomes. Most outcomes available to employees are classified as *extrinsic* outcomes. Extrinsic outcomes have two main characteristics: (1) They are given to the employee by someone else, usually the manager. (2) Employees normally receive extrinsic outcomes *after* they perform. For example, a manager gives bonuses *after* employees turn in a good performance, offers praise *after* a job well done, reprimands employees *after* they violate safety rules, and assigns low performance evaluation ratings *after* employees have performed poorly for a considerable period of time.

Intrinsic outcomes are different. They have two primary characteristics: (1) They are not given to employees by someone else; people give intrinsic outcomes to themselves. (2) They are the *feelings* that come while *doing* the work. The feelings derived from the work itself can be satisfying, like the feelings of an accountant who loves working with numbers, a salesperson who enjoys being with people, or a mechanic who gets pleasure from repairing machinery. The feelings resulting from the work itself can be dissatisfying as well, such as the feelings of an extrovert who hates doing budgets, a shy person who dislikes customer contact, or an energetic clerk who loathes being bound to a desk updating files. Because the outcomes from the work itself (the feelings) come *during* the performance, not after, employees know for certain that they will get those outcomes (feelings) simply by doing the work. Do the work, and get the feelings. In other words, these outcomes are by their very nature tied to performing. Trust is not a problem when it comes to the work itself.

Now, with this analysis in mind, consider: What happens when you put people in jobs where they find the work itself satisfying *and* they naturally do the work well? First, they believe they can perform (confidence is high). Second, they believe they will get certain outcomes, namely the good feelings associated with doing the work (trust is high). Third, they believe the outcomes will be pleasing (satisfaction is high). *The three conditions for motivation—confidence, trust, satisfaction—are met!* Managers find it easy to get good performance out of people like this. Just put them in the right job, get out of their way, and let them perform. Think about how rewarding it would be for everyone if you put all of your employees in jobs that turn them on.

> **LEARNING LESSON**
>
> People perform *best* when the work itself is satisfying *and* they naturally do it well.

SOME OUTCOMES ARE NOT TO BE EARNED

An argument erupted during one of my training sessions when a hard-driving, results-oriented manager firmly stated that all outcomes should be tied to performance. Another manager spoke up in disagreement. "People deserve certain things no matter what," she declared. "I had a manager once who was nice and friendly when you did a good job, but when you made a mistake he would rudely give you the cold shoulder until you worked your way back into his good graces. Everybody resented being treated that way. It made us want to work against him, not for him. It certainly didn't make us want to work harder."

After a moment of silence, a soft voice ended the debate. "My parents were always considerate and caring when I made good grades, but they withheld their affection when I didn't. You don't build relationships that way; you destroy them."

The record shows that people perform better when money, promotions, praise, and recognition, for example, are tied to their performance. However, regardless of performance, every employee deserves fair treatment, kindness, respect (the right to speak, to express opinions, to disagree), and feedback, for example. Think about it.

WHAT SUITS YOU?

GETTING STARTED If you want to discover *solutions* that will work, go to the person with the problem and ask.	Managers evolve into a way of helping people. Some take charge and make decisions for them. Others simply lend an ear. Tenets of motivation management and the Belief System provide a guiding hand. Getting others involved in solving their own problems works! You may want to give it a try.

MOVING AHEAD

Have you thought about how you could move ahead, be more effective, and get better results? I learned how in the middle of the desert on the other side of the world.

MULTIBILLIONAIRE REVEALS THE SECRET TO SUCCESS

I was invited by Secretary of Commerce Malcolm Baldrige to go on a U.S. trade mission to Saudi Arabia in 1982. The two-week trip was led by Secretary Baldrige.

The group consisted mainly of the chairmen or CEOs of U.S. corporations—large ones primarily, men such as Sandy McDonnell of McDonnell-Douglas and T. Wilson of Boeing. We met with Saudi government and business leaders to promote trade with the United States. Basically, we were selling our own wares.

Secretary Baldrige opened doors for us by arranging appointments with practically anyone we wanted to meet. I did not visit with the Saudi king, though some in our group probably did. However, all of us had private meetings with government officials at the next level down, their equivalents of our secretary of defense or secretary of state, and the country's leading businessmen.

Everyone was well educated, tough-minded, and savvy.

The entire trip was fascinating, particularly the cultural differences. Some of the laws were frightening. Two months before our trip, I read that a member of the royal family was found to be having an affair with a young woman; both were stoned to death in public. The punishment for stealing, I was told while there, was to have one's left hand cut off—in public.

The difference in dress was a constant reminder that we were in a foreign land. We wore our standard business attire: suits, white shirts, and ties. The local people were clothed in flowing robes and traditional head coverings, called keffiyah (kuh FEE yuh).

In spite of all the differences, I concluded that the Saudis were a people basically the same as Americans in many ways—although one person in particular was more interesting than all others I met.

He had an unusual depth of insight into human behavior. He was a businessman, a multibillionaire, and the wealthiest person in Saudi Arabia outside the royal family.

I was his dinner guest one evening. I was seated to his left at a table for four, being served an endless stream of delicious food, most of which I did not recognize. Two other members of the trade mission were present. One sat directly across from me, the other to my left.

As dessert was presented, the person to my left, a distinguished and successful businessman in his own right, asked our host, "What is the secret to your success?" His response was something I'll never forget.

He replied, "I have told it many times, but I tell it no more."

We all sat in silence, wondering why. I decided to let someone else take the bait. From my left again, "But why? We would all like to know."

"You are curious, but not enough. Do you really desire to know? And if you did, what would you do? You would have to do different from what you do now."

The person to my left responded, "I don't understand. So what is the secret?"

"But you see, I have already told you."

• • •

CHAPTER 5

Putting It
All Together

"Join the circle of wisdom."

A BRIEFING SESSION

The key to putting it all together—the principles and devices of motivation management and the Belief System—is the *Diagnostic Interview*. The Diagnostic Interview gently forces an accurate diagnosis of problems and causes and substantially increases the prospects of finding good solutions to performance shortfalls.

The secret to diagnosing and solving motivation problems quickly is to put the ball in the employee's court. Rely on employees to help diagnose problems, uncover causes, and come up with solutions.

It takes information to solve problems; and when it comes to motivation problems, employees have the information managers need to make good decisions.

Using the employee-centered approach recommended here will work. You can make it work for you.

THE THINGS WE REMEMBER

Sometimes people ask questions that unsettle my peace of mind.

One that troubled me for a long time came from a potential client: "You're pushing this Belief System stuff, but I'm wondering—how do you get people to openly discuss problems and work together to actually *solve* them?"

I had a dozen ways to explain this, but no one rock-solid answer. After a lengthy search, one of my clients gave me an answer that equaled the question. It happened when I was interviewing him for a book I was writing.

Merrill owned a large, very successful company. He was nearing retirement. An excellent manager, he had unusual insight into human behavior. When I posed the question, "How do you get managers and employees to willingly solve employee problems together?," I had no idea where he would go with it, given his unique way of getting a point across.

He settled back in his chair. "Back in the summer of 1948, when I was almost six years old, we took our first vacation to the beach. Daytona Beach, Florida. We packed our tan '42 Chevrolet the night before and left early the next day.

"By midmorning, the stifling heat was oppressive, blasting our bodies as it whipped in through the rolled-down windows and swirled around inside the car as we headed south on Highway 41. Mom forgot the picnic. We had two flat tires. We ran out of gas and were stranded for what seemed like hours. The engine blew up in the middle of nowhere. The mechanic overcharged us. We had to spend the night in a miserable little motel room filled with suffocating heat and mosquitoes. Mom and Dad argued constantly, alternating between screaming and total silence. Their only words for me were, 'Be quiet.'

"It was the longest two days of my life. I don't remember whether the beach was fun or not. All I remember was the misery of getting there. You know, *the way you get somewhere can dim your view of the destination.* Over the next several years my parents talked about other family vacations, but we never took one.

"I've seen it in business, too. This company, all you see here, was started in 1979. I was 37 years old. My partner and I had the time of our lives getting it off the ground. We worked seven days a week, 15 hours a days. It didn't seem like work. We were financially successful from the start. Then we had a disagreement. It turned into an argument, then a full-fledged conflict. It was brutal. Everything but a fist fight.

"We eventually got the problem worked out, but things were never the same after that. It wasn't long before my partner decided to leave. I don't remember what the conflict was about or what the solution was, but I have a vivid memory of the suffering we went through. I learned that the approach you take to solve a problem can outweigh the solution."

I started to speak, but he was not finished yet.

"Many years ago, one of my executives interviewed a young college graduate. He said she interviewed well, but he was surprised to find that she didn't have any career goals. He quoted her. 'The way you get somewhere can be more important than where you go.' I thought about that in the context of my own life. 'Hire her, George; she can start as my assistant.'

"On her first day at work, we chatted some, sharing ideas, just getting to know each other. I remember asking about her views on managing. One of her comments stuck with me. With the certainty only youth can have, she said, 'You can get people to go almost anywhere with you one time, but to be a successful manager, people have to be on board with you *all* of the time.'

"'And how would you accomplish that?'

"'Easy,' she said. 'People want to travel with you when they expect a pleasant and fruitful journey.'

Merrill looked at me. "Can you imagine? Twenty-two years old."

"Where is she now?" I asked.

"Still here. She's my best executive. She'll take over when I retire." He smiled. "Good decision that was, hiring her. She's done a great job, been a good friend. To use her words, 'We've had a pleasant and fruitful journey.'"

• • •

FORGING A MORE PRODUCTIVE WORKPLACE

To this point, you have learned the theoretical basis of the Belief System of Motivation and Performance (Chapter 1), and you have learned how to identify motivation and performance problems (Chapter 2), how to uncover problem causes (Chapter 3), and how solutions flow from an understanding of those causes (Chapter 4).

Now it is time to put it all together in the workplace. The principles and methods learned previously are but custom-made tools ready for use on a job site. Without a craftsman, they build nothing. You, the manager, are the craftsman. Having learned the use for the tools, you must pick them up and go to work. This chapter is about wielding the tools provided for you to forge a more productive workplace.

THE LONG AND SHORT OF IT

A company I was consulting with had one slot for an executive development program at a prestigious university. A pool of 14 applicants had been narrowed down to three. I was asked to interview them and give a recommendation.

I sat with the first candidate. "Warren, what are the two most exciting new things you've learned recently?"

"Let's see. Ah, ah…okay, neurolinguistic programming and behavior style."

"Could you quickly summarize each of them? Just enough to give me a feel for your understanding of each concept."

Warren was ready to impress me. "Sure. The way I see NLP, we all represent the world with images (visually), sounds (auditorily), and feelings (kinesthetically). Each person tends to be primarily visual or auditory or kinesthetic. If you're trying to teach visual people, for example, or simply communicate well with them, you'll be more successful if you show them pictures, diagrams, things like that, and paint pictures with words."

"Warren, you've given me a good feel for the three 'representation systems,' except for one thing. How do you know which is which?"

He confidently launched into his response. "A visual person uses visual words like see, look, picture, show, clear, vision, imagine, notice. An auditory person uses auditory words such as sound, hear, listen, talk, discuss. The kinesthetic person uses feeling words like feel, grasp, handle, stress, hard, firm, rough, tough, exciting. I see this as something that clearly has value for everybody."

Judging from Warren's frequent use of visual words, he definitely was a visual person. I wondered if he knew what I was. "Warren, this is *exciting* stuff. I *feel* like I have a *handle* on the main point you're *stressing:* if you're alert to the words people use, you can get a good *feel,* or at least a *rough* indication, of whether they're primarily visual, auditory, or kinesthetic. Based on what you know about NLP, have you gotten a *feel* for what my primary representation system is—visual, auditory, or kinesthetic?"

"Well, let me see…I, ah…I guess I haven't noticed."

His response did not surprise me. I had used a lot of kinesthetic words. But he was a visual person, not auditory, and listening was not easy for him. If he read a letter from me, he would quickly see my kinesthetic words; *hearing* me speak them would require some training.

"Do you have a firm grasp of the basics of behavior style?"

Warren jumped into a minilecture. "I like the DISC approach. 'D' is for *dominant*—strong, forceful, and aggressive. Those with the *influencing* style, the 'I' people, they're happy, friendly, and persuasive. 'S' stands for *steady*. The 'S' style tends to be kind, easygoing, and relationship oriented. 'C' is for *cautious*, logical and detail-oriented people with perfectionist tendencies."

"Warren, I have one question…."

"I suppose you want to see if I can apply my knowledge on behavior style, too."

"Could you draw your behavior style graph for me?" The DISC approach stresses that everybody shows *some* of the behaviors of *each* of the four styles. Simple tests are available to gauge this. Numerical scores are generated for each style that indicate the extent to which a person is dominant, influencing, steady, and cautious. Plotting these four points onto a grid produces the person's behavior style graph.

"I'm a 'D,' dominant, that's all I know."

The principal value of behavior style is knowing the *other* person's behavioral tendencies. If that was all he knew about his own behavior style, it was unlikely he knew the style of those around him.

He continued. "Well, I guess I'm looking kind of foolish here."

"I didn't mean to upset you."

"It's not you, it's *me* I'm upset with. I don't like what you've made me see about myself. I'm long on knowledge, short on application." He tapped a fingernail on his desk and stared at some work papers. "You know, it's only when you see your mistakes that you can do better."

He glanced at his built-in cherry bookcase overflowing with books. "I've always known you have to keep on learning. But you have to apply what you learn, too."

I knew I had witnessed learning in progress.

He smiled. "What good is knowledge if you don't use what you've learned?"

Our time was up. I had meetings with the other two finalists.

When we shook hands, Warren held onto mine. "I don't expect you to recommend me for the executive development program, but there's something I want to say. You can be certain that I *will* apply what I've learned here today. Thank you, very, very much."

GETTING STARTED

Learning new tools is not enough. You must pick them up and put them to work.

Warren called me when the company announced who had been selected for the program. "I want to thank you. I can't believe they picked me." When he continued, his words sounded rehearsed and I realized he was speaking *my* language. "I'm really *excited* and it *feels* especially good, after going through a *rough* selection process, to be chosen for the program. The waiting was *stressful* and I know it will be *tough* becoming a student again, especially in a *hard* program, but I'm ready for the *pressure*."

I laughed and felt good. He was the right choice.

• • •

THE DIAGNOSTIC INTERVIEW

Putting it all together comes down to a *Diagnostic Interview*, a structured way for manager and employee to have a face-to-face meeting and collaboratively arrive at solutions to motivation and performance problems that are acceptable to both parties. Throughout this book, you have been implored to *ask the employee* when there is a problem to be solved; you do the asking during the Diagnostic Interview.

There is much about the Diagnostic Interview that is familiar to those in managerial positions, but there is one thing that is quite different. Familiar is the practice of diagnosis itself; it is, after all, basic to any discipline that seeks to remedy problems. In medicine, for example, no doctor would prescribe a medication or procedure for a condition that had not yet been determined. Unfortunately, that is not always true in the management field: Remedies are typically offered before problems have been accurately or fully diagnosed. This is where the Diagnostic Interview is critically different. The very heart of the process is the *belief diagnosis,* the determination of a person's confidence, trust, and satisfaction. With the information gleaned from this unique communication, managers know the problem they are dealing with and its causes, to an extent unobtainable any other way. Thus prepared, managers are much more apt to succeed in their search for a way out of employee motivation and performance problems.

How is a Diagnostic Interview conducted? A simple, yet effective, three-part process is used. First is an important *preparation* phase. Next, the actual *diagnosis* takes place. The process ends with the *problem-solving* phase.

T A B L E 2		
The Diagnostic Interview Process		
Prepare for the Belief Diagnosis	**Rate the Three Beliefs**	**Solve the Belief Problem(s)**
• Document the employee's performance.	• Rate confidence (Belief 1).	• Get employee to identify causes.
• Meet with the employee and state your performance concerns.	• Rate trust (Belief 2).	• Ask employee for solution(s).
• Mutually agree that performance is a problem.	• Rate satisfaction (Belief 3).	• Agree on solution(s).
		• Get and give a commitment.
		• Establish follow-up.
		• Give positive reinforcement.

Managers conduct the Diagnostic Interview, employing the tools of the Belief System, but employees are far from passive players. Indeed, the entire process, including the Belief System itself, is employee centered. Employees are equal partners when it comes to solving motivation and performance problems. Why?

- Employees typically know more about their own performance problems than anyone else. They are their problems, after all.

- Employees generally know what will solve their problems. Since they live with them, you can bet that they have been thinking about how to solve them. They know what will work for them.

- Employees have preferred ways of solving problems they face and tend to resist all others. Keep this in mind.

SECOND-BEST SOLUTIONS

I work, read, or sleep when I travel. Occasionally I get drawn into a conversation.

"What are you working on?" I turned to my left and saw an older man, neatly dressed in suit and tie, smiling. A retired business executive, he later told me. We were on a flight from Atlanta to New York.

"I'm writing a book about motivation management, how to deal with motivation and performance problems."

He motioned to my notepad. "What part are you writing now?"

I smiled and wondered what his reaction would be. "I'm making a pitch for managers to encourage second-best solutions."

He chuckled. "Good line. Grabs your attention." He glanced at my notepad. "Second-best solutions, huh?"

There were several steps in the line of logic that led to the virtues of second-best solutions. I began. "When employees believe in their own solutions, they'll do whatever it takes to make them work."

"I agree. I've seen it many times."

"Employees who believe in their own solutions have a dilemma, though. Let's say an employee has a problem, and she takes it to her manager. The manager is experienced, sees a solution right away, knows how to make it work, and maybe has seen it work before. So, the manager offers *his* solution to her."

He nodded. "Managers seem to think it's their job to solve everybody's problems."

"Yes, and that puts the employee in a predicament, because employees who come with a problem usually come with a solution, too. They come for confirmation, for support, maybe to flesh out a few details—not for the manager to override their solution."

"I couldn't agree more."

"The employee has two solutions now: one she believes in, and one the manager wants her to use."

He lifted his hand and pointed a finger. "Yes, the predicament."

"When the manager hears the employee's solution, he may consider it a good one, but not as good as his own. He's sure his solution will work. He's not certain about hers. Naturally, he judges his solution to be best and hers only second-best."

"Sounds like most of the managers I've known, and I've known a lot in my 72 years."

"When the manager gives his solution to the employee, he makes a dangerous assumption. He assumes the employee can and will make it work."

"Asking for trouble, isn't he?"

"Yes, because managers tend to underestimate the power of employees believing in their own solutions. I've seen some shaky solutions work. They worked because the people who owned them believed in them, and they made them work."

"You're right. I've seen it, too. What will you say in your book about the employee who is sent away with the manager's solution?"

"Two things. Resentment and resistance. She'll be resentful that her boss vetoed her solution in favor of his. And she'll resist using his solution."

> **LEARNING LESSON**
>
> Second-best solutions that employees believe in are better than "best" solutions that cause resistance.

"I agree. Not a good situation."

"No. She owns her solution and believes in it, and she'll do whatever it takes to make it work. Not so with his."

"I'll put my money on her solution."

"That's why I say second-best solutions that employees believe in will yield better results than the 'best' solution pushed on them (even gently) by their manager."

• • •

The manager's role in the Diagnostic Interview is to gather information. That means managers must encourage employees to talk, usually 80 percent of the time, or the process will fail. The manager guides the conversation with Belief System questioning, and then "clams up" to listen and to interpret what is said. This clamming up and paying close, unbiased attention to responses is perhaps the most difficult of the Belief System techniques for managers to master. Obviously, it can be done, and when it is, major breakthroughs in employee motivation often follow. I have seen it time and again.

WHAT I WAS GOING TO SAY...

I walked out of the conference room and headed to my next meeting. Near the elevator a voice behind me yelled, "Wait up!"

I turned and saw Melissa, a unit manager, rushing toward me. She tried to catch her breath and talk at the same time. "John's calling me...on the carpet...at three o'clock today. He said...you'd be there...in the meeting." I was working with John for one reason—a vice president I liked had twisted my arm.

"Yes, I'll be there."

She smiled. "Thank goodness! I may need your help. He's going to come down hard on me, I just know it."

"I'm only there to observe, then do some coaching with John afterward."

Her smile disappeared. "Oh." She reached for a tissue. When she looked up, I saw her tears. "Oh, well." Her voice cracked, then she blew her nose.

"Melissa, we've discussed this. You have to speak up with John. He's a strong personality."

"Speak up—I'll need to shout! He keeps piling work on me, and I'm not getting everything out on time. I'm sure that's what he wants to talk about. I have so many interruptions I can't get everything done. It's completely stressing me out."

In Belief System language, Melissa was telling me she had two problems. There was a confidence (Belief 1) problem, "I can't do it." And a satisfaction (Belief 3) problem, getting something not wanted—too much stress.

"Looks like something has to change."

"You've got that right."

"Do you have anything in mind?"

"Yes, I want to work V-O one day a week."

"Virtual office?"

"Yes, I want to work out of my office at home. A lot of people here do. Having a full day each week without interruptions will do the trick."

"Show John how it will benefit *him*, and be forceful."

"But how can I show him? He never listens."

"Melissa, you can be very persuasive. I've seen you do it."

"Not with him, you haven't." She was right. "Well, thanks for listening. See you at three." She turned and slowly walked away, shoulders sagging.

John started the meeting precisely on time. "Melissa, you've missed several deadlines recently, and I thought we needed to talk about it."

"You're right. It's happened three times. I'm concerned, too."

"What's the problem? Anything I can do to help?"

"I hope so. As you know, my workload has increased recently. It's hard to get everything done with all the interruptions. You know, calls from customers, questions from my staff. I'm really getting..."

"You've always been good with your customers. And your staff, too."

"As I was saying, it's been hectic the last few weeks and I'm get-ting..."

"...stressed out?"

"Yes, and it's hard to get my work done with all the interruptions and I was wondering if..."

"Can't you do something to control the interruptions? Just tell your staff to give you some breathing room."

"They're good about coming to me only when it's necessary. What I'd like to do..."

"Maybe they need some training or something so they can make more decisions on their own. Have you thought about that?"

"What I was going to say was, I feel like I could get more done, and at the same time relieve a lot of stress, if I could..."

"Melissa, sorry to interrupt, but I know exactly how you feel. My job is stressful, too. I started an exercise program and it's been my salvation." He paused. "You know the company runs a fitness center right here in the building. You need to use your lunch hour and get some good exercise to relieve all that stress. Believe me, it'll work."

Melissa stiffened, glared at John, then abruptly closed her notepad. "John, that's a great idea. Thanks so much for your help." I winced at her sarcasm. John didn't seem to notice it.

She stood, reached into her pocket for a tissue, and turned away. She walked quickly to the door and closed it—hard. John jumped. He turned to me. "What was that all about?"

Melissa's stressed-to-the-limit reaction to John's unacceptable behav-ior was not surprising. Neither was John's unawareness of what he had done. The thing that caught me off guard was the sinking feeling I had when the voice inside my head said, "Can I really help him?" I realized I had a confidence (Belief 1) problem.

John had two problems—talking too much and not listening enough. Experience had taught me an unpleasant lesson. People with this combination of weaknesses have a very high mountain to climb. Not Mt. Everest, but close. I had found it easy to teach these people how to listen more effectively but difficult to get them to do it.

I wondered if John would accept my feedback, understand what he was doing wrong, and get a clear picture of the negative consequences. I hoped he would be receptive, as others had been, to a simple, yet profound truth: When you realize others have something important to say, too, you will talk less and listen more.

• • •

WHAT KIND OF MANAGER ARE YOU?

Typical Manager When diagnosing problems, you talk a lot. How else can you help employees, be persuasive with them, and control the conversation so things will not get out of hand?

Motivation Manager You ask, "clam up," and listen—the Belief System way. You know that if you talk more than 20 percent of the time when diagnosing problems, you jeopardize the process—and success.

Now it is time to walk through the Diagnostic Interview process step by step.

Prepare for the Belief Diagnosis

The first phase of the Diagnostic Interview process, the preparatory phase, comprises three steps.

Document Employee Performance

Before meeting with the employee, gather specific information to document his or her performance. Be prepared to show the employee that actual performance is not meeting expectations. Be specific whenever possible. Using examples is helpful. Try to pinpoint symptoms of the problem. Give some thought to what may be causing them. Some things can become fairly obvious with a little Belief System thinking. For example, if the employee recently came from a bankrupt firm that promised much for performance but could not deliver, the person may still believe that "outcomes will not be tied to my performance." A trust problem, perhaps? Just remember this:

It is impossible to resolve performance problems if you cannot convincingly illustrate where the employee falls short of established standards. Do your homework. Here are some examples.

- A manager reviewed recent sales reports and discovered that the number of sales calls Janice made during each of the last two months was roughly 30 percent lower than the targeted number she usually meets. Her actual sales the previous month were down by 41 percent.

- A manager heard about a rift between his operations group and the sales organization. He visited with the sales VP to check it out. The manager learned that Robert, one of his operation's managers, and two of the top salespeople had had a disagreement and had resorted to communicating only by e-mail. This had been causing some delays and mix-ups in shipments to valued customers. The manager confirmed this information through two other sources.

- Last week a manager received a complaint from a customer about Wayne, one of his employees. Wayne had been late completing work for the customer and corrections and changes were needed. The work was returned to the manager, who passed it on to Wayne with a note to take care of it right away. A similar complaint came today from another customer. Same problem.

State Your Performance Concerns

Now, face-to-face with the employee, indicate your concern about motivation and performance. Point out why you are concerned. Be direct and to the point. When doing this, show concern. This is no time for accusations or a threatening manner. Exhibit a desire to help, not punish. Here are some ways to do this.

SAMPLE SCRIPT

Stating Performance Concerns

EXAMPLE A

Manager: Your monthly call reports show a decline in sales activity over the last two months. With your sales performance down, I thought we'd better talk about how you can get back on track.

EXAMPLE B

Manager: There appears to be a breakdown in communication between folks in operations and the staff in the sales department. Good teamwork is critical to meet delivery schedules. I want to discuss what you might do to open up the flow of information.

EXAMPLE C

Manager: As you know, I got a complaint last week about your work. Today I got another one. Same problem as last week. Getting complaints about your work is unusual, so I thought we should talk about it and figure out how you can keep it from happening again.

After opening statements like these to explain the purpose of the meeting, stop and wait for the employee to respond. This gets employees involved in solving their own motivation and performance problems. An employee may be hesitant the first time you approach a problem this way. Be patient. Offer encouragement. Be alert to comments like, "Oh, gee, I didn't know anything was wrong." Responses like this usually indicate a reluctance to talk. Try to eliminate the reluctance with a sincere expression that you want to help.

Mutually Agree that Performance Is a Problem

No progress will occur unless you and the employee agree that there is a performance problem. There should also be understanding and agreement on the disparity between *actual* and *expected* performance. This is where the manager's homework comes in handy. It does no good to say, "Your performance hasn't been up to par," unless you can justify your remarks. So be clear, and be prepared with details of what has brought you to the diagnostic interview.

UNCLEAR EXPECTATIONS HIT HOME

We were getting ready for dinner one night. Our four-year-old son, Eslie, had been outside playing and was dirty from head to toe.

I made eye contact with him (at that age he could hear you only if he looked into your eyes) and said, "Eslie, be sure you've washed your hands before we eat."

"Yes, sir."

Certain that he had both heard and understood, I turned my attention to something else.

Several minutes later we were seated around the table. We all reached to hold hands with those beside us, our custom when we blessed the food. When he put his hand in mine, I could feel the dirt.

"Eslie, did you wash your hands?"

"Yes, sir."

This puzzled me because I was almost certain he had not.

"When did you wash them?"

He looked up at me with an expression of total innocence. "This morning."

• • •

Rate the Three Beliefs

The Diagnostic Interview continues with the beliefs diagnosis. This calls for the manager to rate the employee's three beliefs as described in Chapter 1.

1. Confidence: "Can I do it?"

2. Trust: "Will outcomes be tied to my performance?"

3. Satisfaction: "Will the outcomes be satisfying to me?"

In the Belief System approach to motivation management, the beliefs diagnosis is where the "rubber meets the road." The motivation problem resides in the employee because he or she is the one who is not performing; the solution to the problem generally resides in the employee, too, although he or she may not understand that it does. It makes no difference whether the employee understands or not, however, for employees can do little or nothing to solve their own problem without the manager's intercession.

Unless a trained manager creates the right environment for a solution to emerge, the problem and solution lie fallow in the vessel of the employee. A Belief System manager can turn over that vessel and shake out a solution that will take root, to the benefit of all. Creating the environment that allows this to happen begins with the beliefs diagnosis.

Once agreement has been reached that, yes, there is a performance problem and, yes, manager and employee generally agree on

---

EXERCISE 10

Rating Employee Beliefs

1. Does the employee believe he or she can perform as expected?

1	2	3	4	5	6	7	8	9	10

Cannot perform   Not sure   Can perform
as expected   as expected

2. Does the employee believe outcomes will be tied to his or her performance?

1	2	3	4	5	6	7	8	9	10

Outcomes will not be   Not sure   Outcomes will be
tied to performance   tied to performance

3. Does the employee believe the outcomes will be satisfying?

-10 -9 -8 -7 -6 -5 -4 -3 -2 -1 0 +1 +2 +3 +4 +5 +6 +7 +8 +9 +10

Outcomes will be   Not sure   Outcomes will be
dissatisfying   satisfying

---

its specifics, you can move into the diagnosis of the three beliefs. Use the rating scales to log what you learn. As always in the diagnostic process, ask questions and listen; this is the way to gather the information needed to rate the three beliefs as seen in Exercise 10.

An important tip to keep in mind is this: *Diagnose all three beliefs.* It is a mistake to find a confidence or trust problem, for example, and stop there. You may have more than one belief problem on your hands. Here is how a beliefs diagnosis might unfold:

Managers must look for the answers to three core questions, each one a derivation of the confidence, trust, or satisfaction problem. How the questions are worded can vary, but the objective remains the same: to get specific, truthful answers to these questions.

1. Does the person believe his or her effort will lead to the expected performance? (Confidence)

2. Does the person believe the outcomes will be tied to his or her performance? (Trust)

3. Does the person believe the outcomes will be satisfying? (Satisfaction)

Confidence	Trust	Satisfaction
Effort ······> Performance ······> Outcomes ······> Satisfaction		
"Does the person believe his or her effort will lead to performance?"	"Does the person believe the outcomes will be tied to performance?"	"Does the person believe the outcomes will be satisfying?"

Figure 18 THE THREE CORE QUESTIONS

How should these questions be presented in order to arrive at specific, truthful answers? There are two ways you can approach this, as discussed in Chapter 2. One is to use a list of predetermined questions; the other is to form questions based on what employees are saying and doing.

In terms of predetermined questions, there are three Belief System questions to ask:

1. Can you do the job? (Confidence)

2. Are outcomes tied to your performance? (Trust)

3. Are the outcomes satisfying to you? (Satisfaction)

The three predetermined questions come in many variations. Choose any of the following you want to use. You also can select questions from the lists in Chapter 2 or develop variations of your own. The wording of the questions is a matter of personal preference.

- Variations of *Can you do the job?* (Confidence)

    Can you meet the expectations we have set for you?

    Can you reach these goals?

    Can you handle this okay?

- Variations of *Are outcomes tied to your performance?* (Trust)

  Are you getting what you deserve?

  Is what you get out of your job connected to your performance?

  Are you rewarded when you do a good job?

- Variations of *Are the outcomes satisfying to you?* (Satisfaction)

  Are you getting what you want out of your job?

  Is anything about your job dissatisfying?

  Are you satisfied with the way you are treated here?

Remember from Chapter 2 that questions need to fit the context of the situation. A perfectly worded question asked out of context will not prove effective. Here are some examples of ways to *put your questions in context.* Notice how this makes the questions flow more smoothly.

- Putting confidence questions in context

  "So that's our expectation. *Is that something you can do?*"

  "Those are the new goals. *Do you think you can reach them?*"

  "That summarizes what I'd like you to do. *Can you handle it okay?*"

- Putting *trust* questions in context

  "While we're talking about the reward system, I want to ask you a question. *Do you feel like you're getting what your performance deserves?*"

  "You know, it isn't always easy to give people exactly what they deserve. I was wondering, *do you think we tie rewards closely to your performance?*"

  "Sometimes we get busy and overlook good performance. *Do you feel like you're rewarded when you do a good job?*"

- Putting *satisfaction* questions in context

  "You've been working in this department for six months now. *Are you getting what you want out of your job?*"

  "You've seemed a little unhappy lately. *Are you dissatisfied about something?*"

  "I'm always concerned about making this a good place to work. *Are you satisfied with the way you're treated here?*"

The way managers go about asking questions tends to vary. My experience with the Belief System is that some managers like to rely on and use predetermined questions. Others feel confined doing so and instead prefer to form their own questions, on the spot, based on what they see employees doing and what they hear them saying. This latter approach was discussed in considerable detail in Chapter 2. It can be just as effective as asking predetermined questions, and maybe more so. Notice how the manager in the following sample script forms questions on the spot. All of the needed information is efficiently obtained by asking the employee three simple questions.

SAMPLE SCRIPT
Rating the Three Beliefs

Employee: Seems like everything's been going wrong lately.

Manager : How about filling me in. **What's the problem?**

Employee: I don't know. With all the recent changes in procedures, I've really gotten confused about things. (Analysis: This sounds like a confidence problem that deserves a rating in the 3-to-5 range on the 0-to-10-point rating scale. The probable cause is unclear expectations—not sure what to do and/or how to do it.)

Manager: **Can you give me an example** of what you mean?

Employee: All those new procedures from the engineering department.... A lot of us had trouble understanding them. The staff meeting was short on explanation, and we didn't get any training. (Analysis: Solutions are implied here.)

Manager: **Anything else?** (Analysis: This question takes the discussion beyond the discovery of the confidence problem; there may be a trust or satisfaction problem here, too.)

Employee: Not really. It was smooth sailing until all the changes. I was knocking out the work. Now I'm having trouble getting things done right and on time. It's not a good feeling. (Analysis: There is no evidence of problems related to trust or satisfaction, so ratings of seven or above seem appropriate for both.)

When asking questions around confidence, trust, and satisfaction, I have found that managers are equally adept at uncovering each type of problem. However, managers naturally are more reluctant to uncover motivation problems for which they are responsible. For example, some managers simply do not tie outcomes to performance; they prefer to treat everyone the same. This is a practice that causes trust problems. These managers are unlikely to doggedly focus on uncovering the problems they are creating. It would be wise, of course, for them to do so but hardly expected because it requires going against human nature. Nevertheless, managers who choose to use the Belief System tend to be surprisingly adept at identifying the motivation and performance problems their employees are facing.

Solve the Belief Problem(s)

The third phase of the Diagnostic Interview involves six steps.

Get the Employee to Identify Causes
Once the three beliefs have been rated, the problem (or problems) can be isolated easily. This sets the stage for the next step—uncovering causes—which often gets shortchanged in the urgency to get to solutions. It takes very little time to single out problem causes; often they have already surfaced, although perhaps indirectly. It usually takes only one question to bring them into plain view.

SAMPLE SCRIPT

Getting the Employee to Identify Causes

Manager: Wayne, you've already hinted at this, but tell me again. **What's causing the problem?**

Employee: There were some extensive changes in the procedures we've been using for a long time and they weren't communicated very well to us. There was a 15-minute meeting and we were given the new procedures manual and told to read it. Some of the new stuff is really vague. It's downright confusing. Studying it doesn't help because you can't figure out what it means. I'm not clear on what they expect us to do.

At this point, it is good to summarize your understanding of the problem and its causes. This gives the employee a chance to confirm the diagnosis or to make corrections or additions. The summary should be a brief restatement of the problem (confidence, trust, and/or satisfaction) along with the causes. Nothing else is necessary or desirable. There is no need for finger pointing, sympathy, or lectures. Just summarize the diagnosis. Then wait for the employee feedback to be sure you are correct. Here is an example of summarizing the problem.

SAMPLE SCRIPT

Summarizing Problem Diagnosis

Manager: So what you're saying is that even if you work hard, you can't do the kind of job you want to because you don't fully understand all of the new procedures. (Analysis: The employee is saying, "I can't do it." The cause is unclear expectations—the employee does not know what is expected as outlined in the new procedures.)

Employee: You've hit it right on the head. (Analysis: Now it is confirmed. The employee's confidence level is low, and you know the cause.)

Ask the Employee for Solutions

The next step in solving the employee's belief problems involves the manager *asking the employee for solutions.* Then comes the hard part for many managers: Hold any ideas you may have for solving the problem. Instead, let the employee offer solutions. No manager has all the answers to employee motivation problems; employees do have answers for their own problems. Some employees will be eager to tell you, and others will not. If they seem reluctant, encourage them. You, as the manager, may not agree with the solution, but you are advised to ask. Keep asking until the message is clear, "I really would like to hear your ideas for solving the problem." Hold your own ideas. This is not easy; it is tempting to suggest solutions when you have them and the employee is hesitant, but resist the urge. Try something like the following.

SAMPLE SCRIPT

Asking the Employee for Solutions

Manager: What do you think? **What's the best way to handle this?**

Employee: I'm not sure. What do you think? (Analysis: Managers should resist the temptation to field employee questions that pass the responsibility for the solution back to them.)

Manager: You're good at figuring out things like this. I really would be interested in your suggestions.

Employee: I just need somebody to go over the procedures with me. I know where I'm confused. I know what to ask.

Manager: Do you have anybody in mind to help you?

Employee: I hit it off pretty well with Bob, one of the engineers who developed the new procedures. I'd feel comfortable working with him.

Manager: How much time are we talking about?

Employee: Probably getting together for an hour or so, two or three times, would be enough.

Manager: Anything other than the time with Bob?

Employee: No, that should do it.

End this segment of the discussion by summarizing the employee's suggestions. The purpose is to be sure you understand the key points the employee is making. It is a fatal mistake to seek out solutions and then move ahead without clearly understanding what the employee said. Summarizing is the best check against that happening.

Agree on a Solution

Sometimes the solution recommended by an employee will be completely satisfactory to you, the manager. If so, indicate agreement and move on to the next step. When the solution is not acceptable, what do you do? If the snags are minor, try this: Pose questions about the things that concern you. This often helps an employee see the wisdom of an alternative solution. Consider the following, for example.

Responding to Solutions That Have Minor Flaws

Manager: Let me make sure I understand what you are saying. You want your meetings with Bob to be first thing in the morning when you come in at 7:00. You may not be aware that Bob doesn't get here until 8:00. Do you want me to ask him to come in early?

Employee: Oh, then I guess meeting before 8:00 isn't going to work.

Manager: Maybe you can think about some other times that would work for you. I'll leave it up to you and Bob to agree on that.

The idea is to point out what you are concerned about and why. Ask for alternatives. Get the employee's opinion. Focus on why an alternative is in the best interest of the employee. You likely will find that the employee is inclined to agree with you. Settle on an option that suits both of you.

What if the employee's solution is simply too far off base? This will happen sometimes. What is to be done? Here are three good possibilities:

- Ask the employee for other ideas for dealing with the problem. Keep asking in hopes that an acceptable solution surfaces. If it does, come to agreement.

- Pose questions about the proffered solution that reveal the difficulties with adopting it. For example, "How would you go about implementing this?" Or, "How do you think our customers (other employees or management) will react to this?" Or, "Can we do this given our time and cost constraints?"

- Point out the flaws in the solution, doing so as tactfully as possible. Offer suggestions for overcoming them, and solicit the employee's reaction to the recommendations.

One of these three options normally will work. Try all three, if necessary, but it usually is best to start with option one, and then move to two and three.

REALITY CHECK

Myth Employees prefer open, honest managers who tell it like it is.

Reality Employees prefer to discover the flaws in their own thinking.

Get and Give a Commitment

Once agreement is reached on a good solution to a performance problem, it is vital that both parties make a commitment: The employee commits to solve the problem, and the manager commits to help the employee. Here is the procedure. First, summarize the solution agreed upon. Get the employee to accept the responsibility for its success and to make a commitment to implement the solution. State what the employee is to do and what you are committed to do. Here is an example.

SAMPLE SCRIPT

Getting and Giving a Commitment

Manager: Let me see if I've got this right. You want to meet with Bob two or three times for an hour or so each time.

Employee: That should do it.

Manager: Do you think this will get your performance up to where it needs to be?

Employee: Yes, I think it will solve the problem. I'll certainly dig in to make it work. (Analysis: This is the employee's commitment.)

Manager: Okay, I'll talk with Bob and have him get in touch with you and set up a time for the first meeting. (Analysis: This is the manager's commitment.)

Establish Follow-Up

A commitment from both sides to take action is not the end of the process. How will efforts to solve the problem be monitored? What kind of follow-up will be done by both manager and employee? This must be decided during the Diagnostic Interview. Here is an illustration of how it might work.

SAMPLE SCRIPT

Establishing Follow-Up

Manager: There are a couple of things I want you to do. First, let me know when you and Bob have set a time to get together. Second, after the first meeting, let's get together and discuss how the meeting went and see if you still think this approach is going to get you where you need to be.

Give Positive Reinforcement

How you end the face-to-face discussion is very important. It is helpful to send the employee off on his or her appointed rounds in the best frame of mind possible. Thank the employee for participating in the Diagnostic Interview. Then give positive reinforcement for everything the employee did in the meeting that you would like to see repeated in future discussions. Examples include the person's willingness to talk openly and honestly, to help solve the problem, and to show concern about improving performance. Your closing comments might go like this.

SAMPLE SCRIPT

Giving Positive Reinforcement

Manager: One more thing. Thanks! I'm glad to have you working here. You're always concerned about doing a good job and I appreciate your willingness to work this thing out.

The thanks expressed by employees for the managerial manner just described often surprises new adherents to the Belief System of Motivation and Performance. Instead of the usual one-sided "critique of authority," employees find Belief System managers well prepared to address the problem at hand and legitimately interested in helping to reach mutually acceptable solutions. The effect on motivation and performance is usually apparent in short order.

E X E R C I S E   1 1

Conducting a Diagnostic Interview

1. Identify an employee whose motivation and performance are less than desirable. (Choose a person who will give you the best opportunity of success; save the "toughest" situation for later.)

2. Think about and prepare for each step in the Diagnostic Interview.

3. Schedule a meeting with the employee. (Allow enough time. Choose a time and place so you will not be interrupted.)

4. Conduct the Diagnostic Interview.

5. Evaluate how well you accomplished each step in the interview.

6. Be sure that you and the employee follow through on all commitments made.

MULTIDIMENSIONAL PROBLEMS

Employees can have any combination of the three motivation problems—confidence, trust, and satisfaction—*simultaneously.* This means that solving one problem does not necessarily get employee motivation back on track. A person may have strep throat and a badly sprained ankle; the person is not fully restored when the strep infection is cured, but continues to hobble in pain on the bad ankle. Likewise, an employee's motivation is not fully restored when a confidence problem is solved but a trust problem goes unattended, or when a trust issue is removed but a satisfaction problem quietly undermines the motivation to perform.

It is very important to keep an eye open for multidimensional problems. This need not be done with fear and dread, however. The key is to *diagnose all three beliefs,* as mentioned earlier in this chapter. This point, and an example of its application, was included in the sample script on page 125. The manager in that script diagnosed a confidence problem and then appropriately checked for other problems and found none. In other words, he diagnosed all three beliefs. Another example follows in the form of a sample script.

Diagnosing Multidimensional Problems

Manager: Okay, it sounds like we're in agreement that your performance has fallen off in the last few weeks. The question now is what to do. I'm sure you've thought about it. **What do you think is the problem?** (Analysis: You want to know what the problem is and this question asks that in a simple, effective way.)

Employee: I don't know. I guess I've been discouraged lately. (Analysis: The employee is playing a little hard to get here, but he wants to talk. Otherwise, he would not have dropped the "I've been a little discouraged lately" clue.)

Manager: Discouraged? **What do you mean?** (Analysis: With this question, the manager is going where the employee wants to go, where information is most likely to be found.)

Employee: Things aren't going as well for me now, especially relative to some of my peers. (Analysis: Something has changed. At least part of it relates to his peers. There may be other elements.)

Manager: **What's happened, specifically?** (Analysis: This question moves the employee away from responding in generalities toward giving concrete information.)

Employee: Beth and Jim got their promotions. I didn't. (Analysis: This sounds like a possible trust problem.)

Manager: **So what are you saying?** (Analysis: This question encourages the employee to elaborate.)

Employee: It doesn't seem fair. I've worked as hard as they have and deserve a promotion as much as they do. (Analysis: There are two very important issues here. One, the employee definitely has a trust problem; he does not believe promotions are tied to performance. Two, the manager can easily get tripped up here. It is very tempting to talk about the promotion issue, maybe defend the promotions of Beth and Jim, perhaps try to explain why the employee was passed over. This will not lead to anything good at this point in the discussion. It will only be a diversion from the purpose of this part of the discussion—to identify any and all motivation problems.)

Manager: You feel like you deserved a promotion and didn't get it. **Is that basically what you're saying?** (Analysis: This lets the employee know that the manager was listening and got the message. It also gives the employee a chance to clarify whether the manager has misunderstood what the employee was saying.)

Employee: You got that right. Like I said, it's not fair. (Analysis: This confirms the trust problem. Rather than respond to the fairness comment, it is best to move ahead to diagnose the other two beliefs.)

Manager: We'll come back to that in a minute, but I want to ask you something else first. You said earlier that things weren't going as well for you *now*. **Are there any other issues?** (Analysis: The goal here is to find out if there are any other motivation problems. This open-ended question is an invitation for the employee to tell you. You could ask specifically about confidence and satisfaction problems, but I find that employees respond better to open questions like this one.)

Employee: Since you're giving me a chance to talk, there is one other thing. Sometimes when I'm struggling with something, I feel like I'm in a sink-or-swim situation. I don't have anybody to bounce ideas off of, to get advice from. On top of that, I don't get any coaching or feedback, either. I'll never get promoted if I don't keep on learning and developing my skills. (Analysis: There are three points here. (1) The manager could interpret this as a complaint—"You don't advise me, coach me, or give me feedback; in short, you don't help me." Avoid getting defensive. Now is the time to simply understand what the employee is saying and correctly identify motivation problems. (2) The employee obviously has a satisfaction problem—he is not getting something he wants, namely advice, coaching, and feedback. On the satisfaction rating scale, the problem probably falls in the middle of the dissatisfaction portion of the scale, maybe lower. (3) There is a hint of a confidence problem in the "when I'm struggling" comment.)

Manager: You've mentioned two other problems. You don't have anybody to talk with when you're dealing with difficult problems and decisions. And you aren't getting any coaching and feedback. **Do I have it right?** (Analysis: This question is to confirm the satisfaction problem. The employee has suggested solutions—advise me, coach me, give me feedback. These can be discussed later; talking about them now is a diversion from the task of identifying problems.)

Employee: That's exactly what I'm saying.

Manager: Okay. You mentioned "sometimes struggling with things." **Are you struggling with anything now?** (Analysis: This is a "Can you do it?" confidence question, a follow-up to the employee's earlier comment.)

Employee: Well, I hate to admit it, but, yeah, I guess I am. You know that computer project you gave me, the one I wanted? Well, it's more involved than I thought it would be. I think I'm in over my head." (Analysis: This definitely is a confidence problem, a big one. You can mark it at the lower end of the rating scale.)

Manager: **So you're not sure you can handle it?** (Analysis: This is to confirm the problem.)

Employee: To be honest, I don't think I can. (Analysis: The problem is confirmed.)

The manager in this discussion diagnosed all three beliefs and found five motivation problems: one trust problem (the employee believes promotions are not tied to performance), three satisfaction problems (the employee wants but is not getting advice, coaching, and feedback), and one confidence problem (the employee does not believe he can handle the computer project).

In my experience, this is not an unusual situation. Many employees experience multiple motivation problems. Two to five per employee is very common. This does not necessarily cause employee performance to plummet below an unacceptable level. It does, however, mean that performance is far less than it could be, and that is a problem, especially when multiplied by five or ten employees. It is a serious problem when multiplied by hundreds and thousands.

In the above example, the manager asked nine questions. Except for the first question, none was predetermined; all were formed in response to what the employee said. In addition to asking questions, the manager restated what the employee said on three occasions. Otherwise, the manager hardly spoke. No explanations, no opinions, no defensive remarks—just information gathering. Asking and listening. This is how it should be when a manager is attempting to identify motivation problems and rating the three beliefs, one of the critical steps in the Diagnostic Interview.

MOVING AHEAD

Although the Diagnostic Interview is a logical, step-by-step approach, it can be intimidating. Managers can experience second thoughts during the process, which throws them off track. This occurs the nearer one gets to sitting down with an employee to use it. What will you do if this happens to you?

THE RECIPE

A two-day seminar usually lasts two days. However, I conducted one on motivation management that took a month to complete.

By the end of the second day, one thing had become painfully clear to the attending managers—they had serious problems. They were alarmed. Each of them had at least one employee who was dragging down group performance. They had a nervous, unobstructed view of the potentially disastrous ramifications.

Each manager had agreed that, yes, the Belief System held considerable promise as the remedy they needed. I asked, "So what are you going to do?"

Tom, a very dedicated manager, quickly spoke up. "I'm going to conduct a Diagnostic Interview, face-to-face, to get to the bottom of things and help my operations manager get his performance headed in the right direction before it's too late."

All of the other managers made similar commitments—all except Derek. "Let's be realistic. All of us have good intentions, but, frankly, I'm a little nervous about confronting people head-on about poor performance. Plus, when we get back to the office, we'll be swamped with all the work that's piled up. Chances are we'll use that as an excuse to procrastinate. In all honesty, we may never do anything with what we've learned here."

Everyone stared at me. I looked Derek in the eye and then quickly glanced at each of the other six managers in the group. Finally I said, "My experience tells me that Derek probably has made an accurate prediction."

Harriet, a no-nonsense manager to my left, raised her hand. "I have an idea. I recommend that each of us make a commitment to apply what we've learned here and that you agree to call each of us, let's say in four weeks, to hold us accountable, to see what we've done and how it's worked. And to give us some coaching if we need it."

Ryan, who had proudly told the group his nickname was "Bread Truck" (because of all the rolls he carried around his waist), was seated beside Harriet. A devilish grin appeared on his face. He was bursting to say something to me. "That's a good idea. That way we'll find out what kind of teacher you really are." Lighthearted laughter rippled across the room. Ryan laughed so hard that his upper body shook. I wondered why he had diverted our attention away from a serious, "let's take some action" proposal.

I looked directly at him. "That's not amusing." He lost his smile. Everyone stopped laughing. "And I want all of you to know that I charge extra when I get abused." We all laughed, Ryan the loudest and longest. He loved attention, wanted everybody to love and accept him.

Harriet stopped laughing and got us back on track. "We have a recommendation on the floor."

People began casting their votes. We all agreed to try Harriet's suggestion.

A month later I called everyone. Four of the managers had completed their Diagnostic Interviews. Three were pleased with the results, and one needed more time to be sure. Two had interviews scheduled the next day. One was procrastinating. Guess who? It was Ryan.

"I want to do the Diagnostic Interview, but...ah...I just...."

"Just what?"

"I just don't know if I can pull it off."

"Ryan, I'm wondering if *you really want to do it.*"

"I want to, but I don't know…. Every time I think about it I get cold feet."

"Do you cook?"

"What?"

"Do you cook?"

"No, not really. The wife's a great cook. I probably didn't have to tell you that."

"Ryan, do you like pasta with tomato sauce?"

"Love it. Marsha hates Italian, though. Won't cook it."

"I brought a tomato sauce recipe back from Italy last year. It's proven, been passed down for generations in an Italian family I met. Best tomato sauce I've ever eaten. Want the recipe?"

"Sure!"

"Ready? This is your assignment, a Belief System assignment."

"Shoot."

"Write down these ingredients. One tablespoon chopped onions. Two garlic cloves, chopped."

"What does this have to do with the Belief System?"

"Just write. You'll see." One tablespoon chopped parsley. Two tablespoons extra virgin olive oil. Two 16-ounce cans of peeled, whole plum tomatoes. Salt and pepper. Pasta—your choice. Freshly grated Parmigiano-Reggiano—no substitutes. Red wine."

"Got it."

"Now, the directions. Put the oil in a heavy-based saucepan and let it warm over medium heat. Add the onion, garlic, and parsley. Cook it for about three minutes or until the onion and garlic are translucent. Pour the tomatoes, along with the juice, into a large bowl, and chop them into small pieces. Add the tomatoes and juice to the saucepan and cook uncovered on medium-low heat (just hot enough to barely boil). You'll have to stir fairly often, otherwise it'll stick and burn. Cook it until all the liquid evaporates (no water sitting on the top) and the sauce is thick. Add salt and pepper to taste."

"Got it."

"In another saucepan, add the exact amount of water as directed on the pasta package. Bring the water to a boil, add one teaspoon of salt per serving of pasta, then add the pasta. Cook it only as long as the package directs. Pour the pasta and water into a colander, then put the pasta in a bowl. Stir in just enough tomato sauce to coat the pasta and stir well. That's it. And, Ryan, *follow the recipe."*

"Yesss, sir! You can't see me, but I'm saluting."

"After you've eaten, think about what you've learned. Then call me. Got it?"

"Got it, but...."

"Ryan, bye."

He called me back the following Monday. "Man, it was good! My wife's already an Italian convert."

"That's great. What did you learn?"

"The first thing was, *you can cook anything, if you follow a proven recipe."*

"Good. What else?"

"The 'what else' was tougher. Marsha and I were up until midnight, thinking and talking, trying to figure it out. I got it, I think."

"I'm ready."

"You can accomplish anything, in the kitchen or anywhere, *if you follow a proven recipe."*

"You got it. So what are you going to do, Ryan?"

"Wait a minute. I learned one more thing. I cooked the tomato sauce twice. Burned it badly the first time. Didn't follow the instructions. Got impatient and cooked it too fast. Got lazy and didn't stir it. What a mess. Stunk up the whole house. I learned that you can't just say it, you have to do it—*follow* the recipe."

"Okay, what are you going to do now?"

"I've scheduled the Diagnostic Interview with Rodney for tomorrow morning. I'll review my notes from the seminar later today."

When people suddenly find their confidence, as Ryan had, self-doubt sometimes seeps back in, followed by a flood of anxiety. I wanted to see if that was the situation with Ryan. "Did you say you'd scheduled the meeting with Rodney or that you were going to schedule it?"

"It's already scheduled."

"So, you're really going through with it?"

"Oh, yeah! I wanted to get Rodney's performance back on track all along; I just wasn't sure I could do it. Now that I have the recipe, I know I can do it. I'm looking forward to this, just like I couldn't wait to sink my teeth into the pasta. Thanks for helping me find my confidence. I needed it. Hey, maybe I should write a book: *I Became a Believer at the Kitchen Stove.*"

"Ryan, you'll do fine tomorrow. I know I don't need to say this, but follow the recipe."

• • •

CHAPTER 6

Handling Difficult Problems

"He didn't know he couldn't, so he did."

A BRIEFING SESSION

This chapter shows motivation at its best—dealing with motivation and performance problems at their worst.

A two-step process is presented for solving difficult problems using the Belief System.

Level with employees: Let employees know you do not have a solution to the problem but you are willing to work together to come up with one.

Give the problem to the employee: Put the responsibility for solving the problem in the employee's hands while continuing to provide guidance.

The five tools for solving difficult problems are:

1. *Job matching*—finding job opportunities that are a *good fit* with employee skills.
2. *Substitution*—finding *substitutes* for outcomes that are wanted but not available.
3. *Preference shifting*—guiding employees to *change the preference* they have for certain outcomes.
4. *Offsets*—finding desirable outcomes to *offset* undesirable outcomes that cannot be avoided.
5. *Leveling bold*—letting employees who have gotten by with poor performance know that they can remain in their current position only if they improve their performance.

HOW WE TALK TO OURSELVES

Helen had received four pieces of bad news, all in one day, all from her boss. Most people would have taken that kind of day home with them—to curse it, to toss and turn with it, to be consumed by it. Not Helen.

She thought of her friend, Louise, as she headed home, and chuckled. Louise had said, "Helen, you must feel like the guy who was sky diving and couldn't get his parachute to open."

Helen walked through the front door with a smile and enjoyed cooking a dinner that the family devoured. She cleaned the kitchen; washed, dried, and folded two loads of clothes; and helped the children with their homework. She played with them while they bathed. They snuggled in bed together, talked and giggled, and then she read them a story. Prayers were said and she tucked the children in for the night.

Helen went back into the kitchen, got things organized for breakfast, and made some hot chocolate. She poured two cups and walked carefully into the den. She handed her husband, Joe, a cup over the open briefcase in his lap and softly brushed a hand across his cheek.

Helen sat in her favorite chair, cradled her cup in both hands, and sipped the steaming, soothing liquid. When she looked up and said, "How was *your* day?" she noticed that Joe was watching her.

He did not answer her question. Instead he said, "You always look so calm in the face of adversity." The respect in his voice made her feel good—about herself and about him.

Earlier that evening, while she stood at the stove preparing dinner, she had told Joe what had happened. "My boss sent me an e-mail today saying he wanted to skip my performance review, if it was okay with me—that I was doing fine."

"Of course you're doing fine. But doesn't Mike know how important feedback is to you?"

Mike Taylor was an experienced, competent executive. The results in his unit showed it. He was respected and his opinion carried a lot of weight, especially with Helen. That was why she treasured his feedback, when he gave it.

"Later in the day he dropped by my office and asked me to take over the MicroNet project for a couple of months while Susan's on maternity leave. Mike doesn't realize how big that project is." She paused. "And Susan hasn't told him yet that she isn't coming back to work after the baby's born. The project will be mine until it's wrapped up late next year."

Joe jumped in. "He can't give you another project, not on top of everything else you're doing! How can he be so inconsiderate?" Joe clenched his teeth, shook his head, then let out a long, loud sigh.

"He also told me that the head honcho in executive development had turned down my application to attend the two-week executive development program at Harvard next summer. He said he would approve a similar program at another business school."

"It's not fair. You've waited 10 years to be eligible for the Harvard program! Why can't they let you go?"

"Now where is all that salsa I made last summer?" she mused, as she looked up and down the shelves in the pantry.

Helen calmly set the table. "There was one more problem. Mike has received negative feedback from several credible sources about Jean, the person I hired six months ago. He gave me specifics and it confirms what I've been seeing. Her heart's not in the job. I have to act on it quickly. I'll talk to her tomorrow. She'll tell me what the problem is and together we'll come up with a solution that'll be good for both of us."

"Helen, you've already bent over backwards to help her. I say give her the ax."

Dinner was ready. The discussion had ended.

Joe closed his briefcase and sipped his hot chocolate. The steam fogged his glasses. He looked over the rims at her. "Helen, did you hear me? I said you always look so calm in the face of adversity."

"Joe, being upset is a choice. I choose calm."

Joe sat upright in his chair. "That's it? I hate it when you make things seem so simple. The rest of us mere mortals can't do that."

"Sorry," she said. And she was. "Here's what I do. I defuse potential and actual intensified emotional dissonance with conscious internal dialogue to combat any cognitive impairment that might be produced by the dissonant feelings."

"Honey, that's too intellectual for me. Can you bring it down a notch or two so I can understand? This is important."

"Okay." She paused. "Joe, it all depends on how we talk to ourselves. Your internal dialogue—in other words, what you say to yourself—determines the way you feel, the way you think. If I say, 'They didn't give me what I wanted and they're being insensitive and unfair,' I feel bad. I wallow around in it, and then I feel even worse and I don't think clearly. But if I say, 'I didn't get what I wanted, but maybe I can get the next best thing,' I'm optimistic, positive, ready to take action."

"Okay, so if you can't have what you want, try to get something nearly as good. What else?"

"Two other things. First, if you're stuck with something you don't want, try to find something to make it easier to live with. And second, sometimes you have to leave a dream behind and get another."

"I get it. What did you say to yourself today—what was your 'internal dialogue'?"

"I said, 'Okay, Helen, you wanted a formal performance evaluation, but Mike said no. The next best thing is to get him to do it informally. I'll just get on his calendar for 30 minutes and ask him how I'm doing.' Then I said to myself, 'This may work out even better than a formal review. He'll probably be less guarded, and more open and honest.' "

"That's not what I do, is it?"

She laughed. "I can't hear what you say to yourself, Joe. Lucky me." He laughed. "When I told you about Mike earlier in the kitchen, you were upset. You said he was uncaring, insensitive, inconsiderate, and unfair. If you talk like that out loud, you probably talk like that to yourself."

"What did you say to yourself about the MicroNet project?"

"The first thing I said was, 'I definitely don't want this.' Then I asked myself, 'What would make this extra work easier to live with?' This is what I came up with. I'll go to Mike and tell him how much extra work this is going to be. Then I'll ask if he can get me some exposure with the executive committee so those people can see what I can do. That'd be great for me because it'd give me more career opportunities. Mike can easily get me the exposure, and he'll think it's reasonable compensation, so to speak, for the extra workload."

"And what about the Harvard deal?"

"That was harder, but here's what I said. 'I've been dreaming about Harvard for years. Other options don't come close, but this isn't the end of the world. I can either be miserable about it or I can set my sights on something else.' But I still needed some convincing, so I said, 'Listen to me, Helen, misery is misery. Forget it! Leave that dream alone and get another one.' I don't know what my new dream is yet, but the Harvard dream is fading. I'll be okay with it in a few days."

"It sounds like you're giving up too easily on everything."

"That's a good point. When Mike was in my office this morning, I took the time to feel him out on everything. He didn't want to do the performance review, so I didn't press him. On MicroNet, he said I was his only option. The message was, 'Sorry, but that's the way it is.' He'd already made up his mind. On the Harvard thing, Mike made it clear that they wanted me to go to another program. I don't know why yet, but I'll find out."

"You don't ever whine and cry and complain, do you?"

She walked over, kissed his forehead, and laughingly said, "Only with people who fall for it, like you." She headed for the kitchen with two empty cups to get refills.

He reached to touch her, but she was gone. "You're a remarkable woman."

She yelled over her shoulder, "Yeah, and don't you forget it, either!"

He yelled back, "You just inherited good genes, that's all," and half meant it.

• • •

SOLVING DIFFICULT PROBLEMS

All too frequently, the search for solutions bumps the manager up against problems that have no easy or apparent answers. It is like that with motivation problems. What do you do about the really difficult ones? Problems like these:

- An employee wants a promotion, but there are no immediate opportunities.
- An employee wants more money, but the organization is strapped.
- A manager cannot get approval to fairly reward a top performer.
- An employee dislikes the work, wants to stay, but no other positions are open.
- An employee suffers under pay inequities, but finances prohibit correction.
- An employee with an I'll-sneak-by attitude refuses to increase productivity.
- A manager has inherited a low-producing employee holding on until retirement.
- An employee who is a poor match for the job refuses a transfer.

In cases like these, the Belief System manager simply shifts the hunt for solutions into four-wheel drive; the terrain is tougher, so more torque is put into the climb.

Before wading into the tall grass of motivation problems, it is a good idea for managers to take stock and make sure they know what they think they know about the employee and the problem at hand. Review your earlier findings. Probe to see that you have not missed something or that things have not changed. Could a recent relocation or job assignment have created a different set of motivation problems? Check to see that the premise on which you are proceeding is sound; verify that you and the employee are on the same page. Do the "three-beliefs" ratings still stand up? Would the employee answer today as she did earlier to the key questions, "Can I do the job (Confidence)? Will outcomes be tied to my performance (Trust)? Will the outcomes be satisfying to me (Satisfaction)?" Solutions based on faulty information are no solutions at all.

WHAT KIND OF MANAGER ARE YOU?

Typical Manager   Take stock, review findings, probe...there isn't time. It's better to do something wrong than to do nothing.

Motivation Manager   There's never enough time, but it's better and cheaper to do it right the first time.

There is but one way to address difficult, seemingly intractable problems: head-on. This means managers need to be open and honest with employees and not give up on solving the problem. It may sound simple, but it is not. How would you handle this situation, for example? The company is being acquired, budgets are frozen, and an employee wants a much-deserved raise. No problem being open and honest here, right? Just tell the employee you're sorry, but there's nothing you can do. It's out of your hands. Only that's not true. There very likely are things a manager can do, as I will explain in this chapter. The important point here is that the manager cannot give up so easily on solving the problem.

The Belief System approach to solving extraordinary motivation and performance problems is a two-part exercise in managerial perseverance. The parts are (1) leveling and (2) giving the problem to the employee to solve. Let's get familiar with each.

Leveling

Tell it like it is. Level with people, and tell them honestly and exactly how things are. This is the critical first step in the process of remedying difficult motivation and performance problems. Obviously, at times employees will not want to hear what must be said, but the bedrock of reality must be found, albeit tactfully, before a solution can be constructed that will stand.

At least six situations qualify as "difficult motivation and performance problems" in the Belief System scheme of things. The first two are tougher than the others because the manager has no control over the outcomes—the manager cannot give the employee what he or she wants, in the first instance; and cannot keep the employee from getting something not wanted, in the second (more on this later). Here are the "tough half-dozen:"

1. Employees are performing well but they want something *specific* that you cannot give them. This is a *trust problem*.

SAMPLE SCRIPT

Leveling

Manager: I know you're interested in moving up in the company as soon as possible. We've reached a point where there simply are not any promotion opportunities available. I want to talk with you about why this has happened and discuss some things we can do until the opportunities reappear.

---

2. Employees *generally* are not getting outcomes that their performance warrants, and you can do nothing about it. This is a *trust problem*.

Leveling

Manager: I know you're upset about being a top performer and not getting rewarded for it. To be honest with you, this is not likely to change any time soon due to the company's current financial situation. With that said, I'd like for us to put our heads together on this and see if we can figure out something that will make you happy.

3. Employees are performing well but are getting something they dislike, and you can do nothing about it. This is a *satisfaction problem*.

SAMPLE SCRIPT

Leveling

Manager: I want to thank you for making me aware that you don't like the kind of work you're doing now. At the same time I want to level with you and point out that I don't see any opportunity for that to change in the near future. Let me tell you why, and then we can explore some things that might make a difference.

4. Employees think they deserve more, but their performance does not warrant it. This is a *trust problem*.

SAMPLE SCRIPT

Leveling

Manager: You recently expressed concern about the way you're rewarded here. I'll be glad to review production records with you and the guidelines used for determining rewards. If you've been treated unfairly, I'll do what I can to straighten it out.

5. Employees have been getting by with poor performance and assume they can continue to do so. This is a *trust problem*.

SAMPLE SCRIPT

Leveling

Manager: This is the second time we've discussed your performance. We need to come up with a plan to get this situation back on track, *now*. I think that together we can do that, if you want to.

---

6. Employees simply are not qualified for the job. This is a *confidence problem*.

SAMPLE SCRIPT

Leveling

Manager: We've discussed this situation before and you've told me that the position you're in isn't a good match for you. I agree, and I'd like for us to work together and try to come up with some options that will make sense for both of us.

Clearly, this is sensitive stuff. Handled improperly, it can go painfully awry, but not handling it at all is worse. This is why the surest, safest approach is openness, honesty, and exactitude. It is tough for the employee to refute the truth, particularly when you express it nicely and couple it with a clear willingness to search out a good solution. Those are the important qualifiers—"nicely expressed" (that is, tactful, nonthreatening, sensitive) and "let's find a better way" (that is, "I'm not here to fire you, but to help you").

Giving the Problems to the Employee

Bring employees into the search for ways out of difficult motivation and performance problems; *give them the problem to solve*—this is the real key to success. To do this, most managers must make a critical transition: They must abandon the traditional belief that "It's my job

149

to solve problems; that's what they pay me for" and recognize that employees are the best source of solutions to the problems that affect them.

Leveling precedes the process of "giving the problem to the employee." It goes like this:

SAMPLE SCRIPT

Leveling

Manager: I know you want that raise and, certainly, you deserve it. But my hands are tied. We're in the critical stage of the merger and budgets are frozen. There's just no money. I don't want you to harbor any false hopes about that.

SAMPLE SCRIPT

Giving the Problem to the Employee

Manager: But I don't want to leave it at that. Is there something else we can do that'll make you feel better, something I *do* have control over?

The responsibility for solving the problem is shifted. The employee, with the help and support of the manager, takes up the task.

THE FIVE TOOLS

The Belief System provides five special tools for helping managers and employees solve the three types of difficult motivation problems summarized in Table 3.

Job Matching (for Problem 1)

Employees who do not have the skills to perform their job present a serious problem. They conclude, "I can't do it," and their confidence plummets. When they sense they cannot develop the skills they need, hopelessness envelops them, and they realize, "I'll never be able to do

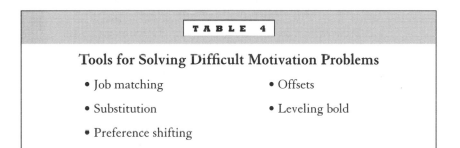

TABLE 3

Types of Difficult Problems

Problem 1 An employee correctly believes, "I don't have, and can't develop, the skills I need for this job (confidence)"; and the manager can do nothing to change the skill level of the employee or the skill requirements of the job. This is a *confidence* (Belief 1) problem.

Problem 2 An employee correctly believes, "I won't *get* the outcome if I perform well (trust) and it's something I *want*," and the manager has no control over giving it. This is a *trust* (Belief 2) problem.

Problem 3 An employee correctly believes, "I'll *get* the outcome if I perform well, but it's something I *don't want* (satisfaction) and the manager cannot keep the employee from getting it. This is a *satisfaction* (Belief 3) problem.

TABLE 4

Tools for Solving Difficult Motivation Problems

- Job matching
- Offsets
- Substitution
- Leveling bold
- Preference shifting

it." This is a sobering, agonizing realization. Employees may not be aware of their skill deficiencies in the short term, but awareness settles on them soon enough.

Managers face a difficult situation when employees do not have, and cannot develop, the skills required for the job. What is a manager to do?

On the one hand, managers feel pressured to replace these employees. The pressure comes from other employees who have to take up the slack. It comes from customers who want better service. It comes from higher-level managers who want stronger results.

On the other hand, managers often feel pressed to turn their back on the problem and keep unqualified employees in place. Why? Managers sometimes feel guilty because they have not helped their employees grow and develop. They find themselves sympathetic to unqualified employees who are loyal. Managers may even discover ways to maintain overall results without discharging a poor performer, the common approach being to place a heavier burden on other members of the team. Managers also may close their eyes to poor performance so they can avoid confrontation and conflict.

LOOKING BACK ON THE FUTURE

My curiosity pushed me to the edge of the chair in Minton's office when he told me, "It's tough enough when you have a poor performer who's arrogant and won't listen, but it's a sticky situation when he's management's fair-haired boy."

That was the kind of mess Minton landed in when he grabbed the reins as the new general manager of a minor league baseball team. The poor performer was Ralph, the coach. "I don't know what to do. As GM, I'm responsible for the success of the team. I have the authority to hire and fire, but you can't ignore the people above you."

There was more. "I inherited Ralph. He was once a major league baseball player, and a good one. After I came on board, he decided without consulting anyone that rather than just coaching, he would become a player/coach." Ralph was strong-willed and Minton was not up to battling with him over it. Minton was also swayed toward inaction because Ralph, as a player, was helping the team win a few games they probably would have lost otherwise.

The problem was that although Ralph was having an outstanding year as a player, he was doing a less-than-stellar job as the coach. Minton was troubled. "One day I think I should bite the bullet and fire him. The next day I wonder if I shouldn't invest and develop him. The big question is whether the investment would pay off."

The owner, who was Minton's boss, thought everything was fine. He liked winning and he liked Ralph. Anything Ralph wanted, Ralph got. "He sees Ralph as a player and doesn't really have a feel for the way he coaches the team."

The players knew, though. "Carlos is our catcher. He's a solid, mature kid, the leader of the team. He says Ralph's just another player—a good one, but he doesn't teach them anything. He says what they need is a coach, and that's not what Ralph is."

Minton had urged Ralph to play less and coach more. But Ralph had said, "No way! Playing's where it's at and that's where I'm gonna stay."

Minton knew that in the long run the owner would hold him, not Ralph, accountable for the success or failure of the team. He had a feeling that the long run was not far away. A gnawing, unsettled feeling set in.

Minton did not like feeling this way.

He asked for my counsel. I did not have the answer, but I would not have given it even if I had. Minton needed to discover his own solution. I thought I could help him find it.

"Minton, are you willing to try some neuro-linguistic programming that my friend Leif Roland taught me?"

He laughed. "Neuro what? Does it hurt?"

"It's a way to clarify your thinking. It could hurt some, but it's well worth the pain."

"Can't be worse than I'm feeling now." He did not laugh this time.

"Okay, let's try it. I want you to go forward in time, and look back on yourself and this situation with Ralph. Now imagine what it will be like if you do nothing." Minton worked his lower lip with his thumb and forefinger, and after 15 or 20 seconds let his eyelids drop. "Let the scene unfold like a movie, and *see* all that will happen if you do nothing. *Hear* what people will say, and what you will say to yourself and others. *Feel* the way you will feel if you do nothing."

Minton frowned. He started grinding his teeth together, working the muscles in his face. His breathing became fast and labored.

When he finally opened his eyes, he looked around, anxious, trying to get his bearings. His brows wrinkled toward a question.

He was troubled and wanted some answers. I suspected that mainly he wanted assurance that his future would not unfold as badly as he had imagined. It probably would. My experience is that most of us have a good sense about the consequences of our behavior. He needed to hold those images, unfiltered by discussion, and let their impact settle firmly into his consciousness.

I said, "Shake your head now, clear everything away, and come back to the present."

He took a deep breath and let it out slowly.

"Let's take the next step. Go to the future once more, and look back again on yourself and this situation with Ralph." Minton was ready.

He already had his eyes closed. "Imagine what it will be like if, instead of doing nothing, you take action. Take your time. Start the movie and *see* all that will happen if you take action. *Hear* people talking and any sounds other than words. *Sense* how you will feel, knowing that you have taken action."

The corners of his mouth turned up slightly and his head nodded agreement. The nodding grew faster, more pronounced. Then it stopped.

Minton opened his eyes and flashed a confident smile.

"Guess I knew all along what I needed to do, huh?" He paused. "I've had a revelation. Wow! Your mind's a wonderful thing if you just let yourself use it."

• • •

Job matching is the tool for managers to use when dealing with the first difficult motivation problem: Someone correctly believes "I don't have, and can't develop, the skills I need for this job" (a confidence problem).

The idea is for employees to move *from* their current job *to* another position that is a good fit for their skills. Job matching usually occurs in four stages. First, employees must become aware that they do not have the skills required for their job. Then they must recognize that they cannot develop the needed skills, at least not in a reasonable time frame. Third, employees must acknowledge the ultimate consequences of their situation—they cannot remain in the current position much longer. And fourth, they must accept the responsibility for getting another job, preferably one that matches their skills. Employees normally are not in a state of readiness to find *another* job until they reach stage three.

> **LEARNING LESSON**
>
> Each person has a unique set of skills, but no one has all of the skills needed to be successful in every situation or the potential to develop them.

Progressing through the four stages is a slow, unpleasant adventure for most employees. They try to make the journey alone, but few are successful. They are gripped in the present by long-held ambitions, reluctance to admit failure, and fear of change. As a result, they stubbornly cling to their current job. There is no wandering eye, no hungry look being cast about for a position that better matches their skills.

It is a delicate matter for most of us to realize that we do not have, and cannot develop, the skills we need. When someone points out our deficiencies, even tactfully, it can be a harsh and heavy blow. Managers will want to create opportunities that allow employees to discover this on their own. The mechanism for discovery can be a thoughtful set of written questions and exercises, or it can be as simple as asking, "Is this job a good match for your skills?"

SAMPLE SCRIPT

Helping Employees Face Their Lack of Skills

Manager: We've talked a couple of times about some of the difficulties you've been having. You've probably been thinking about it a lot. I was wondering, **do you feel like this job is a good match for the skills you have?**

Employee: I've been thinking about this for a long time. Being bound to a desk, analyzing data all day—all that precision and perfection. That isn't what I'm cut out to do. No matter how hard I try, I'm always making stupid mistakes.

Manager: **Do you think you can develop the skills you need** to get that precision?

Employee: I like to think I can learn anything, but the truth is, I'll never develop the precision this job requires. Not in a million years.

Following the employee's self-discovery, managers can use leveling to help him or her see that staying in the present position is not an option. Then it is time to give the problem to the employee. The goal is for employees to be willing, even eager, to leave a job that does not suit their skills and take the responsibility for moving to one that does.

SAMPLE SCRIPT

Leveling

Manager: I agree that this job doesn't really fit your skills. Maybe it's time to discuss some other options.

SAMPLE SCRIPT

Giving the Problem to the Employee

Manager: You probably have some good ideas. **What do you want to do?**

STRIKING A MATCH

Mary Sue was given the responsibility for turning around a struggling 80-person unit, and the timeline was short. A strong leadership team was needed. Gene was the weakest link.

Mary Sue told me what had happened. "I suspected right away that I'd made a hiring mistake. At three months I was certain. Gene was an error in judgment I couldn't afford."

I asked what Gene was doing that made her so sure.

"He's tentative, not taking charge. He wants everybody to like him. I know, I'm that way, too, but he isn't leading his team—they're leading him. It isn't working."

Mary Sue's face was drawn. She felt pressure and did not wear it well. "He's holding back our progress, but it seems unfair not to give him enough time to prove himself."

"You said you were certain at three months that Gene was a mistake. How long ago was that?"

She flinched. She took her eyes off me and rubbed a wrinkle on her skirt. "Two months ago. You're the first person I've discussed it with."

Mary Sue was standing in lonely indecision.

I understood why. She was a kind person. Listening to her dilemma reminded me that considerate people tend to be patient with others, inclined to give them ample time to get on course, often more than ample time. Kind people find it hard to bring the hammer down unless they are certain, absolutely certain, it is the right thing to do.

"Mary Sue, what's Gene's problem?"

"He doesn't have good leadership skills. And he seems preoccupied. Maybe he's lost his motivation. But to answer your question, I'm not sure what the problem is."

She paused and then asked the question that had prompted our meeting. "Thad, what should I do?" She looked down, checked her fingernails, and rubbed one as if doing so would repair a chip in the polish.

I decided to be less direct than her question. "When people aren't performing well, they know it. They suffer because of it. Sometimes they give up. It's hard to tell the boss, unless you make the telling easy."

She got the message. "The Belief System is designed to get people to open up, to talk about where they are, what they want to do. Right?"

"Right."

"Let's use it then."

Mary Sue had Gene complete a set of Belief System questions that would profile his confidence, trust, and satisfaction. The three of us met to talk about the results.

After we pored over his responses, Mary Sue brought the discussion into crystal clear focus with one question.

"Is this job a good match for your skills?"

Gene looked down and tapped a pencil on the notepad in front of him. "I honestly thought it was, until I answered all these questions. I've been in denial. I can see now that I'm probably better suited for something else."

Mary Sue showed surprise at his ready confession. Gene had a serious confidence problem, one more easily cured by getting a job that matched his skills than by struggling to grow into the present one.

She turned to me with a puzzled expression. I had seen that look many times before. Gene had plopped an unexpected gift into her lap. She knew what his problem was, finally. Now what? There was only one thing to do.

She faced Gene, cleared her throat, and moved closer to him. **"I agree with you. This job isn't a good match for your skills. Maybe it's time to discuss some other options."**

I wondered how Gene would react to this. Most people in his situation have been searching for a way out.

He simply said, "I'd like that."

"What do *you* want to do?"

"Find a job that matches my skills better, that's what I want to do."

Mary Sue gave Gene a compassionate smile. She hoped he would not change his mind. "That's a big decision you just made. I'm sure everything will work out fine. This is a big company. You'll find something here if that's what you want. Let me know how I can help you." She paused. "Are you willing to stay for three or four weeks until I can find somebody to replace you?"

"Yes, I am, if I can start looking for something else right away."

"That works for me." She paused. **"Are you okay with where you are now?"**

He assured her that he was indeed okay.

Mary Sue was, too.

She wanted to talk after we concluded the meeting. "I hardly slept last night. I wasn't looking forward to deciding his future. Then midway through the discussion, it hit me—*you have to let people decide their own future.*"

"Yes, and you did it well," I said.

"Do you think he made the right decision?"

"People usually do, when they think through their situation clearly. You helped him do that."

Mary Sue folded her arms on the table in front of her and momentarily rested her head on them. When she looked up, she was refreshed, like a new person. "I love it when everybody wins!"

• • •

E X E R C I S E   1 2

Helping an Employee Who Does Not Have, and Cannot Develop, the Skills He or She Needs

1. Focus on one employee whom you believe does not have all the skills needed for his or her job.

2. List the critical skills that seem to be missing.

3. Do you believe this person could develop these skills in a reasonable time frame if given the opportunity to do so?

4. Meet and get this person to give you his or her view of

   • The skills he or she needs to develop

   • The best way to develop him or her

   • Any skills that cannot be developed to the necessary level in the available time frame

It is a grim reality to discover "I don't have, and can't develop, the skills I need." Whether the discovery comes in our professional or personal life, the stark truth jars us to the core. Our self-confidence and self-worth plunge. Motivation takes a dive. We search the depths of our souls to find a way out. The journey can lead anywhere or nowhere.

Substitution (for Problem 2)

Substitution is a good tool to employ when trying to resolve the second type of motivation problem—someone correctly believes "If I perform well, I will not get something I want" (a trust problem). This technique is aimed at substituting available outcomes that are acceptable to the employee for desired outcomes that are not available. Compensating balances are often found in attractive substitutes.

The goal is to accomplish two things: find substitute outcomes that (1) are within the manager's control to give *and* (2) will compensate the employee for the desired outcome that is not currently available. Get the employee to kick around the possibilities; what he or she comes up with likely will not have occurred to the manager. The manager would hope for a list of things that the employee says would salve his or her wounds and diffuse the problem. The process might go like this:

SAMPLE SCRIPT

Giving the Problem to the Employee

Manager: Let's explore some possibilities that might get you over the disappointment of the current promotion stalemate. I'm willing to work with you on some other options, but I need your help.

It is interesting that when managers start probing in this manner, solutions begin to materialize where before there seemed to be none. The manager's job is to get the employee to identify attractive outcomes that would serve as *substitutes* for the outcome that is desired but not available—a promotion in this case. It can be as simple as asking, "What are some things you want but are not now getting?"

Finding Substitutes

Manager: What is it about a promotion that's really attractive to you?

Employee: A lot of things, I guess. For one thing, I'd have more responsibility. There'd be a greater opportunity for growth and development and more authority, more money, and greater exposure to some of the key people in the organization. That's important to me. I want a chance to show people what I can do.

Ask employees what they want, and in almost every instance, they will tell you, if your intentions are honest and sincere. *Asking* always works better than *telling*, or even *suggesting*. In this example, the employee identified six desirable outcomes. The manager's job then becomes one of deciding, "Which ones can I provide?" The opportunities for giving substitute outcomes appear in a variety of ways, once you have learned what is appealing to the employee. Here is one example.

Finding Substitutes (continued)

Manager: Your comments are interesting. Our department has just been asked to do a special project for the vice president. He wants us to do a feasibility study on the possible expansion of our operation. I need a project leader. It wouldn't involve more money, but it's an opportunity to learn a lot. You'd have a small team working for you, and several of our key executives would have to be interviewed. A lot of responsibility is involved here and it's definitely a chance to show the right people what you can do. This isn't a promotion, but in a lot of ways, it might be even better. What do you think?

There could be little doubt about the employee's reaction to this opportunity. It has multiple outcomes that collectively are more than an adequate substitute for a promotion in the short term.

Preference Shifting
(for Problems 2 and 3)

Sometimes employees want an outcome that would not be as appealing upon receipt as they anticipated. In cases like these, the manager is advised to employ the technique of *preference shifting*. The objective is to shift the employee's preference *away* from the desired, albeit overestimated, outcome and thus remove it as an obstacle to the person's motivation and performance.

The first step with preference shifting is to level with the employee. Then get him or her to think about a more thorough and objective view of the desired outcome. The manager's role is simply to help the employee see the outcome more realistically, to recognize the negatives of a promotion as well as the positives, for example. Once the employee begins to see the whole picture, his or her preference for the unavailable outcome usually begins to wane.

Managers must take care not to pressure employees to shift their preferences. The manager's proper role is that of facilitator, not decision maker. Allow employees the opportunity of their own discovery, the chance to draw their own conclusions. The following scenario gives a Problem 2 problem to the employee to solve and illustrates the use of preference shifting in removing the obstacle to the employee's motivation.

SAMPLE SCRIPT

Giving the Problem to the Employee

Manager: Having the door closed on something you really want is disappointing. I can't tell you what to do or where to go from here, but I can help you think through this if you want me to.

The manager has thrown the preference-shifting ball to the employee. It is in the right hands. Preference shifting cannot be forced. It works only when the employee is willing to explore. Give the problem to the employee to solve, and do it the right way, and you can stimulate a willingness to explore that can pay off handsomely for all concerned. When the employee starts asking questions, you know you're on the right track.

Preference Shifting

Employee: What do you mean? How can thinking through this problem make a difference?

Manager: Well, we've discussed what's good about the promotion, but what about the negative? Have you considered that side of it?

Employee: Not really. What could be negative about a promotion?

Manager: Have you talked to any of the managers at the next level?

Employee: No, but I've seen what's happened to some of them. They don't have any balance in their lives. I'm not interested in that. And I know they have a lot of responsibility and work long, hard hours. That can be pretty stressful.

Manager: Right, and most of our managers travel a couple of days a week.

Employee: I guess I've only been looking at the upside of the promotion I've had my eyes on. The questions you're asking are giving me a more complete picture. Maybe I need to think about this more. Who knows, it might be best to hang onto what I have now and worry about a promotion later on.

Helping employees develop a more accurate assessment of the situation enables them to discover what really is important. The key is for the employee to make the discovery. For a person snagged on a do-or-die proposition that blocks motivation and performance, preference shifting can be a gentle and effective way around the obstruction.

Preference shifting also applies in Problem 3 situations where an employee receives an outcome that seems more unappealing than it really is. Sometimes employees acquire a strong dislike for certain outcomes simply because they are not aware of their full implications. The goal in this situation is to shift the employee's preference to liking the undesired outcome. Fat chance, you say? Maybe not.

On many occasions, employees view outcomes with dissatisfaction, even though they actually offer positive things. Here are a few examples:

- An employee thought a temporary assignment in the marketing department not only was a waste of time but was holding her back. Then she realized she was being prepared for a pending restructuring of her job, rather than downsizing.

- Performing well landed an employee in a special training program that was hard work and not very interesting. This was not the kind of reward the employee was hoping for—until he learned that the program was exclusively for young managers on the fast track to promotion.

- The addition of more work when her plate was already full was not very encouraging to the young assistant until she discovered that "passing the test" could lead to a promotion and more money.

Preference shifting can work wonders for those employees struggling under the misperception that certain outcomes are more undesirable than they really are. Utilization of the technique calls for the manager to lead the employee through the process of self-discovery. Provide information as necessary to help the person fully understand the implications of the outcome. Asking questions rather than telling or suggesting is the best way to lead employees to a more complete and accurate understanding of outcomes. Well-guided employees often shift from being dissatisfied to seeing outcomes as desirable.

The manager's best course of action after "giving the problem to the employee" will depend on the employee's response. But giving problems to employees is a must. When few promotions are available, pay raises are hard to come by, and job security is uncertain, it is absolutely imperative that managers help employees search their hearts and minds for alternative ways to stay motivated.

Offsets (for Problem 3)

Offsets are designed to help correct the third type of motivation problem—someone correctly believes "If I perform well, I'll get something I don't want" (a satisfaction problem). For undesired outcomes that cannot be avoided, offset the dissatisfaction with available outcomes that outweigh the negatives. The employee may not like the undesired outcome, but the offsets can compensate for the disappointment.

Here, too, first level with employees, then give them the problem, and then explore the possibility of offsets. The manager is simply searching the employee's thoughts for outcomes to offset dissatisfaction. Consider outcomes such as these: The more successful the salesperson, the more she has to travel; the better the work done for a client, the more demanding the client becomes; the more valuable the employee's input, the more meetings he has to attend. Solving problems like these runs the risk of "throwing the baby out with the bath water." Your best bet is to try to outweigh the bad with *additional good*—offset the unwanted outcomes with a willingness to make the person's life easier whenever you can. Offsetting may not boost motivation like the removal of the unwanted outcome, but it's better than doing nothing. The effort shows that you are aware of the problem and are doing your best to resolve it. The "thought counts," in this instance; with some employees, it counts a lot.

Helping employees with the "offsetting" option can evolve like this.

SAMPLE SCRIPT

Leveling

Manager: I know you don't like doing the monthly reports. Unfortunately, there isn't anything we can do to change that right now.

SAMPLE SCRIPT

Giving the Problem to the Employee

Manager: But let's not just leave it at that. Although you're stuck with the reports, maybe there's something we can do to make the task easier for you to live with. You're in a better position to determine that than I am. Any suggestions?

In giving the problem to the employee, the manager is searching for outcomes the employee wants but is not getting—outcomes that potentially will offset the dissatisfaction from undesired circumstances. As the employee mentions possible "offsetting outcomes," the manager will be tuned in particularly to those that are within his or her authority to grant.

Listening for Offsets

Employee: I'm always interested in learning new things. There's an in-house computer class I'd love to take. I might get some ideas for doing the monthly reports faster. That could solve my problem. The way it is now, the reports take so much time I can't get my other work done.

Employees usually know what will solve their problems. Managers who get into the habit of asking them for solutions get ahead of the game.

A question that sometimes comes up is, "Could offsets be interpreted as bribing employees to do the work?" I have never, not once, been given the impression that employees have considered offsets as a form of bribery—any more than they view the whole motivation process as a way of bribing them to perform. Instead, employees view both the parts and the whole of motivation management as concern for their welfare in the workplace. My experience is that employees welcome any steps that will improve the *confidence* they have in themselves, the *trust* they have in their manager to give them what they deserve, and the *satisfaction* they find in their jobs.

Notice that in the preceding examples, the manager gives the problem to the employee and leaves it there. While supportive and helpful, the manager does not take the problem back from the employee. This is important. But face it, managers and employees cannot always find good solutions to tough motivation problems no matter how diligent the effort. So all is for naught, the employee is dissatisfied, motivation is down, and performance is headed in the same direction. Is that it? Is that the upshot of the manager's hard work and good intentions? Quite the contrary, I have found. Employees who have watched Belief System managers try and fail to remedy motivation problems overwhelmingly report a considerable liking for the attempt and the way it was done. Here is the reasoning.

- At least my manager *listened* to me.
- My manager obviously *cared* enough to go the "whole nine yards" to solve the problem.
- My manager *showed respect* for me by soliciting my opinion on how best to solve the problem.
- There was obvious *concern* on the manager's part for my welfare.

All of these are positive outcomes that serve at least as partial substitutes for outcomes employees want but are not getting or as partial offsets for outcomes they are getting but do not want.

EXERCISE 13

Finding Substitutes and Offsets

1. Focus on an employee whom you believe is "not getting something wanted" (Problem 2) and/or "getting something not wanted" (Problem 3).

2. Meet with this person and confirm your belief.

3. Use leveling.

4. Give the problem to the employee.

5. Ask and listen for substitutes (for Problem 2) and offsets (for Problem 3).

Leveling Bold

There is one last tactic that may bring forth a solution when all else has failed: *leveling bold*. Here, you go beyond the basic message conveyed in the leveling step described previously—that is, "You have a performance problem, I don't know what the solution is, but maybe you can come up with some suggestions; I'm willing to help you via job matching, preference shifting, substitution, and offsets."

Leveling bold says: "You have a performance problem, neither of us has come up with a workable solution, and I am not willing to live with the problem any longer." The message is "Shape up or ship out." Cruel? It certainly does not have to be. It is not a message to be expressed in anger, but in kindness and with concern for the employee. After all, leveling bold is based on the belief that employees should be given a final opportunity to take control of the situation. What more can employees expect?

GETTING STARTED

If you want to overcome the fear of handling difficult motivation problems, practice handling them.

Furthermore, leveling bold is used only when all other efforts have failed, so the message should come as no surprise to the person involved. The key to this approach is what is said and how it is said. Here is a right way.

SAMPLE SCRIPT

Leveling Bold

Manager: Given what you want, and my knowledge of the situation here, I honestly don't believe we will ever be able to meet your needs, certainly not in the foreseeable future. You have a lot of capabilities. However, your performance is unacceptable and I'm not willing to live with it any longer. Have you considered other opportunities that might give you what you want?

No conscientious manager wants to come to this last resort, but, if your career is long, come to it you certainly will.

REALITY CHECK

Myth Sometimes you should tell employees they have to go, but you can't do it in today's environment.

Reality You can and should terminate certain employees. You just have to do it in the right way.

LIFTING A BURDEN

Sandy was in a hurry when she met with Jack, so she got straight to the point. "You've been one of our top salespeople, and I've decided to promote you. Paul's moving to our Buffalo office and I want you to take over the marketing support position."

Jack's smooth, 26-year-old face beamed.

"You've got big shoes to fill. Paul's done a great job. Let's get together tomorrow and go over your new responsibilities."

Sandy realized later that she had not asked Jack whether he wanted the position. "He must, though, judging from the smile on his face."

The organization Sandy managed had 63 salespeople. They sold technical products in a highly competitive market. Customers bought mainly on price. Pricing was complex, and detailed proposals were required as part of the buying process.

When Sandy met with Jack the next day, she surprised herself because she went to greater lengths than usual covering her expectations. "Your main responsibility is to support our entire sales force in developing proposals. You'll represent our salespeople with the corporate office. You'll have to negotiate with corporate to get their approval on the pricing for each proposal. They're profit minded and tough, but you know that. They want the price as high as possible. The salespeople, obviously, want the price as low as possible. Better chance to make the sale."

She was not sure Jack was listening. He looked anxious to talk, but she had one more thing to say. "The job is filled with conflict. If you push corporate too much on price, they'll be upset with you. If you give in to them, the salespeople will be upset. No way to please both."

She paused. Jack was bursting to talk, and once he started he rambled on for three minutes. Sandy's tension grew. So many words, but she heard only two things: "I understand what you expect," and "I'll do everything I can to make you happy."

Jack's deluge of words reminded Sandy who he was. He was nice, outgoing, and always eager to please. As a salesperson, his strategy was to win customers over with his personality. She remembered that he disagreed with the aggressive, pushy approach used by some of his peers. He did not like the conflict it produced. Attention to detail was not Jack's strength either, but customers forgave him because he was an easy, likable person.

As the weeks passed, everything around the marketing support function started to unravel. The sales force complained that Jack was dragging his feet, caving in to everything corporate wanted, and causing them to lose sales. Corporate said Jack was not responsive to their needs, he overlooked critical details, and his lack of technical knowledge was creating some problems.

Sandy decided to use the Belief System to get to the bottom of things. She called Jack into her office and began summarizing the complaints she had heard. Jack crossed his right leg over his left and started bouncing his foot in short, quick movements.

When Sandy finished she asked him, **"How do you see the situation?"**

He responded in his usual long-winded, ambiguous fashion. The bottom line was, "Gee, I don't know what the problem is," as if nothing were wrong. Sandy took a couple of deep breaths to calm herself.

She shifted gears and tried to get a handle on the problem without blaming Jack. **"Do you feel like we've prepared you for the job?"**

"Sure! Well...I guess you have. I mean, as much as you can for a job like this."

Sandy was thinking a confidence rating of 5 was about right. Jack knew the Belief System, so she asked, "If you think about the Belief 1 rating scale, **where would you put your confidence level?"**

Jack gave a lengthy response and in the end said, "It's on the low side, maybe a 3 or 4."

"Jack, you've been in the job for nearly two months now. **How do you like your work so far?"**

He sat frozen in his chair, except for the foot, and sighed. "It's okay. I guess...I mean...I like it...but it's not what I expected."

"Could you be more specific?"

"It's so different from sales, you know, with all the details and technical stuff, and somebody's always upset. It's just different, but I'm getting used to it."

"What I hear you saying is that you're not comfortable with the job, at least not yet."

Jack started talking, got off track, and zigzagged from one subject to another until Sandy interrupted. "You said your Belief 1 is on the low side and you're not enjoying your work. **What do you want to do?"**

Jack went into a dissertation about how hard he was working, how much he wanted to stay in the job, and how he needed time to "get the hang of things." Sandy wondered if his foot was tired.

Sandy was tough minded, but she still had trouble "pulling the trigger." Like most managers, she had a tendency to give employees more time even though she did not believe they could turn their performance around. She had a good excuse with Jack, though. "I don't have anyone to take his place." She decided to give him more time. That would give her a few weeks to think about who could take over if Jack did not pan out.

"Jack, let's see how your performance shapes up over the next four weeks, and then let's get back together and talk."

Sandy kept her ear to the ground and both eyes on Jack over the next month. His performance got worse, not better. She decided to use the leveling technique with him. "**Your performance hasn't improved** since we talked four weeks ago." She watched him carefully for his reaction. She saw no sign of disagreement, only a tired, defeated expression, and a bouncing foot on his crossed leg. "You have a lot of very good skills, Jack, a lot of strengths, but **I don't believe this job is a good match for you. What do you think?**"

Jack reacted almost before Sandy finished. His voice cracked. "I know, but I've got to prove I can do it. I'm making progress. Just give me a little more time. I'll turn it around."

Jack was like many employees in his predicament. Some people do not fully recognize the skills they need; others are not willing to admit their deficiencies.

Logic told Sandy to say, "No," but her heart won out and she said, "Okay, Jack. Be here at eight o'clock in the morning and tell me your plan to turn your performance around. I'll give you two weeks to show some progress."

They met. His plan was good. His plans always were. Execution was Jack's problem.

When the two weeks ended, Sandy knew she must turn to the leveling bold technique with Jack. She tried to be direct but compassionate. "Jack, you're a talented person, **but your performance isn't where it needs to be. I'm not willing to continue this way. Have you decided what other jobs might suit you better?**"

Jack sat with both feet resting on the carpeted floor and smiled. "This may surprise you, but I feel like a burden has been lifted. I couldn't make the decision myself. You're deciding for me, and I'm fine with that. And, yes, I know what I should do. I'm a salesperson. That's me. I want to get back into sales. The question is where."

"Jack, you look like you're comfortable with this decision. I'd love for you to stay here. We have two or three sales positions that are open. **What do you think?**"

"That's what I'd like to do, stay here."

"Great. Let's get together in a couple of days and decide which sales team would be best for you."

"Okay." He ducked his head, then looked up. "And thanks. I appreciate the way you've handled all of this, from the very beginning."

• • •

EXERCISE 14

Getting Ready to Level Bold

1. Focus on an employee who has performed poorly for too long.

2. Have you leveled with this person?

3. Have you given the problem to him or her?

4. Is leveling bold needed now? If not, might it be in the future?

5. Decide what steps you *should* take.

6. Decide on the steps you *will* take and when.

MULTIDIMENSIONAL PROBLEMS

It is very common for employees to have multiple motivation problems. This was the case with Jack, the employee in the example above. Two points are illustrated in this story, but first, a summary of the problems.

Jack's confidence problem.

Cause: He does not have the skills for the job.

Solution: Get a job that matches his skills.

Jack's satisfaction problem.

Cause: He does not like the work itself.

Solution: Get a job that matches his interests.

The first point is that *problems sometimes have a common solution.* This is the situation with Jack. A different job, the right one, will solve both of his problems.

The second point is that confidence and satisfaction problems sometimes are *interrelated.* Specifically, one or both of the problems can be a partial cause of the other. This is the case with Jack. *Poor performance can lead to job dissatisfaction.* In other words, employees who perform poorly tend to become dissatisfied with the work itself. How can you enjoy your work if you do it poorly? *Job dissatisfaction can lead to poor performance.* Employees who dislike their work find it difficult to perform well. How can you do a good job if you hate your work?

Typically, however, multidimensional problems are not related to each other. This is the situation with Helen in the story that opens this chapter. Helen has three different satisfaction problems. The problems are unrelated to each other; so are the solutions.

Helen's first satisfaction problem.

Cause: She wants but is not getting a formal performance evaluation.

Solution: Substitution—She will get informal feedback from her manager as a substitute for the formal evaluation.

Helen's second satisfaction problem.

Cause: She does not want the MicroNet project, but she is getting it anyway.

Solution: Offsets—She will get exposure with the executive committee, which she wants very much, to offset the extra work on the project and make it easier to accept.

Helen's third satisfaction problem.

Cause: She wants but is not getting an opportunity to attend the executive development program at Harvard.

Solution: Preference shifting—She will shift her preferences; in essence, she will leave one dream alone and get another.

MOVING AHEAD

Managers can pick up some great ideas for solving difficult motivation problems by taking courses, attending training programs, and even reading books like this one. But experienced managers have learned one basic truth, often from the school of hard knocks: Good ideas are not enough to solve difficult problems. It takes more, as the following story illustrates.

WISDOM IN A SMALL PACKAGE

Rufus McMickins took out a handkerchief and dried his wet palms as his CEO approached the microphone to introduce him as the closing speaker at the on-site conference, "New Management for the New Millennium," for the top 100 executives in the company.

He had discussed his speech with Beatrice, his wife. "It's risky."

"Maybe so," she said, "but it's the best way to make your point."

Rufus cleared his throat and felt the wetness under his arms as the CEO began his introduction.

"Rufus McMickins is a man of vision and a man of action—a rare combination. He sees what needs to be done and does it. One idea after another, year after year. His ideas have led us to new products, new markets, and new ways of marketing. His ideas also have streamlined processes, improved our hiring practices, and made this company a better place to work. He is a man I respect very, very much. I am pleased to have him bring our conference to a close. This has been a productive day. You have generated a long list of ideas about new ways for managing and leading our employees into the new millennium. So now, here is Rufus to give all of us some parting words of wisdom."

Beads of sweat dotted Rufus's forehead now. The glowing introduction only added more pressure.

The group applauded as he approached the podium.

"Thank you, Jim, for that generous introduction."

Rufus turned to the audience. He spoke without notes. He noticed that his hands were wet again, but his voice was strong. That was all that mattered.

He paused until the silence drew the attention of every person in the room. He made eye contact with several of the executives in the audience and began.

"We are a talented group. We have many great ideas. But great ideas are a dime a dozen, unless you *act on them*."

He paused, watched people shift in their seats, heard feet shuffling. Then he leaned into the microphone. "Thank you."

Rufus walked to his chair in deafening silence and sat down, hands dripping. He thought to himself, "What in the world possessed me to give a 23-word speech? I must have been crazy."

One person in the audience stood.

"Terrific! Now they're all going to walk out."

But no, the man did not leave. Instead he brought his hands together loudly. Then another, and another, until one by one they all acknowledged a simple but profound truth.

• • •

CHAPTER 7

More Tools
of the Trade

*"Sometimes you have to do what you won't
to get what you want."*

A BRIEFING SESSION

Proactive managers want to address potential motivation issues before they emerge to ruin performance.

Aggressive managers want to push "satisfactory" performance levels to the best-in-class category.

Managers who are leading change frequently face pervasive motivation and performance problems, especially during periods of upheaval.

In each of these situations, where the motivation and performance of every employee needs to be addressed, new tools typically are needed. Motivation management provides them.

This chapter presents three such tools, collectively called the *Belief System Profile.*

These tools are used by employees to develop motivation profiles.

The idea is to identify and solve existing problems, and prevent future ones.

Employees do most of the work, but managers reap the benefits.

SCARING THE DEVIL OUT OF 'EM

Bernie stopped at the traffic light on Peachtree at Piedmont, shook his head, and sighed. "When Floyd starts sloshing Scotch out of his glass, he starts spilling secrets." I was not sure if Bernie was warning me or bracing himself.

We were on our way to meet Floyd. Bernie had hired him two years earlier, and Floyd had just resigned to accept a new job.

I got pulled into this little rendezvous because I had been in Bernie's office, introducing him to the Belief System, when Floyd had come in. "Bernie, you promised to buy me a drink. You ready?" Bernie had asked me to join them. Floyd insisted. "The more the merrier. Meet you at the Ritz Carlton; I'm in my Porsche."

It was noisy as we sat in the busy lounge. I watched Floyd drain his glass as the waitress placed the next one in front of him.

Floyd came across as the type who thrived on corporate politics. I had a feeling he preferred dancing around the edges of the truth, at least when he was sober.

I leaned close to Floyd and spoke over the noise. "So how does it feel being lured away by the competition?"

"Flattering, you know. Good position. They really wanted me." He raised his glass and took one long swig that nearly emptied it.

"So what are you thinking as you leave?"

"About Bernie. He's responsible." Floyd turned to Bernie. "You coached me, developed me. I won't forget." Floyd waved across the room to the waitress; she nodded and he nodded back, satisfied.

"Thanks, Floyd, but that's part of my job."

"Just the same, you did it."

"You deserve that new job, but I hate to lose you."

"I want to do something, to thank you."

Bernie laughed. "You can answer a question for me. You've been on my team for two years, and you know everybody. I'm trying to take them to the next level of performance, but I don't know how. They won't open up to me. Any suggestions?"

Floyd burped, then covered his mouth with his hand. "Bernie, old buddy, you gotta stop what you been doin'...." He paused and took a big swallow. "And that's a fact. You're an extremist. Some of your people, you don't even talk to 'em, so they can't tell you anything. And the others, you haul 'em into your office, throw a million questions at 'em, and expect 'em to open up. All you do is scare the devil out of 'em."

Bernie looked into his glass and said, "So what do I do?" as if the answer were hidden somewhere in the Coca-Cola and crushed ice.

"Not much you can do, really." Floyd burped again, this time covering it with his hand. Floyd saw the waitress approaching, hurriedly finished his drink, and held it out to her. She made a quick exchange. Floyd swirled the Scotch as he lifted the glass. Gold jumped over the edge.

Bernie watched the glass meet Floyd's eager lips. "What do you mean, there's nothing I can do?"

Bernie was about to repeat the question when Floyd answered. "I'm gonna level with you, Bernie." He burped again. No attempt to cover it. "You've got some good people, but they won't ever open up to you. Too many hang-ups, too many secrets in their lives, too much to keep from you.

"Bernie, I probably shouldn't tell you all this, but you need to know. So here goes. Little Miss Sensitive-to-Everything is afraid of you, says you snapped at her once, way back. Mr. Insecure-to-the-Bone says you're so-o-o-o smart, so-o-o-o intimidating, but he wouldn't tell anybody anything anyway."

Bernie glanced at me.

Floyd rattled the ice in his empty glass, sat up straight, and looked anxious until he found the waitress. They waved. He relaxed and continued.

"Mr. Waiting-on-Retirement dodges everybody, trying to hold on. The Big Mama, she'll open up sometimes, but she doesn't trust men because her old man used to beat her. And your new man, Mr. Perfectionist, he keeps his distance, afraid you'll find out he's an alcoholic, like somebody else you know."

Bernie sat frozen in his chair. This was obviously news to him. I wondered if he wanted to know. Too late now. Bernie would never repeat any of it, I was sure of that. The problem was that he would not be able to forget or ignore it.

I looked at Bernie. "Your people are shouldering heavy burdens. Some have serious hang-ups, and some are living with dark secrets. They think they're protecting themselves by not opening up."

Bernie nodded. "I understand. I guess we all do that to some extent."

"Right. And the point Floyd is making is this: The reason your employees don't open up has more to do with *them* than with you."

Floyd raised his glass. "That's 'xactly what I said." Then, in slow motion, the glass wobbled to his mouth.

Bernie frowned. "More to do with *them* than with me? Now that's something to think about."

I sensed that Bernie wanted to talk, but this was not the time or place. He handed me his car keys. "I'll drive Floyd home. It's not far. Can you follow me?"

On the return trip, Bernie was quiet, contemplating. When he stopped to let me out, he thanked me. "I guess you know what I should do with my team."

"Yes, I do." Bernie was leading a team of people who were hiding feelings and avoiding problems. This team was not unusual, and their feelings and problems were not unique. I worked with groups like this every day. One thing I had learned for sure: Hiding feelings and avoiding problems runs counter to performing well. Floyd had opened the door and given Bernie a glimpse of his people. Bernie needed to open the door wider. People needed to get their issues on the table and deal with them.

• • •

THE BELIEF SYSTEM PROFILE

The approaches to motivation management outlined thus far allow managers the flexibility to use the Belief System in the way that matches their own skills, preferences, and circumstances. Managers begin by recognizing that all employee motivation problems can be categorized as *confidence* (Belief 1), *trust* (Belief 2), or *satisfaction* (Belief 3) problems. Then managers take up the solid framework and proven guidelines of the Belief System to expertly steer them through a process that leads to solutions. These approaches are far from rigid; they maintain an informality that allows managers the flexibility to devise their own ways of probing to identify problems, uncover causes, and discover solutions.

There are occasions, however, when managers need more structure to deal with the complexities they face. The Belief System is based on open communication with employees; without it, the Belief System will not work. There are instances when communication is a stumbling block that will challenge the wherewithal of any manager. In these cases, managers need something beyond an informal approach.

The Belief System provides a formal approach that enables managers to crack stubborn communication barriers they face with

TABLE 5
Common Communication Barriers

- An employee puts up protective walls that simply cannot be penetrated.
- A strained manager-employee relationship works against employee disclosure.
- Some employees fear negative consequences of open disclosure.
- The manager or employee easily becomes emotional, defensive, or impatient.
- Many employees lack clarity about their own motivation.
- A low trust level between manager and employee will prevent openness.
- Pressure to perform leaves little time for communication with employees.

employees. The cornerstone is the Belief System Profile, an unusual document designed to create an accurate, in-depth employee motivation profile. The Belief System Profile provides breakthrough access to information about motivation problems, causes, and solutions through its three constituent parts:

- *Confidence* Profile
- *Trust* Profile
- *Satisfaction* Profile

These three tools provide managers a formal, structured way to use the Belief System and successfully address even the most complex situations. This chapter presents these tools and explains how managers can use them independently and without the help of consultants or trained facilitators.

THE EASY WAY OUT

"Why three profiles, if you don't mind me asking?" That was Lyle, early thirties, a first-time manager. He was open minded, curious, still experimenting with different ways to manage. "I mean, doesn't that take a lot of time? Why can't you just ask people what motivates them? That's what I do."

I was leading a Motivation Management seminar with Doris Jean and her team of eight managers. I had just given an overview of the Belief System Profile and its three component parts, the Confidence Profile, Trust Profile, and Satisfaction Profile.

Lyle was the newest and youngest member of the team. The others were seasoned managers. Lyle's question was a good one. Nods from several of the other managers indicated they had the same concern.

"Lyle, what do people usually say when you ask what motivates them?" I did not want to give a lecture or start a debate. I wanted to lead people to some useful conclusions.

"Money, they all say money." The same heads nodded again.

"Is that it? Anything else?"

"Well, no, not really. I assume that money's the main thing that motivates them."

That was exactly the answer I was hoping for—and it was built on shifting sand.

"Lyle, what motivates you?"

"Well, I, ah...money does, I guess."

Two managers started doodling on notepads. One flipped through the pages of the training manual. "You guess?"

"Well, sure, money motivates me."

"Are there two things in addition to money that motivate you? Don't tell me what they are, just think of them."

"Okay, I've got 'em."

"Is either of them more important than money to you at this stage in your career?"

"Yes."

The doodlers looked up.

"Are both of them more important than money?"

"Yes."

The flipper glanced at Lyle.

I had followed this line of questioning with many groups. Things were going smoothly, so far, like coasting downhill on a bicycle. "Lyle, would you tell us what they are, these two things that are more important to you than money?"

He hesitated. Money was a safe topic. "Do you feel uncomfortable sharing them with the entire group?"

"A little, I guess."

"Would you be willing to share them privately with Doris Jean, your manager?"

"Well, I guess." He looked at her. "I guess I would, but..."

"But what, Lyle?"

He squirmed in his chair. "I don't know."

"Okay, everybody, time for an exercise. Make a list of the 10 things that contribute most to your motivation at work, and then put them in order of importance. You have five minutes." The exercise would draw them in, let them experience a few things firsthand, like Lyle. It would get Lyle out of the spotlight, too.

I wandered around the room and looked over shoulders. Most lists were short, some were longer but messy, with words crossed out. Not one was complete.

"Okay, time's up. Anybody have 10 items listed in the order of importance?" No one responded. "Was this harder than you expected?" Several nods. "Anybody have 10 items?" No one did. "Who had money as the most important item on your list?" One hand went up. "Who would feel comfortable sharing his or her list with the group?" Only one person was willing to share.

"Time for another exercise. Take about three minutes and make a list of the things you've learned since Lyle asked his 'Why three profiles?' question."

People dug into the task. Time passed quickly. "Time's up. Who wants to share first? We'll make a list on the flip chart." Everyone was eager to contribute. The sharing and discussion that followed resulted in a short but substantive list.

- People do not always know what motivates them.
- When you ask, "What motivates you?" people tend to say "money," and that can be very misleading.
- While money is important to everybody, other things often are more important.
- Motivation is a personal matter and most people are reluctant to share.

"In view of all of this, what should we do?" asked Doris Jean.

"If you really want to know what motivates people, keep in mind the two problems you face." The note takers readied to write.

"One, *people can't tell you what motivates them until they know.*" Heads nodded.

"Two, *people are reluctant to talk about their motivation.*" That was one of the main reasons we were having this seminar.

"What should you do? *Your job as a manager is to (1) help people understand their motivation and (2) make it easy for them to share it with you.*"

A hand went up. Lyle had a question. "So, how can we do that?"

"That goes back to your original question, 'Why three profiles?' My experience is that the three Belief System tools represent the best way to lead people to both understand and share their motivation with you."

• • •

The Confidence Profile

> **LEARNING LESSON**
>
> You have to *make it easy* for people to share.

The Confidence Profile, easily completed by employees, is chock-full of the unexpected. In fact, managers often are dumbfounded and momentarily speechless. Here are some examples of information that has left managers reeling.

Goals and Objectives

- A manager discovered that an employee did not have a good grasp of the basic goals and objectives of the job and was unintentionally marching in the wrong direction.

- An employee stated point-blank that he understood the goals and objectives of the department but disagreed with them and was deliberately pursuing a different course.

Performance Expectations

- An employee revealed a lack of understanding of the manager's performance expectations, including several critical ones in particular, that would soon leave the manager in a precarious position.

- A manager realized that an employee did not see eye-to-eye with her on performance expectations. They were, in fact, miles apart on some of them, which accounted for numerous performance problems.

Priorities

- An employee was confused about priorities and was neglecting an important, time-consuming assignment with an imminent deadline.

- A manager was dismayed to find that an employee was setting her own priorities even though the manager had clearly spelled them out to her previously.

- A new employee missed two critical deadlines because he was uncertain about priorities, but he was embarrassed to ask the manager because his previous boss had always made him "feel stupid" when he asked questions.

Skills

- An employee confessed that the Confidence Profile had helped her realize that her skills were not a good match for the job and she intended to find a more suitable opportunity.

- A manager probed and uncovered serious skill deficiencies that, coupled with extreme insecurity, had led an employee on a long course of lies and deception to protect his job.

- An employee had been agonizing over a lack of skills, and although he knew a solid, low-cost solution, he was afraid to discuss it with his manager.

These examples are a reminder that while confidence problems are pervasive, employees often do not come forward with them. The pot may be hot, employees may be in a stew, but remove the lid they will not because self-doubt might bubble into view. Even so, managers are but a short step away from significant performance improvement. All it takes is quick action. Seek out the silent plea of employees who want to develop the confidence to be all they can be. The Confidence Profile is a sure way for managers to hear this plea.

Remembering that *confidence* (Belief 1) refers to beliefs people have about their effort leading to performance, the Confidence Profile is designed to reflect those beliefs about each of the various components of the employee's job. Take a close look at the Confidence Profile in Exercise 15. Notice that the employee makes a list of the most important parts of the job, and then uses rating scales to indicate the amount of effort expended and the performance level achieved in

Confidence Profile

What Are the Most Important Parts of Your Job?	What Level of *Effort* Do You Normally Give?			What *Performance* Level Do You Normally Achieve?		
	Low	Average	High	Low	Average	High
1.	0 1 2 3 4 5 6 7 8 9 10			0 1 2 3 4 5 6 7 8 9 10		
2.	0 1 2 3 4 5 6 7 8 9 10			0 1 2 3 4 5 6 7 8 9 10		
3.	0 1 2 3 4 5 6 7 8 9 10			0 1 2 3 4 5 6 7 8 9 10		
4.	0 1 2 3 4 5 6 7 8 9 10			0 1 2 3 4 5 6 7 8 9 10		
5.	0 1 2 3 4 5 6 7 8 9 10			0 1 2 3 4 5 6 7 8 9 10		
6.	0 1 2 3 4 5 6 7 8 9 10			0 1 2 3 4 5 6 7 8 9 10		
7.	0 1 2 3 4 5 6 7 8 9 10			0 1 2 3 4 5 6 7 8 9 10		
8.	0 1 2 3 4 5 6 7 8 9 10			0 1 2 3 4 5 6 7 8 9 10		
9.	0 1 2 3 4 5 6 7 8 9 10			0 1 2 3 4 5 6 7 8 9 10		
10.	0 1 2 3 4 5 6 7 8 9 10			0 1 2 3 4 5 6 7 8 9 10		

11. Even when my level of effort is high, I do not always perform well on the following parts of my job:

a. My effort does not always pay off because:

b. The thing that would help most is:

12. My level of effort is not high and consequently I do not perform well on the following parts of my job.

a. My effort is lacking because:

b. The thing that would help most is:

each. These ratings reveal employee confidence levels as well as other useful information.

What do managers learn when they review employee responses to the initial question in the Confidence Profile, "What are the most important parts of your job?"

- Managers invariably discover that employees do not have a complete and accurate understanding of goals and objectives, performance expectations, and priorities. The confusion appears in the lack of clarity about certain parts of the job, the omission of parts the manager deems important, or the inclusion of parts the manager does not intend for the employee. Communication is the culprit. The Confidence Profile reveals these problems and gives the manager an opportunity to clarify.

- Managers sometimes find that employees have a clear understanding of goals and objectives, performance expectations, and priorities, but the employees disagree with the manager's view. The danger is not in the disagreements, but in the manager's lack of awareness. The Confidence Profile reveals these disagreements and allows managers to take steps to resolve them.

What do managers learn from employee responses to the effort and performance rating scales in the Confidence Profile? Four combinations of responses are of particular interest.

- *High Effort, High Performance*

  The manager can see from this combination of ratings that there is no confidence problem. The employee is saying, "I work hard and do a good job. No problem."

- *High Effort, Low Performance*

  There is a problem when performance is low. The question is, "*What* is the problem?" The message here is, "I put out a lot of effort, but my performance isn't where I want it to be." This suggests a confidence problem; when effort does not lead to performance, employees conclude, "I can't do it." When managers see this combination of ratings in the Confidence Profile, they will want to know "What is causing the problem?" and "What solution would work for you?" For answers to these questions, the manager's job is straightforward; simply turn to item 11 in the Profile and read what the employee has to say. Employees usually know what is causing problems and have a solution in mind that will work for them.

- *Low Effort, High Performance*

  This is a combination of ratings that gives managers a special insight. The employee is saying, "I perform this part of my job well, and it doesn't take much effort." This happens when employees are very experienced and/or have a natural ability for the job. Managers find this information handy when delegating work to employees. It allows employees to perform well by letting them do what they do best.

- *Low Effort, Low Performance*

  Again, when performance is low, there is a problem. The employee is saying, "I'm not trying and I'm not performing." Low effort and low performance obviously means the employee has a motivation problem. Is it a confidence, trust, or satisfaction problem? This combination of ratings signals only that there is a problem. The manager will have to determine what the problem is, what is causing it, and what will solve it. This generally is easy; just turn to item 12 in the Confidence Profile and read. Employees who have been living with "low effort, low performance" generally know what their problem is, what is causing it, and what will solve it for them.

	TABLE 6	
Using the Confidence Profile to Diagnose Employee Motivation		
Effort	**Performance**	**Diagnosis**
High	High	No problem
High	Low	Confidence problem
Low	High	No problem
Low	Low	A problem—could be confidence, trust, or satisfaction

Stop and think about it. Will employees *really* disclose confidence problems that usually set them squirming? My experience is that, yes, with the Confidence Profile, they will. Managers, however, have to answer this question for themselves, and there is only one way to know for sure—give the Confidence Profile a try.

A LITTLE COMMUNICATION GOES A LONG WAY

Belinda called me before meeting with Bob, her manager, to discuss her Belief System Profile. "Are you going to be there tomorrow for my session? 'Cause if you're not, I'm not going."

"Yes, I'll be there." Bob had asked me to meet with them. She did not respond. "Are you okay?"

"I just finished my preparation, getting everything on paper and all. I don't have any big issues to deal with, but I'm afraid Bob will. You know how he is. He can skin you alive before you know it."

"Belinda, I won't let *anything* like that happen. We may have to tackle some tough issues, but I'll work with you on them."

We chatted for several minutes. I listened until she talked her anxiety away. "I feel better now. I just wanted to be sure you'd be there. See you tomorrow."

Belinda was a kind, gentle, cautious person. Bob was dominating, direct, and fearless. These oil-and-water styles were the foundation of Belinda's concerns and would make the session interesting and challenging for me as the facilitator.

When we began the discussion the next morning, Belinda looked as anxious as she had sounded over the phone. I was not concerned. Most people, including the manager, came to such meetings full of apprehension.

"Belinda, what have you heard about the other sessions?" Her answer would be feedback for Bob.

"Nothing much, really, except they've all been good."

That was what I expected, and I wanted Bob to hear it. He had received some criticism in his first three sessions. He had handled it well. The themes were consistent. He was becoming a better manager already because he had listened to and acted on some solid suggestions.

"Belinda, Bob's willingness to meet with you today is his way of saying 'Help me help you.' But you have to let him know *how* to help."

"And Bob, you know how important it is for you to listen and be receptive, and to hold your dominant tendencies in check, given Belinda's easygoing manner. My job is to be sure the session goes well for both of you. Let's start with the Confidence Profile."

Bob finished reading Belinda's Confidence Profile quickly and went out to refill his coffee cup. Belinda was hard at work jotting down a few last-minute notes on her copy in green ink. I marked one item in red.

In the discussion that followed, Bob acknowledged that Belinda was doing good work and focused on clarifying his expectations of her. She took copious notes.

When he had finished, Bob said, "Doesn't look like we have any confidence problems here."

"No, I don't think so. And thanks for clarifying things for me. As long as I know what you expect, I'll do a good job."

Belinda smiled, but not for long.

I had a couple of questions. "Belinda, let's go back to your Profile, the first page, item 5, for a minute. I have a couple of questions."

She squirmed in her chair. "I thought we'd already finished with that."

When they had discussed item 5 earlier, Belinda had told Bob she was overloaded with work and simply had not focused on streamlining the processes. He said it was not a problem yet, but it would be if she didn't give it immediate attention.

What Are the Most Important Parts of Your Job?	What Level of *Effort* Do You Normally Give?			What *Performance* Level Do You Normally Achieve?		
	Low	Average	High	Low	Average	High
5. Streamline all processes in my unit to maximize effectiveness.		X			X	
	0 1 2 3 4 5 6 7 8 9 10			0 1 2 3 4 5 6 7 8 9 10		

Figure 19 CONFIDENCE PROFILE (PARTIALLY SHOWN)

Bob watched me closely as I continued. "Belinda, since you're planning to give a high priority to streamlining the processes, how would you mark the two rating scales for that now?"

"My effort certainly will be at the 8 to 10 level now—let's say a 9." She circled the 9 on the rating scale, and then she stopped. Tears formed. She blinked them away.

Careful not to let Belinda see, Bob pointed at me. With as much gentleness as possible, I said, "Belinda, what are you thinking now?"

"I don't know if I can streamline the processes. They're complex. The people two levels below me work directly with them. I never have. I've put off the streamlining because I don't know what to do."

"Bob, do you expect Belinda to literally streamline the processes by herself? Or do you expect her to make sure the streamlining gets done?"

"The latter, definitely. Belinda, I know you don't have time to roll up your sleeves and get buried in the details of all those processes. You're a great manager, and the streamlining is just another activity for you to manage, not do yourself. I guess I didn't make that clear before. Sorry."

"That's a relief," Belinda sighed.

"Belinda, look back at item 5 and the two rating scales. If your effort is at the 9 level, as you marked, how well do you expect to perform, given Bob's expectations?"

She circled the 9 on the performance scale and smiled at Bob. "I think I can handle it now."

He flashed a smile back.

I was happy, too. Her confidence problem was solved. "Anybody ready for a break?"

"Yes, but I want to say something first." Bob turned to me. "I've been reminded that little miscommunications can lead to big problems. I'm speaking for myself, but I think it applies to all managers. You need a process that forces you to slow down and communicate better."

• • •

The Trust Profile

Whereas the Confidence Profile focuses on the employee, the spotlight is on the manager in the Trust Profile. Employees are given the opportunity to provide feedback that lets managers know how well they are tying outcomes to performance. In other words, the Trust Profile tells managers how much they are trusted to give employees what their performance deserves. This trust level, of course, has a direct bearing on employee willingness to work hard and do a good job.

Managers hold their breath when reading the Trust Profile, a report card on their managerial practices. They may receive high marks for fairness in the way they treat employees. However, the Trust Profile can signal problems, as was the case in the following situations.

- A manager discovered that a hardworking, high-performing employee was looking for employment elsewhere because he felt mistreated, overlooked, and unimportant. He said he was rewarded no differently than anyone else, that all employees were treated the same regardless of their performance.

- A poor performer made it clear he had no interest in improving performance because the same system that failed to reinforce good performance offered no incentive for poor performers to change.

- A manager learned why performance had slipped and cooperation had turned to indifference for a once dependable worker. Initially happy with a pay raise, the employee was struggling with feelings of anger and resentment because less deserving employees had received similar pay increases.

- A manager knew his employees were concerned but was caught completely off guard when he discovered that they were outraged because a poor performer was "continually getting by with murder" and nothing was being done about it.

- A busy manager realized why employees were no longer responding to his directions and requests. He had developed the habit of issuing orders without following up and holding people accountable.

These examples are a reminder of the seriousness of trust problems. The consequences are damaging and there is no instant remedy. Lack of trust is like a medical problem that takes weeks, even months, to cure. Managers must consistently give people what their performance merits until trust is restored, and they must continue doing so to maintain a healthy trust environment.

Keeping in mind that *trust* (Belief 2) refers to beliefs about outcomes being tied to performance, the Trust Profile is structured to mirror employee beliefs in three ways. Do employees believe outcomes are tied to performance (1) specifically for themselves, (2) generally in the organization, and (3) explicitly for poor performers? Examine the Trust Profile in Exercise 16. Notice that item 12 reflects the trust level for the employee, items 1 through 3 and 8 through 11 for the organization, and items 4 through 7 for poor performers.

Managers learn a great deal from employee responses to the rating scales. The bottom line is this: The Trust Profile allows managers to see themselves through the eyes of the employee. Specifically, managers learn how much employees trust them to tie outcomes to performance.

- *Trust Regarding the Employee*
  Managers often begin near the end when reading an employee's Trust Profile. The rating on item 12, "Outcomes are tied to *my* performance," is a clear indication of how much the employee trusts the manager. Managers can breathe a sigh of relief when the employee's rating is in the 8 to 10 range, indicating, "Yes, you are giving me what my performance merits."

  When ratings are at the other end of the scale, managers are faced with the stark realization that employees firmly believe they are not getting what they deserve on the basis of their performance. Discussion of the trust issue can open the

Trust Profile

Do You Agree or Disagree with These Statements as They Apply in Your Organization?

	Disagree	Agree

1. People who do a good job get what they deserve.

   0 1 2 3 4 5 6 7 8 9 10

2. High performers get bigger pay raises than others.

   0 1 2 3 4 5 6 7 8 9 10

3. Promotions are based on performance.

   0 1 2 3 4 5 6 7 8 9 10

4. Poor performers would be the first to go during downsizing.

   0 1 2 3 4 5 6 7 8 9 10

5. People who perform poorly do not get by with it for very long.

   0 1 2 3 4 5 6 7 8 9 10

6. Poor performers are not treated as well as high performers.

   0 1 2 3 4 5 6 7 8 9 10

7. Poor performers are under a lot of pressure to improve.

   0 1 2 3 4 5 6 7 8 9 10

8. People who do a good job are rewarded better than others.

   0 1 2 3 4 5 6 7 8 9 10

9. Praise and recognition are reserved for those who perform well.

   0 1 2 3 4 5 6 7 8 9 10

10. Rewards are tied to performance rather than to other factors like politics.

    0 1 2 3 4 5 6 7 8 9 10

11. People get what they deserve on the basis of their performance.

    0 1 2 3 4 5 6 7 8 9 10

12. Outcomes are tied to my performance.

    0 1 2 3 4 5 6 7 8 9 10

13. How does your *trust* level affect your motivation and performance?

14. Any suggestions to *increase* your trust level?

15. How would you be affected if these suggestions were implemented?

floodgate for an outpouring of emotion. Managers often are, and should be, jolted into action when they learn they are not tying outcomes to employee performance. Employees who come to their manager with a Trust Profile that reflects trust problems are expected to share their thinking and suggest solutions; this is found in their responses to items 13 through 15.

- *Trust Generally in the Organization*
  Employee ratings on items 1 through 3 and 8 through 11 provide a clear indication of the employee's view of the extent to which outcomes generally are tied to performance in the organization. While one employee may have a distorted perception based on limited information, managers find it difficult to refute ratings that run consistently across the group completing the Trust Profile. The collective feedback can be invaluable to the manager, either reinforcing current management practices or calling for changes across the organization that will improve employee motivation and performance.

- *Trust Relative to Poor Performers*
  Employees who work hard and do a good job tend to have disdain for workers who consistently perform poorly. These same employees have little respect for managers who tolerate those poor performers. Employee ratings on items 4 through 7 in the Trust Profile, and the discussion that follows, provide clear feedback to managers on this issue. In some cases, employees praise managers for the way poor performers are handled; in others, managers get a good feel for the seriousness of the problem.

TABLE 7
Using the Trust Profile to Diagnose Employee Motivation

Item Analysis	Diagnosis
Items 1–11: These ratings reflect the employee's beliefs about the extent to which outcomes are tied to performance generally in the organization (items 1–3, 8–11) and specifically for poor performers (items 4–7).	Ratings of 6 or below on several of these items indicates a serious, or potentially serious, trust problem *throughout the organization.*
Item 12: This is the most important rating in the Profile. It shows the extent to which the employee believes outcomes are tied to his or her performance.	A rating of 6 or below indicates that *this employee* has a serious, or potentially serious, trust problem.

Under normal circumstances, employees seldom take trust issues to their manager. They do not want to be seen as complaining, disgruntled employees. They are unsure whether the manager will receive them favorably. They often expect that more harm than good will come of it. However, these concerns seem to evaporate when the Trust Profile is used; I have witnessed it with hundreds of employees. The Trust Profile overcomes employee reluctance to voice trust problems. Employees find it easy to mark the rating scales and show them to their manager. Equally important, managers are receptive. They welcome the feedback. Why? They quickly learn that the Trust Profile makes their life easier. It provides valuable information that yields solutions to existing problems and prevents future ones. Seeing is believing, and managers may want to take a look for themselves. Doing so is simple—use the Trust Profile a couple of times and see what happens.

FINDING THE COURAGE

Madge and her employee, Dottie, zipped through the Confidence Profile in record time. "Was Dottie just easy on me or what? I didn't expect to sail through it like this."

I laughed uneasily. "We haven't finished yet."

There had been little for Dottie and Madge to discuss because Dottie was a high performer. She was a perfectionist who also was good with people. This made her a good match for the job of customer service representative.

Madge had been the customer service supervisor for the last nine years. Ten customer service reps, all women, all in their twenties, were under her direction. Two things stood out about Madge: She wanted to be liked, and she avoided conflict at any cost.

The Trust Profile was next. Madge and I quickly scanned Dottie's rating scales.

Dottie rested her elbows on the table, eager to get started. This time Madge instinctively backed away.

I braced for the trouble that lay ahead. Although Dottie felt that outcomes were tied to her performance, a problem was evident in four other items on her Trust Profile.

Do You Agree or Disagree with These Statements as They Apply in Your Organization?

	Disagree	Agree
4. Poor performers would be the first to go during downsizing.	X 0 1 2 3 4 5 6 7 8 9 10	
5. People who perform poorly do not get by with it for very long.	X 0 1 2 3 4 5 6 7 8 9 10	
6. Poor performers are not treated as well as high performers.	X 0 1 2 3 4 5 6 7 8 9 10	
7. Poor performers are under a lot of pressure to improve.	X 0 1 2 3 4 5 6 7 8 9 10	
12. Outcomes are tied to my performance.	X 0 1 2 3 4 5 6 7 8 9 10	

Figure 20   TRUST PROFILE (PARTIALLY SHOWN)

Madge sighed and leaned forward. "Dottie, I'm not sure what to say about these low ratings. If you don't mind, it'd be a big help to me if you'd get us started on this."

"You know I like my job, Madge, everything about it really, except for one thing: Latisha. She's been here for two years and doesn't know our products yet. She doesn't answer her phone unless she feels like it, and she handles only half as many calls as the rest of us. You know this; you put the numbers together every week. Half the time she either can't answer the customers' questions or she gives them the wrong information. Then when they call back, we have to deal with their anger and frustration. Nine reps work harder every day because of her, and we're fed up with it."

Madge sat motionless. The color left her face. She was under the gun to get her department shaped up. Top management had discovered the importance of customer service and was screaming for a quick fix.

"In the language of the Belief System, Dottie, you're telling me we have a trust problem, is that right?"

"Yes, a *pervasive* trust problem."

Madge looked at me. "I feel like I'm caught in the undertow and can't get back on my feet. This has to be fixed, doesn't it?"

"Yes, it does. You don't have a choice."

"What should I do?"

"Madge, what do *you* think you should do?"

Silence. I needed a few minutes alone with Madge. I had two questions for her. Depending on the answers, the solution could be obvious.

"Dottie, would you excuse us?" Reluctantly she left the room.

"Now, about Latisha. **Does she have the skills to do the job?**"

"No, she doesn't."

"Can she develop the skills?"

"She's tried and, no, she can't."

"Madge, **what should you do?**"

"Fire her, but it's not as easy as you think. She's a troublemaker."

"Madge, who would be upset if you fired Latisha?"

"Nobody, except Latisha."

"Who would be happy?

"Everybody. All of the reps for sure. And Randy." Randy was her manager. "He's been pushing me to deal with Latisha for a long time."

"Madge, I've seen situations like this before. Latisha knows she's not right for the job. She'd be happier somewhere else."

"I agree. But believe me, she won't go quietly."

"Do you have a human resources department and a legal department that can help you with this?

"Well, yes, but..."

"The thought of confronting Latisha obviously is very unsettling to you. But you're under the gun from top management. Just imagine their reaction when they discover that Latisha has been a serious problem for a long time and you still haven't dealt with her. And you know they'll find out. It's just a matter of time. You're under the microscope. What will they do, Madge?"

"I expect they'll fire me."

"Do you believe that?"

"Yes. I have to move fast, don't I?"

"Yes, Madge. **What are you going to do?**"

"Meet with Randy first, then HR, and then the legal staff. I won't be able to sleep until it's over, so I want to move fast."

"You sound determined."

"I am."

"Okay, Madge. Should we bring Dottie back in now?"

"Yeah. I'll tell her I'm working on the Latisha issue. We can start with Dottie's Satisfaction Profile."

"Fine."

"One more thing. Dottie and most of the reps have talked to me about Latisha, but this Trust Profile, it's different. Seeing the way Dottie marked those rating scales, well, that just hit me hard. It made me realize how unfair I've been to everybody. And why? Because I've been afraid. Well, that's history now. I've realized that you can find the courage to do what's right."

• • •

Satisfaction Profile

When we work closely with people, we tend to *think* we know them. We make judgments and reach conclusions. We do this by engaging in casual conversations, noticing the way people react in different circumstances, and watching them perform under pressure. Over time, we build a reserve of information. Eventually we say, "I've got him pegged," or "I have her sized up." For the most part, however, we know little more than people want us to know.

Most employees are unwilling to share what they like and dislike about their job; most managers are not trained to find out. This leaves both parties at a distinct disadvantage. How can employees perform at their best when faced with mounting dissatisfaction? How can managers solve such problems when they are unaware of them?

The Satisfaction Profile offers a simple solution. It gives employees a welcomed opportunity to dispel false assumptions and let the manager *accurately* know them. It takes managers below the surface and provides in-depth knowledge of employees. Managers often say, "Finally I know what makes this guy tick," or "Now I understand why she reacts that way."

Managers are keenly interested in the Satisfaction Profile. It confirms much about the employee, solidifies hunches, refutes incorrect assumptions, explains puzzling behaviors, reveals unrecognized strengths, and uncovers well-kept secrets. It also unveils satisfaction problems that are holding back employee performance. Several examples are shown below. Two crucial steps then are taken—(1) employees identify, as part of the Satisfaction Profile, what is causing the problem, and (2) employees recommend a solution that would work for them. Here are some examples of disclosures in Satisfaction Profiles that enabled managers to quickly get employees on performance improvement tracks.

- A busy, dominating manager assumed all was well with a new employee who had not complained or asked for help. It was an eye-opener when the manager discovered that the perfectionist employee felt extremely uncomfortable in his loosely defined job. His Satisfaction Profile indicated a need for greater clarity about performance expectations, more structure in his job, and less uncertainty regarding the direction he should take. His performance was floundering and his job dissatisfaction was high.

- A steady-performing, dedicated employee who could not say "no" had accepted additional work from her manager during the last year. Her workload had become unreasonably heavy and the pressure to perform was intense. This had translated into long hours, high stress, and little time for family, according to her Satisfaction Profile. Her manager, a friendly, caring person with a hands-off management style, was stunned when the employee broke down and cried and told him she could not continue working under the present circumstances.

- A happy, fun-loving employee developed a reputation for working hard and fast and performing well on any and every project assigned to her. Gradually she became the person everyone turned to for work requiring data analysis and number crunching. She wanted everybody to like her, so she accepted project assignments without complaining. Her manager was shocked to discover how depressed and unhappy she was in her job. Her Satisfaction Profile showed too much routine and detailed work, not enough task variety, and too little work calling for her creative abilities.

- An experienced manager was promoted and pushed everybody hard to perform without getting to know the capabilities of each member of his new team. One of his team members was a young, capable, high performer. The manager was shocked when this employee bluntly stated that he was planning to leave if he continued to be underutilized. His Satisfaction Profile clearly indicated he wanted more meaningful work, an opportunity to make significant contributions to the department, and additional authority and responsibility.

- A manager knew he was long overdue for a heart-to-heart discussion with a hardworking employee who did her best but always struggled to get the job done. He kept procrastinating because he felt she was not the right person for the job, but he did not know how to tell her. Her Satisfaction Profile said it all. She wanted a job that matched her skills and interests, and she planned to leave the company to find one. She had been miserable in her job for months; the manager had gotten poor performance for months.

You will recall that in the Belief System, *satisfaction* (Belief 3) refers to the belief people hold about outcomes leading to satisfaction. With this in mind, the Satisfaction Profile is designed to reflect employee beliefs about 50 workplace outcomes. For each of these outcomes, employees use two rating scales to indicate (1) how satisfying or dissatisfying the outcome would be *if* they had it, and (2) the extent to which they currently are getting the outcome. The complete Satisfaction Profile follows in Exercise 17.

Satisfaction Profile

	Dissatisfying If I Had It	Satisfying If I Had It	Do Not Get It	Do Get It

1. Money

-10 -8 -6 -4 -2 0 +2 +4 +6 +8 +10   0 1 2 3 4 5 6 7 8 9 10

2. Promotion

-10 -8 -6 -4 -2 0 +2 +4 +6 +8 +10   0 1 2 3 4 5 6 7 8 9 10

3. Job Security

-10 -8 -6 -4 -2 0 +2 +4 +6 +8 +10   0 1 2 3 4 5 6 7 8 9 10

4. Benefits

-10 -8 -6 -4 -2 0 +2 +4 +6 +8 +10   0 1 2 3 4 5 6 7 8 9 10

5. Meaningful
   Work

-10 -8 -6 -4 -2 0 +2 +4 +6 +8 +10   0 1 2 3 4 5 6 7 8 9 10

6. Achievement

-10 -8 -6 -4 -2 0 +2 +4 +6 +8 +10   0 1 2 3 4 5 6 7 8 9 10

7. Job That
   Matches
   Abilities

-10 -8 -6 -4 -2 0 +2 +4 +6 +8 +10   0 1 2 3 4 5 6 7 8 9 10

8. Fast Pace

-10 -8 -6 -4 -2 0 +2 +4 +6 +8 +10   0 1 2 3 4 5 6 7 8 9 10

9. Respect

-10 -8 -6 -4 -2 0 +2 +4 +6 +8 +10   0 1 2 3 4 5 6 7 8 9 10

10. Routine

-10 -8 -6 -4 -2 0 +2 +4 +6 +8 +10   0 1 2 3 4 5 6 7 8 9 10

11. Fair
    Treatment

-10 -8 -6 -4 -2 0 +2 +4 +6 +8 +10   0 1 2 3 4 5 6 7 8 9 10

12. Feedback

-10 -8 -6 -4 -2 0 +2 +4 +6 +8 +10   0 1 2 3 4 5 6 7 8 9 10

13. Recognition
    from Boss

-10 -8 -6 -4 -2 0 +2 +4 +6 +8 +10   0 1 2 3 4 5 6 7 8 9 10

	Dissatisfying If I Had It	Satisfying If I Had It	Do Not Get It	Do Get It

14. Competition
    with Others
        -10 -8 -6 -4 -2 0 +2 +4 +6 +8 +10   0 1 2 3 4 5 6 7 8 9 10

15. Friendly
    Co-workers
        -10 -8 -6 -4 -2 0 +2 +4 +6 +8 +10   0 1 2 3 4 5 6 7 8 9 10

16. Teamwork
        -10 -8 -6 -4 -2 0 +2 +4 +6 +8 +10   0 1 2 3 4 5 6 7 8 9 10

17. Detailed
    Work
        -10 -8 -6 -4 -2 0 +2 +4 +6 +8 +10   0 1 2 3 4 5 6 7 8 9 10

18. Ideas
    Encouraged
        -10 -8 -6 -4 -2 0 +2 +4 +6 +8 +10   0 1 2 3 4 5 6 7 8 9 10

19. Independence
        -10 -8 -6 -4 -2 0 +2 +4 +6 +8 +10   0 1 2 3 4 5 6 7 8 9 10

20. Clarity
        -10 -8 -6 -4 -2 0 +2 +4 +6 +8 +10   0 1 2 3 4 5 6 7 8 9 10

21. Pleasant Work
    Environment
        -10 -8 -6 -4 -2 0 +2 +4 +6 +8 +10   0 1 2 3 4 5 6 7 8 9 10

22. Customer
    Contact
        -10 -8 -6 -4 -2 0 +2 +4 +6 +8 +10   0 1 2 3 4 5 6 7 8 9 10

23. Job That
    Matches
    Interests
        -10 -8 -6 -4 -2 0 +2 +4 +6 +8 +10   0 1 2 3 4 5 6 7 8 9 10

24. Task Variety
        -10 -8 -6 -4 -2 0 +2 +4 +6 +8 +10   0 1 2 3 4 5 6 7 8 9 10

25. Prestige
        -10 -8 -6 -4 -2 0 +2 +4 +6 +8 +10   0 1 2 3 4 5 6 7 8 9 10

	Dissatisfying If I Had It	Satisfying If I Had It	Do Not Get It	Do Get It
26. Considerable Responsibility	-10 -8 -6 -4 -2 0 +2 +4 +6 +8 +10		0 1 2 3 4 5 6 7 8 9 10	
27. Creativity	-10 -8 -6 -4 -2 0 +2 +4 +6 +8 +10		0 1 2 3 4 5 6 7 8 9 10	
28. To Be Kept Informed	-10 -8 -6 -4 -2 0 +2 +4 +6 +8 +10		0 1 2 3 4 5 6 7 8 9 10	
29. Opportunity to Learn New Skills	-10 -8 -6 -4 -2 0 +2 +4 +6 +8 +10		0 1 2 3 4 5 6 7 8 9 10	
30. Authority	-10 -8 -6 -4 -2 0 +2 +4 +6 +8 +10		0 1 2 3 4 5 6 7 8 9 10	
31. Time Off	-10 -8 -6 -4 -2 0 +2 +4 +6 +8 +10		0 1 2 3 4 5 6 7 8 9 10	
32. Recognition From Peers	-10 -8 -6 -4 -2 0 +2 +4 +6 +8 +10		0 1 2 3 4 5 6 7 8 9 10	
33. Time for Family	-10 -8 -6 -4 -2 0 +2 +4 +6 +8 +10		0 1 2 3 4 5 6 7 8 9 10	
34. Perfection	-10 -8 -6 -4 -2 0 +2 +4 +6 +8 +10		0 1 2 3 4 5 6 7 8 9 10	
35. To Help Others	-10 -8 -6 -4 -2 0 +2 +4 +6 +8 +10		0 1 2 3 4 5 6 7 8 9 10	
36. Fun at Work	-10 -8 -6 -4 -2 0 +2 +4 +6 +8 +10		0 1 2 3 4 5 6 7 8 9 10	
37. Pressure	-10 -8 -6 -4 -2 0 +2 +4 +6 +8 +10		0 1 2 3 4 5 6 7 8 9 10	

	Dissatisfying If I Had It	Satisfying If I Had It	Do Not Get It	Do Get It

38. Contact
    with People
    -10 -8 -6 -4 -2 0 +2 +4 +6 +8 +10   0 1 2 3 4 5 6 7 8 9 10

39. Flexible
    Hours
    -10 -8 -6 -4 -2 0 +2 +4 +6 +8 +10   0 1 2 3 4 5 6 7 8 9 10

40. To Do
    Things Well
    -10 -8 -6 -4 -2 0 +2 +4 +6 +8 +10   0 1 2 3 4 5 6 7 8 9 10

41. Relationships
    -10 -8 -6 -4 -2 0 +2 +4 +6 +8 +10   0 1 2 3 4 5 6 7 8 9 10

42. Caring Boss
    -10 -8 -6 -4 -2 0 +2 +4 +6 +8 +10   0 1 2 3 4 5 6 7 8 9 10

43. Job Structure
    -10 -8 -6 -4 -2 0 +2 +4 +6 +8 +10   0 1 2 3 4 5 6 7 8 9 10

44. Long Hours
    -10 -8 -6 -4 -2 0 +2 +4 +6 +8 +10   0 1 2 3 4 5 6 7 8 9 10

45. Lots of Stress
    -10 -8 -6 -4 -2 0 +2 +4 +6 +8 +10   0 1 2 3 4 5 6 7 8 9 10

46. Uncertainty
    -10 -8 -6 -4 -2 0 +2 +4 +6 +8 +10   0 1 2 3 4 5 6 7 8 9 10

47. Quality Work
    -10 -8 -6 -4 -2 0 +2 +4 +6 +8 +10   0 1 2 3 4 5 6 7 8 9 10

48. Opportunity
    to Contribute
    -10 -8 -6 -4 -2 0 +2 +4 +6 +8 +10   0 1 2 3 4 5 6 7 8 9 10

49. Competition
    with Self
    -10 -8 -6 -4 -2 0 +2 +4 +6 +8 +10   0 1 2 3 4 5 6 7 8 9 10

50. Time for Self
    -10 -8 -6 -4 -2 0 +2 +4 +6 +8 +10   0 1 2 3 4 5 6 7 8 9 10

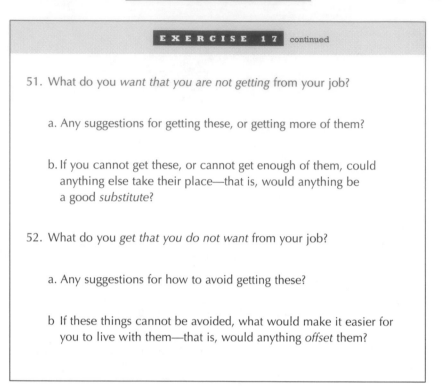

EXERCISE 17 continued

51. What do you *want that you are not getting* from your job?

   a. Any suggestions for getting these, or getting more of them?

   b. If you cannot get these, or cannot get enough of them, could anything else take their place—that is, would anything be a good *substitute*?

52. What do you *get that you do not want* from your job?

   a. Any suggestions for how to avoid getting these?

   b If these things cannot be avoided, what would make it easier for you to live with them—that is, would anything *offset* them?

   The Satisfaction Profile gives managers marvelous insight into each and every employee's motivation. With the two rating scales, four possible combinations of ratings are possible, all interesting and helpful to the manager.

- *Get and Want*
  The rating scales in the Satisfaction Profile will indicate that employees are getting certain outcomes they find satisfying. No motivation problem here, but this is valuable information for the manager. The employee's message is, "I like what you're doing. Keep it up."

- *Get but Don't Want*
  In other cases, the rating scales may show that employees are getting outcomes that are dissatisfying. *This is a problem.* When employees identify problems of this type in the Satisfaction Profile, they are asked to identify solutions that will work for them (item 51a in the Profile). However, since dis-

TABLE 8

Using the Satisfaction Profile to Diagnose Employee Motivation

Is the Employee Getting the Outcome?	Is the Outcome Satisfying or Dissatisfying?	Diagnosis of Employee Motivation
Yes	Satisfying	Get and Want— No Problem
Yes	Dissatisfying	Get but Don't Want— A Satisfaction Problem
No	Satisfying	Don't Get but Want— A Satisfaction Problem
No	Dissatisfying	Don't Get and Don't Want— No Problem

satisfying outcomes cannot always be removed, employees also are asked to identify desirable outcomes that *are* available that would *offset* the dissatisfaction (item 51b in the Profile).

- *Don't Get but Want*
  The Profile may show that employees are not getting outcomes they want. *This is a problem.* Employees are requested to recommend solutions they prefer (item 52a in the Profile). Since employees cannot always get outcomes they want, they are asked to identify desirable outcomes that *are* available that would be acceptable *substitutes* (item 52b in the Profile).

- *Don't Get and Don't Want*
  The rating scales often reflect a situation in which employees are pleased that they are not getting certain outcomes. This is not a problem. Managers will want to take note of this and continue to shield employees from these unwanted outcomes.

The Satisfaction Profile is powerful because it is accurate and comprehensive. Are employees reluctant to be truthful when completing the rating scales? I have never witnessed it—not once. Is the list of outcomes complete? I believe it is. A list of 49 stood unchallenged for more than seven years until item 50 was added. Managers who have used the Satisfaction Profile find it valuable because (1) it identifies motivation problems and yields solutions for them, and (2) it provides an abundance of information to prevent problems in the future. The Satisfaction Profile offers many benefits to the manager, if you choose to use it.

I WON'T FORGET THIS DAY

Preston and his manager, Henrietta, were circling the track, going in opposite directions. Resentment and anger would soon collide. I ran through the emergency procedures and waited. We were in the middle of their session on the Belief System Profile. They'd had productive discussions about Preston's Confidence and Trust Profiles. Each had given the other opportunities to cross the line and get to the real source of their difficulties. Neither had done so, yet.

Henrietta had provided the first occasion. "I was wondering, do you think people can sometimes be given too much independence?"

"No, but not having enough sure can make you angry," Preston retorted.

She had not pursued it. This brief exchange was eye-opening to me. Preston was aggressive and blunt. Henrietta was meek and indirect. They refuted the notion that opposites attract. The road was paved for disaster, unless something changed.

Later, she said, "Oh, by the way, I noticed you were in O. D.'s office last week." O. D. was her boss.

"Yeah, so?" He looked at her scornfully. "Which time?"

"Let me see, I think it was Thursday, yes, Thursday morning."

"Yeah, well, that was the *first* time. He wanted my opinion about the new direction the company's going in. I asked if I could be on the long-range planning committee. He said yes."

"Preston, I wish you would...go through me on things like that. I just feel like you...well...step out of bounds a lot, and it makes me, I don't know...I guess I resent it."

Preston shrugged. "Whatever."

Characteristically, Henrietta dropped it. Preston was the snarling dog, and Henrietta was cowering. I had seen this many times.

	Dissatisfying If I Had It	Satisfying If I Had It	Do Not Get It	Do Get It
12. Feedback		X	X	
	-10 -8 -6 -4 -2 0 +2 +4 +6 +8 +10		0 1 2 3 4 5 6 7 8 9 10	
19. Independence		X		X
	-10 -8 -6 -4 -2 0 +2 +4 +6 +8 +10		0 1 2 3 4 5 6 7 8 9 10	

Figure 21   SATISFACTION PROFILE (PARTIALLY SHOWN)

Now our attention was on Preston's Satisfaction Profile. Henrietta pored over it. Preston buried his head in a report unrelated to the discussion. I had scanned his Profile quickly and spotted the only two satisfaction problems. He wanted more feedback and greater independence. In my experience, the fewer the problems, the bigger they are.

Henrietta marked something on every page of Preston's Profile. Preston tapped a finger on the tabletop. The sound reminded me of a ticking bomb.

When Henrietta gently laid his Profile on the table in front of her, she appeared calm, all emotion hidden. "Preston, I believe I understand what you've marked here. It looks like there are two main issues. Where would you like to begin?"

"Item 19. I want more independence."

"Preston," I interrupted, "could we start with item 12, the one on feedback?"

"Fine with me." He looked at Henrietta. "Same thing. I want more feedback."

"I hear what you're saying, but I don't know, it just seems like when I give you feedback, you don't always act like you really want it. I mean, you don't make it easy. You don't seem...How can I say it? Well, receptive, I guess, is the word."

Preston leaned into the fray. "What do you mean? I always want feedback. Just tell me one time when I wasn't receptive."

Henrietta looked at me and swallowed. The dog had growled, and Henrietta was ready to retreat. She turned to Preston. "Well, now, maybe."

"What are you talking about? I'm just trying to understand you."

"Oh, right." Henrietta slumped back in her chair and backhanded the ball to me. "You tell him."

My approach with Preston was based on his dominating personality. He preferred feedback that allowed self-discovery. He did not like being *told* what to do.

"Would you like my feedback, Preston?"

He hesitated. "Well, sure. Why wouldn't I?"

"Just checking. Is it easier for you to accept feedback from people you respect?"

"Absolutely."

"What about feedback from people you don't respect?"

He stole a quick glance at Henrietta. "Well, I, ah…it's hard to respect what someone says if you don't respect the person."

This surely sent Henrietta reeling. There was no visible reaction.

"Preston, how do you react when you get feedback from someone you don't respect?"

The question got his attention. He switched to his analytical mode and searched for an answer. His concentration was not interrupted when someone tapped lightly on the door and handed a note to Henrietta.

"I react in one of three ways. Sometimes I just stop listening. Other times I listen, and then I discount what the person said. And sometimes I attack, challenge everything. I probably come across as defensive."

"In other words, not receptive."

"Well…yes, not receptive."

"What's going to happen the next time someone *could* give you feedback, even if it's something you might find valuable?"

He studied his hands. "Nothing. They'll leave me hanging."

Henrietta watched him. I had a feeling she sensed the value that could come from his introspection.

"Preston, what are you thinking?"

"That I'm learning a valuable lesson. The point is this: People can't help you if you won't let them. I definitely need to be more receptive to feedback." He frowned. "Wait a minute. Is that why you wanted us to deal with the feedback issue before we discussed my independence problem? So I'd be more receptive to Henrietta's feedback?"

"Yes."

"How did you know?"

"People with dominant tendencies like you have a strong need to be respected and also a tendency not to respect people who *appear* weak. Like you said, it's hard to respect what a person says if you don't respect the person."

Henrietta lurched forward. "Is that the way you feel about me, Preston?"

"Well, I...."

"Sure it is. You don't respect me, do you? You think I'm weak. Well, you're sadly mistaken. Just because I'm not dominating like you doesn't mean I'm weak and incompetent. You'd better find a little respect in a hurry, otherwise you can be disrespectful somewhere else. And just for the record, I don't have much respect for your arrogant, roll-over-every-body-that-gets-in-the-way style."

The cowering had ended. The growling dog would respect her for fighting back. If she held her ground, his respect would grow.

"Preston, tell Henrietta what she can do to gain your respect."

"I need guidance and direction, and a firm hand when I get out of line, like you're giving me now. That's what I want."

"Fine, if that's what you want, I'll be more than happy to start with this independence business. I have to tell you, your work is suffering because you leave others out. You don't brief them, you don't get input from them, and you go around them to get things done. Your independence is causing problems. People are reluctant to work with you. You have a great career ahead of you, but not if you try to go solo on everything."

"You see, that's the kind of feedback I need to hear. Now let me be sure I understand. What you're saying is this: Everybody needs help to be successful."

"You've got it."

"You're telling me that I've done a lot of damage. Is it too much to repair?"

Henrietta smiled. "No, I don't think so. You just have to get people involved, keep them informed, and realize they can help you produce better work, if you'll give them a chance."

Preston looked at me. "What do you think?"

"I don't know, Preston. What do *you* think?"

"I think...no, I *know* I'll react differently to feedback now, be more receptive to it. I'll stop letting my need for independence interfere with getting the job done. On the respect issue, I'll work on that from two sides, earning more and showing more. Please know, I won't forget this day. Thanks."

It struck me how often the Belief System leads people to embrace change.

• • •

MOVING AHEAD

GETTING STARTED

Go ahead and tackle those motivation and performance issues. Choose to use the *Belief System* Profile.

The Belief System Profile is a manager's tool box containing three instruments. Managers who endorse motivation management can use the Profile to (1) get employee performance back on track, (2) push solid performers to new levels of achievement, or (3) prevent anticipated motivation and performance problems. The Belief System Profile can be used with either full teams or larger organizational units.

Why the *Belief System* Profile? Think about it and remember this: There are many ways to drive a nail, but a hammer works best because it is designed for the task.

THE DISAPPEARANCE OF CHARLIE SUMMERS

Lucinda was ecstatic when she discovered that Roland, her 50-year-old manager and mentor, had once worked with the mysterious Charlie Summers.

Stories handed down over the years had painted two pictures of Charlie: one a creative genius, the other just plain stubborn. What was the truth? And whatever happened to Charlie, anyway? Lucinda wanted to know.

She had asked Roland to discuss Charlie at their next weekly meeting. He had agreed. The meetings were Roland's commitment to his newest employee's professional growth and development.

They took an outside table at the popular coffee shop in a quirky old house down the street from their office. Both were coffee fanatics, and they looked forward to meeting there each week.

"What's our topic for discussion today?"

"I keep hearing about Charlie Summers. I don't know if the stories are fact or fiction, but they're definitely intriguing."

"Charlie and I were in college together, came into the company at the same time. We worked side by side."

Lucinda took out her notepad, ready.

"Charlie would breezily say, 'I'm intelligent, witty, charming. All the potential in the world.' It was true, Charlie had it all, almost."

"Give me an example."

"Charlie arranged for a helicopter pilot to take a potential client from D.C. to a beautiful spot in the Shenandoah Valley and leave him in an open field. Minutes later Charlie, who had taken skydiving lessons at company expense, 'dropped in' on the CEO. The best French chef in New York City was there to prepare an elegant lunch. In one day, Charlie combined the three passions of this guy—mountains, French food, skydiving. He loved it. An expensive sales call you might say. Never asked anybody for approval. Just did it. That was Charlie. Won the business, though."

"That's great, I love it!"

"Top management had told Charlie not to pursue the business. The unpublished fact was, the client's company was in financial trouble. When Charlie brought in a signed contract, management reluctantly signed it. Big mistake. The company folded, and we lost a bundle."

Lucinda wrote *Charlie wouldn't listen!* "What else do you remember about Charlie?"

"We had a new CEO at the time. He made it clear that advancement in the company would favor those with an MBA degree. Charlie loudly proclaimed, 'MBA programs are a waste of time.' A lot of us agreed, but we went back to school anyway. We got promoted, and Charlie didn't. It wasn't just the MBA business, although Charlie wanted everybody to think it was. If the truth be known, Charlie wasn't keeping up with the latest technology, new processes, and advanced management techniques. Charlie usually wiggled out of training programs, and if forced to go, pretended not to be there. Charlie always acted like, 'I already know everything that matters.'"

Lucinda scribbled *Charlie wouldn't learn!* "It was getting too late for Charlie to recover, wasn't it?"

"Charlie wasn't even 30 years old then, not too late to turn one's career around."

"I agree, but isn't it hard for a person like that to change?"

"Ah, now that's true. People liked Charlie, so they gave advice, offered encouragement. Change a little here, a little there. Communicate more, argue less, live by the rules. But Charlie was Charlie and it fell on deaf ears."

Charlie wouldn't change! "Why?"

"Not a question I can answer. Why does anybody refuse to listen and learn and change?"

"What happened to Charlie?"

"Didn't show up for work one day. Didn't call in. No communication of any sort. I called the apartment. The phone was disconnected. I finally went by, got the super to let me in. The place was empty. No fowarding address. The only trace of Charlie was the familiar perfume."

"Perfume? Charlie was a woman?"

"Yes."

"Ever hear from her?"

"No, not a word."

• • •

CHAPTER 8

Motivation
Management at Work

*"The Belief System is for managers who won't settle
for being ordinary."*

A BRIEFING SESSION

Some managers like informal approaches to motivation management; others prefer formal ones. Some want structured approaches; others insist on the freedom to be flexible.

Motivation management offers five approaches that range from informal and loosely structured approaches to those that are very formal and highly structured.

In this chapter you will learn about the five approaches and how to make choices that suit you best.

I'M A SLAVE TO MINE

Jerry said he wanted to discuss a problem with me. I had worked with several executives in his company but never with Jerry. I had heard he was a likable person and a hard worker, and that his performance was adequate. I did not know what to expect when I walked into his office.

After a few minutes of chitchat, he cleared his throat. "I want you to analyze some things for me."

"Okay."

"I'll describe a situation and you react to it."

"Looking for anything in particular?"

"Just your reaction, first impression. Be honest."

I had no clue where this was going. "All right."

"A manager had a great opportunity a few years ago. Chance of a lifetime. New job, new company, new part of the country. Turned it down." He stopped and looked at me.

"You want me to react to that?"

"Yes."

"Fear of change."

"I agree. Another manager had a chance to head up a challenging, high-profile project. Would've been great for his career. He didn't take it."

"Fear of failure." That was my first reaction, though the person certainly could have had other reasons for saying no.

"You got it. This other manager, he wants everybody to like him. So he tends to make the popular decision rather than do what's right."

"Fear of rejection."

"Okay. Another manager. He won't deal with the tough problems, like people who aren't getting the job done. Never has fired anybody."

"Fear of conflict."

"Right. Then there's the manager who likes everything to be black and white. When things get gray, it paralyzes him, and makes him procrastinate. Decision by indecision, I call it."

"Sounds like fear of uncertainty."

"Right again.

"Jerry, are these examples all the same person?"

He hesitated. "Yes."

"Is this person you?"

"Yes."

"Everybody has fears."

"I know, but...." He slumped in his chair.

Jerry's fears were fairly normal. His response to them was not. He caved in every time and would continue to do so.

He continued. "I don't get good performance reviews and I get passed over for promotions. People are losing confidence in me and I'm losing confidence in myself. I've blown some great opportunities."

"So how is fear causing all that, Jerry?"

"With the fear, I'm not making good decisions."

"Does it have to be that way?"

"I, ah...well... I don't know. I mean, fear is so powerful. It clouds your thinking. And the worst part is, when you give in to fear, you have a lot of lost opportunity. And, believe you me, the could have beens, the should have beens, they haunt you."

"Jerry, how would you like to deal with your fears?"

"I don't know. I honestly don't know. What should I do?"

"What would you *like* to do?"

"I want to be more rational, not let fear influence my decisions so much."

"Have you ever been overwhelmed by something that you success-fully dealt with?"

He took a deep breath. "I used to be overweight. I'd get hungry and immediately reach for food. Finally I learned to let the hunger be a cue to think rather than reach."

"Is that what you want to do with fear—let it be a signal to think, rather than be driven by it?"

He sat up straight and smiled. "Yes!"

"Did it work with food?"

"Lost 20 pounds. Kept it off, too."

"Do you think you can make it work again?"

"I don't see why not."

"Yes, I believe you can do that. Now, when feelings of fear remind you to think, what will you think about?"

"What I need to do is...think about the consequences of giving in to fear, especially lost opportunities."

"Jerry, you've been giving in to fear for a long time. I'm wondering if you believe this approach will work."

"Yes, I believe it will."

I did, too. I had seen it work many times with other managers.

My experience is that when you have a fear about using new tools and techniques, you can use this same approach.

•••

APPROACHING MOTIVATION MANAGEMENT

There are five approaches to motivation management. They range from very informal to formal, loosely structured to highly structured. You can select the approach that best matches you and your circumstances.

It is appealing to have several approaches to motivation management from which to choose. Take a look at them, get a feel for each one, then *choose what will work for you.*

All five approaches stand on the same solid foundation of knowledge. First, three conditions must exist for employees to be highly motivated (Chapter 1).

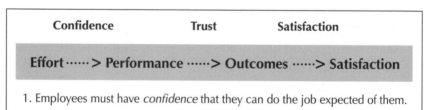

Confidence	Trust	Satisfaction

Effort ·····> Performance ·····> Outcomes ·····> Satisfaction

1. Employees must have *confidence* that they can do the job expected of them.
2. Employees must *trust* their manager to tie outcomes to their performance.
3. Employees must find *satisfaction* in the outcomes they receive.

Figure 22 CONDITIONS FOR MOTIVATION

When motivation and performance fall short, you will know that one or more of these conditions—confidence, trust, and satisfaction—are not being fully met.

Second, motivation and performance problems stem from a handful of causes that logically point to a small number of solutions (Chapters 3 and 4). It helps to keep a close eye on them.

	TABLE 9	
	Common Causes and Solutions at a Glance	
Motivation Problem	**Most Likely Causes**	**Most Practical Solution Approaches**
Confidence (Belief 1) *"I can't do it."*	• Inadequate skills • Unrealistic expectations • Unclear expectations • History of failure	• Training, coaching • Find more efficient methods • Clarify expectations • Be supportive
Trust (Belief 2) *"Outcomes are not tied to my performance."*	• Outcomes are not tied to performance	• Tie outcomes to performance
Satisfaction (Belief 3) *"The outcomes aren't satisfying to me."*	• Not receiving desired outcomes • Receiving unwanted outcomes • The work itself is not rewarding	• Give people outcomes they find satisfying, when appropriate • Withhold outcomes that are dissatisfying, when appropriate • Get people into jobs that match their skills, interests, *and* needs

Third, the information managers need for motivation management can be found outside of themselves. Managers only need to watch what employees do, hear what they say, and sense what they feel. It is there, *within the employee*, that managers will understand problems, uncover causes, and discover solutions often not found elsewhere.

How often have you seen a problem suddenly erupt and cause damage beyond repair, like a dish that drops and breaks into smithereens, impossible to put back together? And as you examine the pieces, you remember seeing the dish carelessly resting at the edge of the table, and you say, "I should have seen it coming."

Employees always give warning signs. They want solutions; they do not want motivation and performance issues to develop into full-fledged problems. So, they say, often in a quiet, subtle way, "Look at me! A problem is brewing. I need help." Managers who keep their eyes open, and ears tuned in, will see the warning and hear the plea before the damage is done.

Employees with motivation and performance issues always come to the manager's door. They tap, perhaps softly at first. You may not hear. But tap they will. They may go away, but they will return another day. Eventually they will be heard.

When you hear their plea, set aside whatever you are doing, open the door, and invite them in. Make them welcome. Lend an ear. Treat them like a trusted friend, a close relative, who appears at the door unexpectedly, troubled. Let them talk. React to their situation. No stock answers. Let the nature of the situation determine the way you respond. The goal is to help them find an answer. This is the first approach to motivation management. Strengthen an individual's motivation to perform by quickly and adeptly *responding to the situation*.

Sometimes people appear at the door at the most inopportune times, when the world is crashing around you. You ask them to come back in a couple of hours. Things will be calm by then. Plus you will have a few minutes to clear your mind, collect your thoughts, and get prepared for a problem-solving discussion. You will guide the conversation and all will turn out well. This is the second approach to motivation management. Strengthen an individual's motivation to perform by *preparing to deal with problems effectively*.

Perhaps meeting with the employee in two hours does not give you enough time to prepare. The discussion could be very difficult, and it is certainly important. You need more time. No problem. Better to be ready. Think through the situation carefully. Decide how to guide the discussion. Determine what you will say. Develop a plan. Then, when you are ready, meet with the employee. This is the third approach to motivation management. It calls for thorough preparation, *going the extra mile to get ready* to meet with the employee.

There are occasions when some major changes are taking place and people are riled up. They do not like the way things are going. Complaints are flying, attitudes have taken a turn for the worse, and expected productivity gains are not materializing. What are you to do? Quickly inviting everyone to a meeting is not going to soothe the ruffled feelings; words will not turn this situation around. You must develop a plan to reach all of your employees, hear their concerns, and take action that gets their motivation and performance on track. This is the fourth approach to motivation management. Strengthen the motivation to perform for an entire team, or a larger organizational unit, by creating a master plan that will *address the concerns of one and all.*

These four approaches to motivation management are planted in common ground. They do not center on abstract, overly academic, pie-in-the-sky notions. Instead, they all focus on *solving problems.* The idea is to see the early warning signs, hear the gentle tap on your door, and know when storms are brewing. Now you can act. You can uncover causes. You can discover solutions.

Only one thing is better than effectively solving motivation problems: having fewer problems to solve. This is the fifth approach to motivation management. Strengthen employee motivation to perform by taking aim at *prevention.* Set your sights on making decisions with motivation in mind. The idea is to make decisions that, to the extent possible, create confidence, trust, and satisfaction—the three conditions required for motivation. In other words, turn motivation and performance problems away before they begin.

Contingency Approach

Using motivation management is easier than you might expect, especially with the first approach. I call it the contingency approach because the way you handle motivation and performance problems depends on the situation. Specifically, the way you respond is contingent on what the employee says and does. The idea is to let the problems come to you. The key is to recognize problems when they first appear, and quickly respond to what you see and hear. "What does that sigh mean?" "You seem upset. What happened?" "You look discouraged." Be alert for early warning signs. Check them out.

If you are holding a ticking bomb with 15 seconds left on the clock, your options are limited. When the clock shows 15 *minutes,* you have more choices. The same is true with motivation problems.

The clock is always ticking. The sooner you find the problem, the sooner you can start working on it. Set responses, no. Just quick-on-the-feet responses to the situation. Guidelines, yes.

In a nutshell: (1) Identify the problem, be it confidence, trust, and/or satisfaction (Chapter 2); (2) uncover the causes (Chapter 3); (3) discover solutions that will work (Chapter 4); and (4) turn to the employee for the answers—remember, all of this information is within the employee.

The contingency approach to motivation management appeals to managers who (1) prefer dealing with problems informally as they arise; (2) enjoy the challenge of being put on the spot, making quick decisions, taking a risk; (3) find excitement in difficult, unpredictable situations; and (4) like the flexibility of not being pinned down to a set way of doing things. It is intended for use when managers are faced with isolated motivation and performance problems.

The contingency approach has a natural three-step process.

TABLE 10

Using the Contingency Approach

Three-Step Process

1. *Stop,* look, and listen to what employees are doing and saying.

2. *Respond* quickly to what you see and hear.

3. *Follow through* to identify problems, uncover causes, and discover solutions.

Step 1—stop, look, and listen—does not mean you actually have to stop, but slowing down is essential if you want to see and hear all that stands before you. Keep your eyes and ears open. Spot those confidence, trust, and satisfaction problems. Notice employees who are moping, dawdling, or brooding; listen for the curt comment, the hint of anger, the sign of frustration. All are signals that something is amiss. These are the ways employees quietly tap on the door, hoping it will open, wishing for an understanding heart and a helping hand.

Step 2—respond to the situation—comes on the spot. There is no set way to react, no standard format. The way to respond is contingent on the situation, specifically, on what the employee says and does. There are two guidelines. First, respond to what you see. "You look upset." "I see no one is helping you." "You seem to be discouraged." Second, respond to what you hear. "You sound anxious." "You say you're ready to give up. What do you mean?" "Sounds like you're irritated with the changes we've made."

Responding like this opens the door and clearly communicates, "I want to listen if you want to talk." That is exactly what employees are looking for when they toss out warning signs: they want to talk. Revealing thoughts and feelings is their way of tapping on the manager's door, hoping to be invited in, wanting to share a problem and find a solution.

The goal of Step 2 is to open the door, get the employee talking, and get the ball rolling toward a solution. And remember, even if it does not work, you still get benefits. The employee knows you were willing to listen. This will pay off later.

Step 3—follow through—keeps the ball rolling. Set your compass on PCS (problem, cause, solution) and do not waver from the path. The goal is to get employees to identify problems, point out the causes, and suggest solutions that will work for them.

Chapters 2 through 4 provide an in-depth guide, including sample questions, that managers can use when they choose the contingency approach.

10-Step Formula Approach

Some managers prefer slightly more structure than that offered by the contingency approach to motivation management. The 10-step formula approach offers structure without confining managers who want to be free to be flexible.

Like the contingency approach, the 10-step formula approach is designed to be used when managers are leading teams with occasional rather than pervasive motivation and performance problems. This approach works best when there is an open, trusting relationship between the manager and the employee. It may be unrealistic to wait for openness and trust to catch up with the urgency of the problem, but the 10-step formula approach still offers an excellent structure for guiding the discussion.

The 10-step formula is a collection of *questions to be answered.* The answers must come from the employee. This is consistent with the repeated theme of the book: Employees know the problems they are facing, they know what is causing them, and they know solutions that will work for them. Chapters 2 through 4 provide guidelines managers can use to obtain the information called for in the 10-step formula.

The 10-step formula approach follows a three-step process: I call it *ready, set, go.*

TABLE 11

Using the 10-Step Formula Approach

Three-Step Process

1. Get *ready* to meet with the employee.

2. Get the employee *set* for the discussion.

3. *Go* through the 10-step formula.

Step 1—get *ready* to meet with the employee—calls for managers to set aside preconceived notions about the problems employees are facing, what is causing them, and what solutions might work best. It works better to be open-minded and receptive to whatever employees may have to say. It also is helpful to review the 10-step formula, at least until you have committed it to memory—which, by the way, is easy to do. Finally, choose the questions you will use and get comfortable with them. (See Chapters 2 through 4 for suggested questions.)

Step 2—get the employee *set* for the discussion—refers to the manager's opening comments. What exactly will you say to begin the discussion? The purpose is to prepare employees and encourage them to play a leading role in solving their own motivation and performance problems. Perhaps you will find it helpful to rehearse your introductory comments. What you say and how you say it are particularly important when employees do not have an open, trusting relationship with you. These initial remarks always are important and often are critical to the success of the 10-step formula.

TABLE 12

10-Step Formula—Questions to Be Answered

Getting Started

1. What performance expectations is the employee not meeting (or in danger of not meeting)?

Focus on Confidence (Belief 1)

2. Does the employee believe "I can do it?"

3. If not, then why not—that is, what is *causing* the problem?

4. What *solution* would work for the employee?

Focus on Trust (Belief 2)

5. Does the employee believe "Outcomes are (or will be) tied to my performance?"

6. If not, then why not—that is, what is *causing* the problem?

7. What *solution* would work for the employee?

Focus on Satisfaction (Belief 3)

8. Does the employee believe "The outcomes are (or will be) satisfying to me?"

9. If not, then why not—that is, what is *causing* the problem?

10. What *solution* would work for the employee?

Step 3—*go* through the 10-step formula—begins with being clear about any performance expectations the employee is not meeting or may not meet in the future. The 10-step formula then moves quickly to PCS—problem, cause, solution. Is the employee experiencing a confidence, trust, and/or satisfaction problem? What are the causes? What solutions will work for the employee?

Chapters 2 through 4 provide extensive preparation, including many sample questions, to guide the manager's walk through the 10-step formula.

Diagnostic Interview Approach

The Diagnostic Interview, described in Chapter 5, is the last of three approaches intended for managers who must deal with occasional motivation and performance problems. This approach is a well-planned, step-by-step process for identifying problems, causes, and solutions. It is an option that appeals to managers who (1) like to think through things in advance, (2) feel comfortable following procedures and structured approaches, (3) prefer planning and prevention, and (4) want to control circumstances rather than be controlled by them.

The structure of the Diagnostic Interview is shown below.

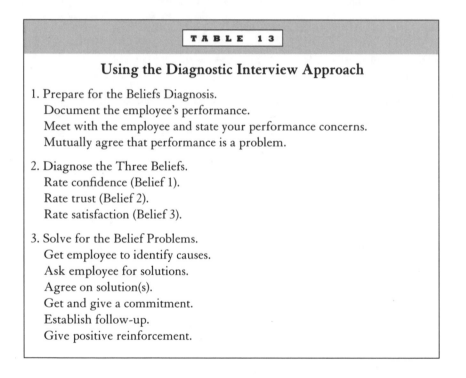

TABLE 13

Using the Diagnostic Interview Approach

1. Prepare for the Beliefs Diagnosis.
   Document the employee's performance.
   Meet with the employee and state your performance concerns.
   Mutually agree that performance is a problem.

2. Diagnose the Three Beliefs.
   Rate confidence (Belief 1).
   Rate trust (Belief 2).
   Rate satisfaction (Belief 3).

3. Solve for the Belief Problems.
   Get employee to identify causes.
   Ask employee for solutions.
   Agree on solution(s).
   Get and give a commitment.
   Establish follow-up.
   Give positive reinforcement.

This approach is thoroughness at its best. It gives managers strong support for motivation management. At first glance, it can seem intimidating. A closer look reveals that a set of fundamental steps simply have been assembled in a logical, systematic way. In other words, structure has been added to make the problem-solving process more ordered and less haphazard. Remember that detailed guidelines and suggestions for conducting the Diagnostic Interview are provided in Chapter 5.

Belief System Profile Approach

The Belief System Profile is designed for a single team or a larger organizational unit when (1) motivation and performance problems are pervasive, and (2) upheavals in motivation and performance are expected as a result of large-scale organizational changes such as reorganizations, reengineering, turnarounds, and downsizing. These circumstances call for a formal, structured approach that can be systematically used with all employees. The Belief System Profile is such an approach to motivation management. I have seen it used successfully with countless organizations, large and small, experiencing motivation and performance problems of every kind you can imagine.

Four steps provide end-to-end assurance that employees will place nagging motivation and performance issues squarely on the table and offer practical solutions that will work, solutions that can be equally supported by both manager and employee. The four-step process is shown below.

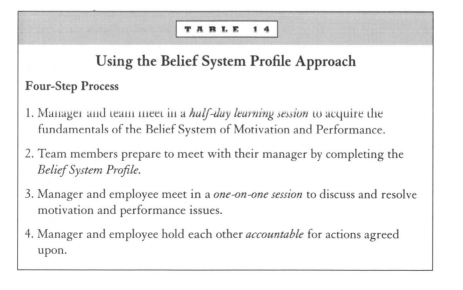

TABLE 14

Using the Belief System Profile Approach

Four-Step Process

1. Manager and team meet in a *half-day learning session* to acquire the fundamentals of the Belief System of Motivation and Performance.

2. Team members prepare to meet with their manager by completing the *Belief System Profile*.

3. Manager and employee meet in a *one-on-one session* to discuss and resolve motivation and performance issues.

4. Manager and employee hold each other *accountable* for actions agreed upon.

Step 1—*the half-day learning session*—is adequate to give this approach to motivation management a solid foundation. The focus is on the team; consequently, sessions are best conducted in small groups, one team at a time. The aim of the session is for the manager and his or her team to (1) acquire the fundamentals of the Belief System of Motivation and Performance, (2) learn how the Belief System Profile will be used, and (3) understand the full range of benefits that can be derived from open, honest dialogue about motivation and performance issues employees are facing.

Step 2—*preparation for the one-on-one session*—takes place after the half-day learning session. Each team member completes the three parts of the Belief System Profile—the Confidence Profile, the Trust Profile, and the Satisfaction Profile. This typically requires two to four hours. Why so much time? The total set of questions is quite comprehensive, and many of the questions are surprisingly thought-provoking. In short, employees find themselves, perhaps for the first time, making a thorough assessment of their motivation to work. The clarity that results often has profound and everlasting value.

Step 3—*the one-on-one session*—provides the opportunity for employees to meet individually with their manager to discuss the motivation and performance issues they are facing. The employee gives the manager a copy of the completed Belief System Profile, the manager reads it, and discussion begins. The role of the employee is to lead the discussion on the question-by-question, page-by-page march through the three Profiles. The role of the manager is to listen and ask questions to ensure understanding.

The first goal of the one-on-one session is for motivation and performance problems to be identified and solutions to be agreed upon. The second goal is for the manager to gain in-depth knowledge of the motivation of the employee with the aim of *preventing* problems from occurring in the future.

I offer three suggestions based on my experience with one-on-one sessions. First, allot approximately two hours for each session. In some cases, less time will be required; in other cases, more will be needed. It depends on the number of issues to be discussed and how troublesome they are to resolve.

Second, both manager and employee should make a list of steps that will strengthen the employee's motivation and performance. This keeps the focus of the discussion on *action*. When the one-on-

one session is completed, it is advisable for the manager and employee to exchange copies of the personal to-do lists they have made.

Third, consider using trained facilitators to enhance the effectiveness of discussions that are expected to be difficult. The facilitator's role is to keep the discussion on track, help the manager and employee work through emotional issues and disagreements in a productive way, and ensure that commitments to action are made that will benefit both manager and employee.

Step 4—*accountability*—is perhaps the most important step in the four-step process. Everything can go well in the half-day learning session, the preparation, and the one-on-one session, but the ultimate measure of success is improvement in employee performance. My experience is that accountability is the key to performance improvement. One approach that seems to work well is for the manager and employee to hold each other accountable. This can be done easily and effectively with periodic, short meetings in which manager and employee review the respective to-do lists generated during the one-on-one session.

When motivation and performance problems are widespread, regardless of the reasons, the Belief System Profile is an excellent tool to systematically reach every employee and address every issue that is holding back their motivation to perform. Use the Belief System Profile in this way and you will see that motivation management works.

Decision-Making Approach

There is an inevitable connection between motivation and performance. Strengthen motivation and performance improves; turn motivation down and performance declines with it.

There is another important connection. Consider this: What happens if you move a person into a job she hates? Or assign work to someone who does not have the required skills? Or promise a pay raise and fail to give it? What impact will these three decisions have on the motivation to perform? Now, multiply the impact by tens, hundreds, even thousands of people in your organization. Imagine what the rumbling sounds like, feel the tremors, get a clear picture of the net effect. This can happen any time large-scale decisions are made—decisions such as downsizing, reengineering, reorganizing, and others that cause sweeping changes.

Consider more decisions. Move a marginal performer into a job he loves. Delegate work that matches a new employee's skills. Give a high performer the rewards she deserves. What impact do decisions like these have on the motivation to perform? Again, do the multiplication. Do it just for the team you manage. Then do it for the larger organization. Imagine how people would react. Consider what they would say. Envision the cumulative effect. Suppose you make up your mind to consistently make decisions that motivate. How would the results make you feel?

Managerial decision making and employee motivation *are* linked. Because of this, managers hold a wonderful opportunity in their hands. *Every* decision has the potential to make a positive impact on employee motivation. That potential is opportunity. It gives you the wherewithal to lead others to new heights in performance. This holds true for any decision, whether it is a decision to make a change or to keep things the same. It always pays off when you make decisions with motivation in mind.

Just follow a simple two-step process.

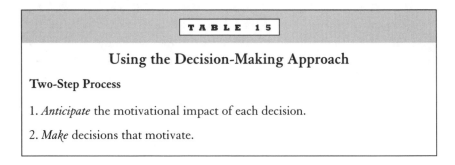

TABLE 15

Using the Decision-Making Approach

Two-Step Process

1. *Anticipate* the motivational impact of each decision.

2. *Make* decisions that motivate.

SHIP IN A STORM

Free advice is worth exactly what it costs.

At least it seemed that way. When I finished an interview for one of my books with Walter, vice president of operations, he briefly described a project he was leading. "We're about to wrap up the planning and things are going pretty well, I guess, but I was wondering, what do you think? Will it work?"

Executives exalt you when you tell them what they want to hear. But I can never make myself do that.

"No, Walter, it won't."

"Why not?"

"You're reengineering two vastly different jobs into one. Employees won't like the new job."

He stiffened his back. "They never do, do they?"

"They won't perform well either, *won't be able to.*" My comment begged for a question. I waited and did not get one, so I continued. "The reengineered job calls for people to have incompatible capabilities. It's an impossible task. Employees are smart. They'll see the handwriting on the wall."

"Employees get upset over every little disruption. They'll get over it."

"Good point. The question, then, is whether they will see this as a 'little disruption.' I expect you'll have a riot on your hands *before* the change actually takes place. Afterward you'll have disgruntled, unmotivated employees whose performances will be marginal at best. Turnover will be high immediately before and after the change and, of course, high performers will be the ones to go. They have options."

"Well, it has to work. We've already made the decision, we're committed to it, and we're paying a group of consultants a bundle to make it work."

I said, "Good luck," and meant it. Then I thanked him for the interview.

He walked me to his door and shook my hand.

Something about the way he looked made me decide to tell him a story. "Walter, I once knew a strong, forceful, intelligent man who had a dream one night. He dreamed he was a paratrooper and realized that once he jumped he couldn't turn back. He woke up in a panic and then breathed a sigh of relief. 'Thank goodness, I'm the captain of a ship. I don't have to be afraid. When you're the captain you can *listen to the forecast, change directions, and avoid the storm.*'"

As I walked across the large reception room, I noticed Walter's lanky frame still standing in the doorway. I wondered what he would do and if I would ever know.

A week later in the terminal of Logan International Airport in Boston, I checked my voice mail. "This is Walter Johnson, ship captain, on the edge of a storm. Have to make a decision soon. Do we weather the storm or change directions? I need an update on the forecast. If you're available, call Monica, my secretary, and get on my calendar for an hour as soon as possible."

Three days later, he welcomed me and offered a chair. "You irked me, you know, when you were here before. I got over it when I realized why. The truth hurt. Anyway, tell me more about what's in store."

Walter's plan was to combine two departments—the Help Desk and the Research Department—and achieve cost savings through downsizing and reengineered jobs for greater efficiency.

My experience is that executives always make better decisions when they understand the impact their decisions will have on employee motivation and, consequently, on performance. My plan was to help Walter gain this understanding.

"Walter, **what qualities do your high-performing Help Desk employees have?**"

"Hmm...let me walk through this. The best employees soothe angry callers and deal with their complaints, mainly about shipping problems and product defects. They're also good at answering tedious technical questions and getting complete and accurate information on problems they pass along to the Research Department. They're good listeners, relationship oriented, make people feel good."

I was impressed. "Anything else?"

"They're detailed, precise, sort of perfectionists."

"Okay, they have to be good with people and detail oriented. **What qualities do high performers in the Research Department have?**"

"They're good problem solvers, quick decision makers, aren't afraid to make a mistake. They have to call customers and tell them what we'll do to solve their problems, and the good ones persuade customers to like the solution."

"Good, problem solving and persuasion are key."

Next I explained the basics of the Belief System to Walter. He got it quickly.

"Walter, if you combine the two departments and the two jobs, each employee will take on the functions of *both* departments. In other words, employees who are good with people and detailed oriented also will have to be quick problem solvers and persuasive—and the problem-solving, persuasive types will have to be good with people and details. **Will these employees enjoy their new job?**"

"Well, I guess they won't. The quick decision makers won't have the patience to deal with complaining customers, and the employees who are good with people will get stressed under the hurry-up pressure to solve problems quickly and make risky decisions. We'll definitely have some satisfaction (Belief 3) problems. You can't provide good service without people who like coming to work."

"I agree, and few, if any, of your employees will find the work satisfying. **Will they feel equipped for their new job?**"

"No, not for the new functions. Serious confidence (Belief 1) problems, I'd say. You can't train a risk-taking problem solver who makes quick decisions to slow down and give attention to all the details, can you?"

"No, afraid not. Can't change a leopard's spots. If combining departments and reengineering the jobs leaves employees dissatisfied and ill-equipped to do the work, **will you get the performance you want?**"

"Definitely not. Motivation problems become performance problems. Not a pretty picture, is it?" He paced back and forth in the open space beside his desk.

"Walter, when you call everybody together to explain the plan to combine departments and jobs, **how do you expect your employees to react?**"

"That's a question I can answer. We did that last week. The consultants explained the plan to everybody. Pandemonium. That's what prompted our meeting today."

"What are you going to do?"

"I've decided not to continue steering the ship into the storm. Beyond that, I don't know."

"What do you *want* to do?"

He ran his fingers through his dark hair. "I still need a solution to the cost problem, but I don't know what to do?"

"What's the best way to find a solution?"

"I've racked my brain and keep coming up with zilch."

"Would your employees have any good ideas?"

Walter's head jerked up. "That's exactly what someone shouted in the employee meeting last week. 'You don't have to pay consultants, we know what's going on, and we can tell you how to reduce cost.' One of the few suggestions sandwiched between angry complaints."

"Would you feel comfortable asking them?"

"Why not? It's a great idea. Nothing to lose."

"And maybe a lot to gain."

"I'll do it."

"So, Walter, if you look at the big picture, what are you taking away from this conversation?"

"Remember the employee. Make decisions that motivate."

• • •

USING APPROACHES IN COMBINATION

Most managers choose to use more than one approach to motivation management. Three of the approaches—the contingency approach, the 10-step formula approach, and the Diagnostic Interview approach—are designed for similar circumstances, namely, when managers are faced with a limited number of motivation and performance problems among their team members. The three approaches are progressively more structured, and most managers tend to lean toward one of them on that basis. This is a matter of personal preference.

When problems escalate and become more widespread, the Belief System Profile is the more appropriate approach to use. Some managers choose to use it in other circumstances as well. The Belief System Profile, for example, has a proven track record in transforming average work groups into high-performing teams.

Decision making with motivation in mind is an approach that can be used when making any decision. It is advisable to use it for every decision. All you have to do is ask yourself a simple question: If I make the decision *this* way, how will employee motivation be affected?

There you have it. Five approaches to motivation management. Each one is solid, simple, and practical. Pick one or more to match your needs and preferences. You have the knowledge to choose. You have the skills to use. Only one thing remains.

MOVING AHEAD

Now is the time to jump in and get your feet wet. Time to stop making mouth music and do something about it. Go ahead and give motivation management a try. That is the only way to determine if you can make it work for you.

TABLE 16		
Deciding How to Approach Motivation Management		
Approach	Key Feature	When to Use
Contingency Approach	Very informal, loosely structured	Use when problems are *limited* in number.
10-Step Formula Approach	Informal, some structure	Use when problems are *limited* in number.
Diagnostic Interview Approach	Formal, structured	Use when problems are *limited* in number.
Belief System Profile Approach	Formal, highly structured	Use when problems are *pervasive*.
Decision-Making Approach	Informal, little structure	Use when making *all* decisions.

WISDOM

No one moved.

I had concluded the Motivation Management seminar. I thanked the group and offered words of encouragement and praise. They thanked me with applause, long and warm.

The attendees kept their seats. That happened sometimes. They were overwhelmed with what they had learned. Minds reeled with opportunity. They wanted something more but weren't sure what. I waited.

"Dr. Green, any final words of advice?"

"How about a story? I was in Tampa, Florida, working with a client a couple of years ago. Long-time friends, Jay and his wife, Sandy, invited me to stay with them. I'd been to their beautiful lakeside home many times. They'd built on a five-acre lot carved from a flourishing orange grove. Fresh-squeezed orange juice every morning, 10 minutes from tree to glass. And fresh asparagus, one of my favorites, 15 minutes from garden to plate.

"Jay and I walked to his garden, an irrigated plot bursting with produce ready for harvest. His trained eye quickly found the single

> **GETTING STARTED**
>
> Take a close look at the motivation and performance issues and decide whether the Belief System will help you.

asparagus spears that had emerged from the dark gray, sandy soil around the bushy asparagus plants. Jay deftly plunged a knife into the earth and cut the succulent young asparagus shoots one inch below the surface.

"When did you first plant asparagus?" I asked.

"He laughed and said, 'Too late. I'd always wanted asparagus in the garden, but it doesn't produce until the third year. I was too impatient to wait, so, every year I had no asparagus. Finally, I got around to planting some—just a few plants. And look at it now. Asparagus everywhere!'

"There was a valuable lesson in his words. It doesn't matter whether you're dealing with fruits and vegetables, relationships or leadership, success or failure, one truth stands out:

You reap what you sow,
more than you sow,
later than you sow.

"When you apply this to management and motivation, it becomes crystal clear: Now is the time to sow."

• • •

Data Supporting the Belief System

"An opinion is just that."

A BRIEFING SESSION

Choosing tools for motivation management is not easy. Tools often fail to deliver what they promise. What is a manager to do?

One option is to listen to the promises, but ask for *proof.*

If there is no proof, well...

When you find tools that offer proof, evaluate the proof. Shake it up. Sift out the truth.

The Belief System has been tried and tested. Data have been collected.

The Belief System is not standing on false promises and illusions.

Review the research findings and draw your own conclusions.

PUTTING NEW TOOLS TO WORK

When considering new tools, managers have to sift through lofty promises, evaluate the opinions of others, and eventually make their own decision, usually without any hard evidence in support of the tool. Not so with the Belief System. Empirical data are available.

I have conducted research on the Belief System since 1977, initially to develop the model, later to fine-tune it and measure its effectiveness. None of the research was of the academic type—no artificial environments, no experimental and control groups, and no sophisticated statistical analyses. All of the research was conducted in organizations that were using the Belief System. All evaluation methods were suggested and endorsed by those organizations.

Conducting research in organizational environments is limiting, however. Work must go on, and research is secondary. Employee promotions and new job assignments are not put on hold to accommodate research. The frequent changes in team composition make it difficult to collect sufficient meaningful data. Longitudinal studies are impossible.

Nevertheless, research on the Belief System has yielded considerable data. The research findings presented here are significant. You will find this information useful, and you'll see why I believe so firmly in the advantages of using the Belief System.

SOWING THE SEEDS

Managers who used the Belief System in the studies presented here all followed the same implementation model. Specifically, they used a three-step process that I believe represents the ideal conditions for planting the seeds of the Belief System.

1. Two-day learning session

2. One-on-one application session

3. Team meeting

The *two-day learning session* is intended for a single team—one manager and all team members. The learning is designed to accomplish three purposes: (1) to help the team learn the basics of the Belief System model, (2) to prepare manager and employee to meet one-on-

one to apply the Belief System, and (3) to motivate the team to take full advantage of this opportunity to improve their situation at work.

The *one-on-one application session* is designed to bring manager and employee together to discuss what can be done to strengthen the employee's motivation and performance. The Belief System Profile, as described in Chapter 7, is completed in advance by the employee and serves as the basis for the discussion. There are two goals for the session: for the manager to learn what motivates the employee, and to solve any existing motivation and performance problems the employee is experiencing. Both manager and employee leave the session with to-do lists that represent steps for improvement.

The *team meeting* brings the full team together after the manager has completed a one-on-one application session with each employee. Common themes that appeared across the majority of the one-on-one sessions are shared with the team. Recommendations are made for improving individual and team performance. Decisions are made regarding a variety of other applications of the Belief System. Two of the most common ways to continue the momentum generated by the initial implementation of the Belief System are (1) accountability sessions between the manager and each employee to verify that to-do list items are being completed; and (2) follow-up, one-on-one sessions that address any new issues and concerns. Additional programs include Motivation and Behavior Style, Hiring with Motivation in Mind, Belief System Selling, and Motivation Management for Executive Decision Making.

REAPING THE HARVEST

The acid test of the Belief System is not what happens when it is applied, but what transpires afterward. In other words, the proof of value is in *results*, not *process*. The Belief System sows a variety of seeds, yields an assortment of crops, and produces a bountiful harvest. This chapter is about the harvest. Research findings are presented to show what sowing the seeds of the Belief System produced in relation to each of the following:

- Leadership effectiveness
- Motivation and performance

- Job satisfaction
- Managing teams
- Managing change
- Downsizing
- Turnarounds

Leadership Effectiveness

Employees who participated in the Belief System research spoke frankly with their managers; the Belief System Profile and one-on-one sessions promoted this open communication. The end result was honest feedback from employee to manager, a rare occurrence under normal circumstances. A trained facilitator was present during the one-on-one sessions to guide the discussion. Employees were not critical and demanding; instead they simply offered feedback and suggestions for the manager's consideration. Managers got reinforcement for what they were doing correctly and learned what they might do differently for better results. This feedback provided managers with the opportunity to make adjustments and become more effective leaders.

To measure the impact of the Belief System on leadership effectiveness, employees were asked to evaluate their manager on 25 leadership behaviors before and after the use of the Belief System. Employees used the following rating scale to indicate the extent to which their manager showed each behavior: never, rarely, infrequently, frequently, usually, or always. The latter three ratings were considered to be "favorable responses" when tabulating the results.

Data were gathered from 100 percent of the employees on 12 teams before the Belief System was implemented; 109 employees responded. One hundred of the same respondents also completed the survey approximately three months later, after all one-on-one application sessions were completed. The results are shown in Table A.1.

It is clear from the aggregate results that these employees saw positive changes in leadership effectiveness. The average score jumped 16 points—from 69 before the Belief System to 85 after. One measure increased by 43 percentage points, another by 30 points, and 10 by 20 to 29 points.

TABLE A.1		

Leadership Effectiveness Before and After the Belief System

The Extent to Which Your Manager	Percentage Favorable Before	After
1. Links performance and outcomes so that rewards are obtained when performance is achieved.	81	93 (+12)
2. Understands what employees desire when performance exceeds expectations.	65	93 (+28)
3. Recognizes employees for high productivity.	85	97 (+12)
4. Builds the skills of employees in order to raise their performance.	51	80 (+29)
5. Sets difficult yet attainable performance goals.	86	94 (+ 8)
6. Motivates employees to achieve results.	65	89 (+24)
7. Provides desired outcomes for performance.	67	92 (+25)
8. Substitutes desired but unavailable rewards with others that are desirable to employees.	45	74 (+29)
9. Adapts management approach to the style of the employee.	39	82 (+43)
10. Effectively resolves employee problems.	68	94 (+26)
11. Quickly recognizes symptoms of performance problems.	69	85 (+16)
12. Accurately identifies performance problems.	74	89 (+15)
13. Uncovers the causes of performance problems.	51	77 (+26)
14. Involves employees in solving their own performance problems.	63	93 (+30)
15. Chooses appropriate solutions to address performance problems.	61	88 (+27)
16. Implements solutions to performance problems.	62	79 (+17)
17. Follows up on solutions to performance problems that are implemented.	56	79 (+23)
18. Recognizes when effort decreases.	77	83 (+ 6)
19. Deals with declines in employee satisfaction.	52	69 (+17)

TABLE A.1 continued		
Leadership Effectiveness Before and After the Belief System		
The Extent to Which Your Manager	Percentage Favorable Before	After
20. Prevents undesirable consequences from occurring for high performers.	67	81 (+14)
21. Matches employee skills with the skill requirements of the job.	80	90 (+10)
22. Determines the skill levels of employees.	83	92 (+ 9)
23. Provides necessary tools to get the work done.	69	90 (+21)
24. Provides assignments that satisfy employees.	74	89 (+15)
25. Offsets undesirable outcomes with desirable ones.	58	83 (+25)
Average score	69	85 (+16)

I worked closely with all of these managers and employees. I watched the managers change. I observed employee reaction, and I listened to what they had to say. What was my conclusion? There was little room for doubt: The Belief System improved leadership effectiveness dramatically for each manager.

Motivation and Performance

Did managers change in other ways as a result of the Belief System? What impact did the Belief System have on employees? Data were gathered to answer these questions. An 18-item instrument was used with the same employees who completed the leadership effectiveness survey plus one additional team. Employees rated 18 statements using the following scale: strongly disagree, disagree, agree, or strongly agree. The results from 104 responses are presented in Table A.2.

The findings show that both managers and employees made remarkable changes as a result of the Belief System. While all of the results are impressive, one is extraordinary: *Seventy-four percent of employees indicated that they were performing better as a result of the*

| TABLE A.2 |

Motivation and Performance Before and After the Belief System

As a Result of the Belief System Training and Application	Percentage Agree/ Strongly Agree
1. My manager understands me better.	96
2. My manager treats me better.	81
3. My manager makes better decisions about me.	90
4. My manager adapts more to my style.	86
5. My manager is more effective with me.	88
6. My manager has more respect for me.	82
7. My manager and I communicate better.	91
8. My manager and I have a better relationship.	86
9. My manager and I are more open and honest with each other.	88
10. My manager and I work better together.	87
11. It is safer to say what I think to my manager.	84
12. I like my job better.	68
13. I am more confident in my future.	68
14. I am more motivated.	74
15. I am performing better.	74
16. This is a better place to work.	71
17. The Belief System has been well worth the time I have invested in it.	93
18. The Belief System has been a breakthrough experience for me.	74

Belief System. The managers of these employees, in a separate survey, confirmed that three of every four employees had indeed improved their performance. An independent survey by a state university verified both managers' and employees' views on the Belief System's impact on performance.

DEEPER THAN THAT

I cried when I read it.

Bernetta had stopped me in the hallway. She had been through the Belief System twice—once with her manager, and then with the team she supervised. She was a good student, and I remembered that she had read and liked my first Belief System book, *Performance and Motivation Strategies for Today's Workforce.*

"I was hoping to see you today. Here." She handed me two pages from a spiral notepad. "See you later." She smiled and walked away.

I unfolded the pages and began to read. The first thing that caught my attention was in the upper right corner following the date— "4:20 A.M." Here is what the letter said:

> I don't know what inspired you to write your book, but I believe it was because you care about people and have been blessed by God with the Gift to do something about it.
>
> I am very excited because of progress I have already been making with my manager, my group, and the office in general. Your Belief System has really changed me and them.
>
> It is very hard for me to have a conversation with anyone without using what I learned from it.
>
> I am also driven by a need to help people, and this tool enabled me to bring this effort to a high level.
>
> I'd like to personally thank you for bringing the Belief System to our company. I know you are successful and always will be— because your basic desire is to be of help!
>
> GOD Bless Thad Green

I always have been struck more by the impact the Belief System has on the *person* than on performance.

A few days later, I dropped by Bernetta's office to thank her for the note.

"You're welcome. You know, people are astonished that they can easily learn the Belief System *and* easily apply it *and* get good, tangible results in a hurry. But the impact goes deeper than that. You know what I mean?"

"Yes, I do."

"It changes the way you see others, the way you see yourself, the way you feel about yourself. It gives you new skills, builds your self-confidence, gives you power in a world that's racing out of control. It fills a gap, provides a missing link, completes the whole. I know I'm running on a bit, but that's my take on it. The Belief System *will* make you different...and you'll *like* it."

• • •

Job Satisfaction

Employee opinion surveys are commonly used as a measure of job satisfaction. Many of my clients conduct these surveys annually. The results provided an opportunity to gauge the impact of the Belief System on employee satisfaction.

The data presented in Table A.3 on page 244 represent survey results for two consecutive years in an 80-person unit of a large corporation. The results in the first year indicated that the unit had serious morale problems; that was, in fact, the primary motivating factor in the decision to use the Belief System.

Implementation of the Belief System began in the middle of the following year and was completed before the employee opinion survey was administered again. The Belief System was the only intervention of any kind during this time period. Although it is possible that other factors could have influenced the survey results in the second year, management and employees alike attributed the changes fully to the Belief System.

The survey results in the second year were remarkable for two reasons. First, the *magnitude* of favorable responses was exceedingly high. With a favorable response rate of 65 percent or higher considered "world class" by corporations using this employee opinion survey, 8 of the 16 categories in the Belief System study fell in this high norm level, as did the average for all 16 categories. Second, the *increase* in favorable responses over the previous year was extremely high. The average score nearly doubled, with an increase of 27 percentage points. The shift in scores as a result of the Belief System is shown in Table A.4 on page 245.

TABLE A.3

Employee Opinion Survey Before and After the Belief System

Category of Questions	Percentage Favorable Before	After
1. Management Leadership	17	66 (+49)
2. Respect	21	61 (+40)
3. Teamwork	43	61 (+18)
4. Dedication to the Customer	38	65 (+27)
5. Integrity	54	83 (+29)
6. Empowerment	27	56 (+29)
7. Quality Process	22	55 (+33)
8. Supervision	53	80 (+27)
9. Performance Management	32	64 (+32)
10. Job Satisfaction	58	72 (+14)
11. Recognition	34	69 (+35)
12. Pay and Benefits	47	59 (+12)
13. Employment Security	35	57 (+22)
14. Operating Efficiency	41	56 (+15)
15. Competitive Position	58	76 (+18)
16. Company Satisfaction	25	68 (+43)
Average score	38	65 (+27)

Managing Teams

The formal application of the Belief System is designed for use with teams. The intent is to maximize team performance by strengthening individual performance. This is accomplished with a focus on leadership effectiveness. Existing teams that need to elevate performance find the Belief System helpful because it quickly identifies and solves existing motivation and performance problems. The Belief System is particularly applicable when teams have undergone changes in leadership and membership and when teams are newly formed. When

	TABLE A.4

Shift in Employee Opinions After Belief System Implementation

Percentage Favorable Responses	Number of Categories Before	After		
80–89	0		2	
70–79	0		2	
		0		11
65–69	0		1	
60–64	0		3	
50–59	4		5	
40–49	3		0	
30–39	4		0	
		12		0
20–29	4		0	
10–19	1		0	
Total	16		16	

either team leaders or team members are new, the Belief System promotes a rapid information exchange between manager and employee that escalates individual motivation and performance.

THE BEST PART WAS...

"How'd you do it?"

That was a question Wayne was being asked a lot. Two years earlier, his company had decided to consolidate functions that were being performed in multiple locations across the country. A new location was selected, five key managers were named, and *then* Wayne was chosen to lead the consolidation effort that would bring 500 employees together under one roof. And lead it he did, making the consolidation a big success story in the company.

Wayne answered the often-asked question in the following letter he sent to me:

I have been reflecting on all that has happened in the 15 months since you introduced the Belief System of Motivation and Performance to my team. I wanted to pass my thoughts along to you.

As you know, I had never met any of the five managers I inherited. The Belief System Profile and the one-on-one sessions you and I had with them greatly accelerated my understanding of how to best communicate, motivate, and work with each of them. Invaluable stuff. It would have taken me a year or longer to learn all that came out about each person in the one-on-one sessions.

The five managers not only were new to me, they were new to each other. I was pleased that they were willing to share their Belief System Profiles with one another in an open forum. It was a quick way to build understanding and develop relationships. That was the day we became a team.

The consolidation task we faced was essentially a start-up operation. Nobody on the team, including myself, had experienced getting a new venture off the ground. The Belief System helped me realize that everyone would have confidence problems. I learned a lot about myself, and it taught me how to make decisions to minimize *their* self-doubt and spot it quickly when they questioned *themselves*. Everybody was able to run full speed without being afraid that failure was lurking around the next corner ready to ambush them.

I had made a big deal with the team about creating a performance culture and rewarding them based on merit. I meant it. The Belief System made me aware, however, that when it comes to trust, words mean little; action is what counts. As a result, I decided to recognize good performance immediately and deal with poor performance the minute I spotted it. This got their attention—and their trust.

The Belief System showed me that when it comes to employee satisfaction, everybody is different. Certainly my five managers were as different as day and night in what they wanted. The old me would have treated everybody the same way. Knowing the handful of things important to each person was instrumental in maintaining a high level of job satisfaction, particularly during the first year of long hours and intense pressure.

The adage that "knowledge is power" has taken on new meaning for me. The Belief System pointed me in a new direction. I did not become a different person; I did not make a 180-degree turn in my management style. I did shift my way of thinking, though, and changed my style enough to become a more effective manager and leader. The best part was that with the knowledge of the Belief System, it is easy to change.

All things considered, the consolidation was a tremendous success. How did we do it? A lot of hard work and a few good decisions. The decision to use the Belief System goes at the top of the list. Why? Because when you manage to motivate, you get results.

• • •

Managing Change

Managers typically say that the single most important factor in managing change is *people*, yet in most cases, people problems abound. Why? Management often gets distracted and does not focus on the people side of change. Even when managers do focus on people, they are faced with an endless array of motivation and performance problems.

Often these managers simply do not have the skills necessary to effectively deal with the people issues. And managers who have the skills find that their efforts fall short, and nagging motivation and performance problems persist.

One reason for this is that managers consistently overlook one key element of change: how people react to change *emotionally*.

Emotions *always* accompany change. The threat of change alone fills people with fear and anxiety. The change process causes a flood of negative emotions that can, and often do, become a destructive force. Effectively addressing people problems, particularly those charged with emotion, is important to success when managing change.

One organization that was anticipating emotional upheaval during a major change effort elected to use the Belief System as the primary vehicle to focus on the people issues. The vice president responsible for this organization, an 800-person unit within a larger corporation, first used the Belief System with his team of eight managers, and six of those managers subsequently implemented the Belief System with their own teams of managers. Data were collected in this organization over a two-year period to determine the impact of the Belief System on managing change.

In terms of *leadership effectiveness* when managing change, aggregate scores for the six managers who used the Belief System with their teams are shown in Table A.5 on page 248.

TABLE A.5

Leadership Effectiveness Before and After the Belief System When Managing Change

The Extent to Which Your Manager	Percentage Before	Favorable After
1. Links performance and outcomes so that rewards are obtained when performance is achieved.	86	95 (+ 9)
2. Understands what employees desire when performance exceeds expectations.	67	90 (+23)
3. Recognizes employees for high productivity.	86	98 (+12)
4. Builds the skills of employees in order to raise their performance.	53	81 (+28)
5. Sets difficult, yet attainable performance goals.	88	91 (+ 3)
6. Motivates employees to achieve results.	70	88 (+18)
7. Provides desired outcomes for performance.	70	91 (+21)
8. Substitutes desired but unavailable rewards with others that are desirable to employees.	52	72 (+20)
9. Adapts management approach to the style of the employee.	45	77 (+32)
10. Effectively resolves employee problems.	75	97 (+22)
11. Quickly recognizes symptoms of performance problems.	69	81 (+12)
12. Accurately identifies performance problems.	73	84 (+11)
13. Uncovers the causes of performance problems.	56	68 (+12)
14. Involves employees in solving their own performance problems.	66	95 (+29)
15. Chooses appropriate solutions to address performance problems.	61	86 (+25)
16. Implements solutions to performance problems.	63	72 (+ 9)
17. Follows up on solutions to performance problems that are implemented.	58	74 (+16)
18. Recognizes when effort decreases.	80	83 (+ 3)
19. Deals with declines in employee satisfaction.	63	74 (+11)

The Extent to Which Your Manager	Percentage Favorable Before	After
20. Prevents undesirable consequences from occurring for high performers.	70	79 (+ 9)
21. Matches employee skills with the skill requirements of the job.	88	91 (+ 3)
22. Determines the skill levels of employees.	81	93 (+12)
23. Provides necessary tools to get the work done.	69	93 (+24)
24. Provides assignments that satisfy employees.	84	93 (+ 9)
25. Offsets undesirable outcomes with desirable ones.	63	84 (+21)
Average score	69	85 (+16)

The results showed improvement on *all* 25 leadership behaviors when managing change. The average "favorable" rating score increased from 69 percent to 85 percent, with an increase of 32 percentage points on one item and increases of 20 to 29 points on nine items.

How long do managers sustain leadership effectiveness when managing change? Data have suggested that the improvement is long term. For example, the vice president who used the Belief System with his team received a favorable rating by all of his managers on only one of the 25 measures when the survey was first administered. However, when the one-on-one sessions were completed three months later, his scores soared and remained high a full year later, as shown below.

Sustaining Leadership Effectiveness When Managing Change

Before the Belief System	After three months	After 15 months
100% favorable response on one of 25 measures	100% favorable response on 10 of 25 measures	100% favorable response on eight of 25 measures
	Improvement shown on 23 of 25 measures	Improvement shown on 20 of 25 measures

A second survey that focused on motivation and performance during the change effort was administered after the six managers had completed their one-on-one sessions. The results corroborate the positive findings from the leadership effectiveness survey. The survey results are shown in Table A.6.

TABLE A.6

Motivation and Performance After the Belief System When Managing Change

As a Result of the Belief System Training and Application	Percentage Agree/ Strongly Agree
1. My manager understands me better.	93
2. My manager treats me better.	73
3. My manager makes better decisions about me.	86
4. My manager adapts more to my style.	79
5. My manager is more effective with me.	80
6. My manager has more respect for me.	75
7. My manager and I communicate better.	88
8. My manager and I have a better relationship.	79
9. My manager and I are more open and honest with each other.	86
10. My manager and I work better together.	80
11. It is safer to say what I think to my manager.	82
12. I like my job better.	59
13. I am more confident in my future.	59
14. I am more motivated.	61
15. I am performing better.	64
16. This is a better place to work.	64
17. The Belief System has been well worth the time I have invested in it.	88
18. The Belief System has been a breakthrough experience for me.	61

All of these results were impressive—one in particular: *64 percent agree that as a result of the Belief System "I am performing better."* This is a noteworthy achievement. Managers, take notice. Imagine what would happen if you could improve the performance of *two-thirds* of your workforce during a major change effort.

What was the impact of the Belief System on *employee satisfaction* when managing change in this 800-employee organization? The employee opinion survey described earlier was administered before and after the Belief System. The results, summarized below in Table A.7, showed a quantum leap in job satisfaction across the organization.

TABLE A.7		
Employee Opinion Survey Before and After the Belief System When Managing Change		
Percentage Favorable Responses	**Number of Categories**	
	Before	**After**
70+	0	3
65–69	1	3
	6	15
60–64	3	1
50+	2	8
40+	6	1
30+	3	0
20+	1	0
	10	1
10+	0	0
Total	16	16

Downsizing

One of my clients had seen his division shrink from more than 900 employees to about 300 during a time when 100,000 employees were being laid off companywide. He knew the aftermath of downsizing could be devastating and that recovery could be a long and painful journey with no guarantee of success. "Some of my counterparts are taking a wait-and-see attitude. They plan to let the dust settle, assess the damage, and then figure out what to do. I'm not willing to do that in my division. I want to prevent as many problems as we can."

What was the state of mind of his workforce after witnessing the division drop to one-third its former size? He described it. "People are afraid. They don't believe the downsizing is over. They're angry, angry that their friends and co-workers are gone, and angry that workloads have increased. Anxiety levels are high. People aren't sure they can handle more responsibility, new methods and procedures, and increased performance standards. I tell you, we're a catastrophe waiting to happen if we don't do something to prevent it."

He elected to use the Belief System and took it to every level in his organization. "If we can't find out what the problems are, we can't fix them. The Belief System's the best way I know to get people to open up and share their concerns, to give us a chance to deal with them. If we work together on this, we'll be as strong as ever—maybe stronger—but we have to work together."

The Belief System was implemented first with the division head and his team, and then it cascaded throughout the 300-person organization over a two-year period. The measured results that show the impact of the Belief System are presented below.

The people value added by the Belief System. Where a favorable response rate of 65% for any one of the 16 categories of questions is considered "nirvana" by management, the Belief System registered the results as shown in Table A.8.

The customer value added by the Belief System. The division landed the highest customer satisfaction marks ever as people responded as follows:

- Delighted   55%
- Satisfied, Very Satisfied, or Delighted   95%

The economic value added by the Belief System. The bottom line in the division increased dramatically when a significant increase in revenue was accompanied by only a modest increase in expenses:

Projected business	$35.7*
Actual business	$43.1*
Increase in revenue	20%
Increase in expenses	8%

*Figures expressed in millions

	TABLE A.8		
Employee Opinion Survey Before, During, and After the Belief System in a Downsizing Organization			
Percentage Favorable Responses	Number of Categories Before (Year 1)	Number of Categories During (Year 2)	Number of Categories After (Year 3)
70–79	1	4	5
65–69	4 7	2 8	6 13
60–64	2	2	2
50–59	5	4	2
30–49	3 8	3 7	1 3
10–29	0	0	0
Total	15	15	16

"We were able to determine that the principal cause of these results was the Belief System and the impact it had on the personnel of the division and the improvements in motivation and performance they experienced," the division head explained. "I have contended since year

one that the Belief System was changing the way this organization conducted business. Now we are seeing the tangible results of that change. This confirms my belief that if you take care of your people, they will take care of your customers, and the bottom line will take care of itself."

Turnarounds

Organizations sometimes end up in trouble, performance sinking far below acceptable levels. Ineffective leadership and poor management practices generally are to blame. These organizations are characterized by a lack of direction, poor communication, and interpersonal conflict. Employees are not motivated, not held accountable, and not performing. Putting a troubled organization back on course is a tedious process, like straightening an onerous tangle of barbed wire.

My experience is that every organization in a turnaround mode has one element in common: Employees have plenty to say and they want to be heard. And every successful turnaround effort has one factor in common: Managers listened to employees and acted on what they heard.

The Belief System is designed to make it easy for employees to talk, for managers to listen, and for action to follow. I have used it with many clients in turnaround situations. The example that follows is a representative application.

NEVER A SINGLE SIMPLE ANSWER

Bryan was hired to orchestrate the turnaround of an organization that was deeply in trouble by every conceivable measure of performance. Here is a letter I recently received from him:

Dear Dr. Green:

It has been several years since I was introduced to you and the Belief System. As you will recall, I had assumed the leadership of a large geographically dispersed network engineering group, which, at the time, was in "last place" in our organization with respect to the Employee Opinion Survey.

Our Leadership Team met following my arrival and we characterized our group as follows: "People who are disengaged, disempowered, and disspirited, where conflict, emotion, and scar tissue are pervasive and there is only nominal teamwork with fear and insecurity influencing behavior...."

We were in search of a comprehensive tool that would revitalize the group and lift the Employee Opinion Survey results and the rest of our measured results out of (our then) last place position. You were instrumental in convincing me and, subsequently, our leadership team that the Belief System of Motivation and Performance was a tool that had a track record of demonstrated results and we committed to its adoption.

In the last three years our Employee Opinion Survey results have increased dramatically. From last place, we have progressed to best-in-class in our regional organization. In addition, our team is now in the Domestic High Performance Norm (or better) in all but *one* of the measured categories; and there is not a statistically significant difference between our score in *that* category and the Domestic High Performance Norm.

With reference to our district's operational results, our measures of internal customer satisfaction have been at 100 percent for the last two years and we have produced two consecutive years of financial results which have far exceeded our commitments.

In short, we have achieved the turnaround and revitalization of the district team that we were seeking when we first met three years ago. We have achieved the status of High Performance Team and the strength of the team continues to develop.

While I am sure we will all agree that there is never a single simple answer to the very complex and pervasive performance and motivation problems that characterized this organization, our commitment to and investment in the Belief System has been a key element to our success.

Very sincerely,
Bryan

• • •

WHY DOES THE BELIEF SYSTEM WORK?

The research data presented in this chapter paint a clear picture: The Belief System works.

- Managers become more effective leaders.
- Employees are more motivated.
- Individual, team, and organizational performance improves.
- Workers find greater job satisfaction.
- Teamwork is strengthened.
- Managing change runs more smoothly
- Downsizing works.
- Turnarounds are more successful.

TABLE A.9				
Why the Belief System Works				
Percentage of Response				
A Minor Reason the Belief System Works		A Major Reason the Belief System Works		
Elements of the the Belief System	1	2	3	4	5
1. Belief System Model	1	6	24	37	32
2. Two-Day Learning Session	1	15	26	43	15
3. One-on-One Application Session	0	0	6	21	73
4. Team Meeting	0	14	19	53	14

Why does the Belief System work? There are many ways to approach this question. I was interested in the views of people who have used the Belief System. What do they think? Their responses are summarized above. The findings as shown in Table A.9 are based on responses from 11 teams—75 employees and their 11 managers.

The data, I believe, point out two reasons the Belief System works: (1) All four elements are essential. They have a logical flow; they depend on each other. In short, they constitute a *system*. (2) The one-on-one application sessions between manager, employee, and facilitator offer the greatest value.

Annotated
Bibliography

Green, Shannon. *Unleashing the Motivation to Perform*. Atlanta: The Belief System Institute, 1998. In this book, Green takes readers on an intimate journey into discussions between managers and employees who are interacting one-on-one to resolve debilitating motivation problems. She shows the ease with which managers skillfully use the Belief System of Motivation and Performance to remove stubborn barriers that block performance. The book gives managers a sense of the far-reaching impact they can have on how hard employees work and how well they perform, all achieved simply by managing with motivation in mind.

Green, Thad B. *Performance and Motivation Strategies for Today's Workforce: A Guide to Expectancy Theory Applications*. Westport, Conn.: Quorum Books, 1992. This book presents the first application model that gives practical value to the expectancy theory of motivation. It provides techniques and tools managers can use to identify, diagnose, and solve motivation problems at work. Included are specific guidelines on what managers should say and do to resolve problems before they get out of hand, and a framework for involving employees in resolving their own motivation and performance problems.

Green, Thad and Bill Barkley. *Manage to the Individual: If You Want to Know How, Ask!* Atlanta: The Belief System Institute, 1996. This book provides a step-by-step course of instruction on the Belief System of Motivation and Performance. Detailed guidelines are presented that show managers how to use the Belief System to manage to the individuality of their employees. The approach focuses on applying the principle, "If you want to know, ask." The book provides research data on the application of the Belief System in the corporate environment that documents the irrevocable connection of bottom-line results to employee motivation.

Green, Thad B. and Raymond T. Butkus. *Motivation, Beliefs, and Organizational Transformation.* Westport, Conn.: Quorum Books, 1999. Basing his work on the pioneering research of Victor Vroom, Green, assisted by coauthor Butkus, introduces a new management tool to facilitate the people aspects of change: the Belief System of Motivation and Performance. Their book shows that managing change requires building support from a highly motivated workforce; that most strategies today overlook the emotional factor in change; and that only by addressing the motivational and emotional problems associated with change can management implement change successfully.

Lawler, Edward E. *Motivation in Work Organizations.* Monterey, Calif.: Brooks/Cole, 1973. Dealing extensively with both theory and practice, this book was written for students of organizational behavior as well as for managers who must deal with the day-to-day motivation problems that occur at work. Discussing various influences on motivation and performance—including job design, leadership style, and pay systems—Lawler claims that the ability to analyze work situations from a motivational perspective is critical for managers if they are to effectively resolve the many complex performance problems they confront on the job.

University of Michigan Survey Research Center. *Michigan Organizational Assessment Package: Progress Report II*. Ann Arbor: University of Michigan Institute for Social Research, 1975. Drawing on the work of Victor Vroom and Edward Lawler, a broad-gauged employee attitude survey instrument is presented that can be adapted to different work settings and used to measure employee attitudes and feelings about a wide variety of organizational issues. Consisting of 10 standardized modules, the survey instrument includes about 350 items that address such areas as job satisfaction, leadership style, work motivation, performance outcomes, and employee beliefs and values.

Vroom, Victor H. *Motivation in Management*. New York: American Foundation for Management Research, 1965. This study was one of the first to focus on the interplay between motives and work among managers. It summarizes existing research on the motivational patterns that distinguish managers from hourly workers and other occupational groups. Some of the major issues discussed include how the desires of managers differ from those of other members of the labor force, what motivational differences exist among levels of management in various fields, and the effects of management behavior on the job satisfaction and performance of subordinates.

Vroom, Victor H. *Work and Motivation*. New York: John Wiley & Sons, 1964. In this landmark book in organizational psychology, Vroom broke new ground by integrating the work of hundreds of researchers to present a new conceptual model of workplace behavior. Joining theory with empirical research, Vroom examines a variety of issues related to work and human behavior, including occupational choice, work satisfaction, and the role of motivation in work performance. (The 1994 edition, published by Jossey-Bass, includes a new introduction by the author.)

Index